This page intentionally left blank

Wallasey – Days Gone By

By Tony Franks-Buckley

Dedication

This book is dedicated to all my friends and family who have supported me through my life and help me achieve the goals that I have reached. I also dedicate it to my loved ones who are gone but not forgotten.

Joyce Dennett

Norman Spearing

Derek Franks

Mabel Buckley

Acknowledgements

I would like to thank Paul Wirral and his hard work at providing and creating Wallasey Memories Facebook group and his website www.historyofwallasey.co.uk Also I would like to thank Mike Kemble who also has a useful site of www.wirralhistory.net And last but not least I would like to thank Gavin Chappell whose previous work on Pirates in the area has helped me considerably as well as the help he has also given me elsewhere.

About the Author

Wallasey Historian and Author that completed BA Honours Degree in Modern History at Liverpool John Moores University under the guidance of fellow author Prof Frank McDonough, Dr Mike Benbough-Jackson and a host of others.

Main interests in history are from the Industrial Revolution era in Britain, which was the beginning of the modern day Britain as we know it today. Also holds a keen interest in World War II due to being taught about the war through Uncle, who served in the Royal Navy and was involved in the D-Day landings.

As well as graduating from university, previously attended Wirral Metropolitan College in Birkenhead and gained A Level results through an Access to Higher Education Diploma in English Literature, History and Environmental Studies which allowed advancement to University.

Other Books and Research Papers

The History of Wallasey – A Small Suburb with a Large History

The History of Birkenhead & Bidston

Liverpool during the Industrial Revolution 1700 – 1850

To What Extent did the EU Unite Europe by the end of the 20th Century?

Was the Great British Reform Act of 1832 Truly "Great"?

How effective were poor law reforms and philanthropy in reducing the causes of poverty in Britain during the 19th Century?

Was there an "American Indian Holocaust" from English Migration to America?

How effective was Nazi Propaganda?

To what extent did Britain experience an "Agricultural Revolution" between 1750 – 1830?

Globalisation in the Modern World.

Find me on Twitter @TonyFrBuckley

My Blog Site http://tonyfranksbuckley.blogspot.co.uk/

Introduction to the Borough of Wallasey

The name Wallasey is derived from the Old English pronouncing "Wealas Eye", which when roughly translated means Welshman's or Stranger's Island, due to at high tide the settlement was cut-off from the rest of the Wirral Peninsula. Even today Wallasey is still an island of sorts. It's impossible to travel to or to leave from the town without crossing over (or under) water of some description, whether it be Liverpool Bay, the River Mersey, the River Birkett or Wallasey Pool... now known as Wallasey and Birkenhead Docks.

In the past, the main feature that cut-off Wallasey from the main land, making it an island was Wallasey Poole. This is a natural inlet running from the River Mersey across the north-western corner of the Wirral Peninsula. At high tide, the water level in the Pool rose to such an extent that it stretched across the marshland that is now known as Leasowe, joining Liverpool Bay and thus, bisecting the tip of the peninsula. Such was the height and strength of the tide that the water also travelled up the Rivers Birkett and Fender, swelling both so that an area stretching as far as Bidston Moss, Woodchurch and as far as Prenton Dell became a marshy flood plain. At the furthest point... what is now Prenton, the Prenton Brook sprang from the hill at the top of what is now Prenton Hall Road and powered Prenton Mill (hence Prenton Mill Road) before running down to Prenton Dell which became a brackish lake at high tide and marshland at low tide. This flooding was to occur twice a day with every tide until a barrage was constructed across the mouth of Wallasey Pool and another tidal barrier or embankment was constructed between Leasowe and Wallasey Village to prevent the Pool joining Liverpool Bay. Entrance locks were constructed at the mouth of Wallasey Pool to allow craft access to what was to become Wallasey and Birkenhead Docks. Prior to the taming of the Pool, the only way across the water was either by boat or by a rickety bridge near to what is today Bidston Moss that was supposedly constructed from the bones of a stranded whale.

The value of Wallasey Poole as a natural harbour has long been recognised, its banks have been home to many marine connected activities and a primitive dock was located close to what is now Kelvin Road which used to transport the finished articles from Seacombe Pottery to various parts of the country. Seacombe Pottery was founded by John Godwin (formally of the Crown Works in Longton, Staffordshire and well known for his "Pearl ware" pottery) in 1852. The other activities included smuggling (something that Wallasey has long been notorious for), fishing, ferries and ship building. William Laird founded his first shipyard on the banks of Wallasey Pool prior to moving to land reclaimed from the Mersey adjacent to Birkenhead Priory where his ship building business flourished up to the latter part of the twentieth century.

The foundation stones of the docks were laid in the early part of the nineteenth century with the Alfred Dock entrance locks being opened in 1866 but the main design and construction of today's docks was undertaken by Jesse Hartley, who also constructed many of Liverpool's docks. He completed construction of the locks, retaining walls and the land reclamation schemes in the 1890's.

Two ship canals have been proposed to connect with the pool. The first was an extension to the Bridgewater Canal from Sale to West Kirby and the second was an extension to the Pool, cutting across Bidston Moss to Leasowe where it would have connected with Liverpool Bay. Thomas Telford, the renowned canal builder and civil engineer was reputedly consulted for both schemes and when inspecting Wallasey Pool he is supposed to have said… "Look… they've built Liverpool on the wrong side of the river!" His inference was that the natural harbour of Wallasey Pool should have been taken advantage of instead of reclaiming land from the Mersey to construct the Liverpool dock system. Neither of the ship canal schemes came to fruition but the one that was to have connected to the Bridgewater Canal did pre-date the Manchester Ship Canal by seventy years

From when the construction of the docks was completed they were successful. Goods from all over the North West were transported to ports in every country on the planet. It was not until containerisation and bulk transport was introduced in the 1960's that the port's importance began to diminish, leaving only a few berths in regular use today. The Morpeth Dock, which was one of the earliest docks constructed on the Birkenhead side of the Pool, has been isolated from the main system by a dam and it's bascule bridge ("D" Bridge) removed and replaced by a causeway.

In August 1984 the Tall Ships visited the River Mersey for the first time. Wallasey and Birkenhead Docks were moorings for the first visit from the Tall Ships. Some of the ships were moored in Wallasey and Birkenhead Docks as well as in Liverpool Docks In subsequent years, the Tall Ships have returned to the River Mersey but their moorings are usually concentrated in the Liverpool North Docks and Albert Docks. Trade has shrunk to such a low level that other parts of the Pool have been in-filled. Wallasey Dock, situated between the Morpeth Dock and the Alfred Dock entrance locks from the Mersey, was once a tidal dock having its own entrance from the river and known as the Great Low Water Basin. In this form it was unsuccessful. The river entrance was filled-in; the dock connected to the main dock system and renamed Wallasey Dock in 1877. This dock was lined with warehouses... one of which was occupied for many years by "Barry No-shoes" who ran a successful car spares outlet.

After the warehouses were demolished the dock was in-filled during the spring of 2002 and the land used as a marshalling area for vehicles waiting to board the new Irish roll-on-roll-off ferry terminal that was constructed on the site of the old Wallasey Landing Stage. The ferry service operates from the new terminal and floating landing stage in the river built in 2002. At the far end of Wallasey Dock is situated a pumping station responsible for "topping up" the water levels within the dock system with water drawn from the River Mersey. During the in-filling of Wallasey Dock, the water from the pumping station was diverted into a new culvert constructed beneath the surface of the lorry park and out-falling adjacent to the now fixed number three bridge

On the river side of Wallasey Dock, close to the pumping station was situated Wallasey Landing Stage which was used mainly for the importing of livestock. An elevated walkway was constructed allowing animals to walk to the Woodside Lairage abattoir situated next to Woodside Ferry. Next to the elevated walkway or cattle walk as it was known locally was the "One O'clock Gun". These small cannon would fire at precisely one o'clock to indicate the end of lunchtime to the dock workers.

Opposite the now dammed, entrance to Egerton Dock is the East Float Dock. The entrance to this arm of the docks was once spanned by a swing bridge connecting the Birkenhead side of the docks to a man-made island known as Vittoria Quay and Dock which accommodates warehousing and additional shipping berths. In later years the dock has been home to laid-up Isle of Mann Steam Packet Company ships, Fishery Protection vessels and even a company building and repairing tugs and small ships. Adjacent to the entrance to the docks from the Birkenhead side, where the roundabout is today was a police station. It was close to "D" Bridge and backed onto Egerton Dock. Opposite were the Mersey Docks and Harbour Board workshops. This location is now occupied by the Tower Quays business development.

Between the Four Bridges and Duke Street Bridge is an expanse of water known as the East Float. On the North bank, adjacent to the remaining Spiller's Flour Mills was situated the Warship Preservation Trust's Historic Warships Museum. Here were moored the following ships... HMS Onyx and HMS Plymouth, both of the 1982 Falkland Islands War fame, U534... a resurrected German U Boat - U534 brought back from the Mediterranean where it was sunk during World War Two, LCT 7074... the last surviving LCT (Landing Craft Tank) that took part in the D-Day landings, the "Planet" LV23... a retired Mersey Bar Lightship that guided ships into the Mersey Estuary for many years (not part of the Historic Warships Collection but shares their moorings) and HMS Bronington, M1115... a wooden minesweeper built in 1954, permanently moored at Trafford Wharf on the Manchester Ship Canal until July 2002, when it was acquired by the Trust for the collection. Another recent addition to the collection is not a ship but a scale model of the "Liberator" bomber that sunk "U534", constructed and donated by Martin Kinnear... a local enthusiast and model-maker.

Wallasey Village

The village has a mixture of popular mostly 20th century semi-detached and detached housing, a pleasant shopping street, with a floral roundabout in the centre. It's considered the wealthiest area of Wallasey. St Hilary's church is an ancient foundation; the old tower is all that remains of a 1530 church building which burned down in 1857. At the north end of Wallasey Village, the main street leads to the promenade and coastal park, and two golf courses. The promenade passes here, running from the 'Gun site' around to Seacombe, a total of over 7 miles.

New Brighton

New Brighton was a popular seaside resort after the mid-19th century. At one time it houses an enormous tower which stood higher than Blackpool and was the North West's premier coastal resort. Sadly it declined after the tower and pier were demolished, finally hitting its low point in the 1950s from which I do not believe it will ever revive. Nevertheless, the marine promenade is part of a popular walk and the areas near the sea offer a much improved beach and many leisure activities. The recently rebuilt Floral Pavilion plays host to regular productions and national stars such as Ken Dodd, and Vale Park is a beautiful public park. Housing here ranges from large villas near the sea to suburban semi-detached homes, while there are some less attractive terraces in parts of the area. New Brighton is served by a railway station of the same name. New Brighton promenade is the UK's longest promenade.

Poulton

Poulton was originally a small fishing and farming hamlet beside the Wallasey Pool from which it derived its name. It developed with the growth of the docks, mainly as an industrial and terraced housing area. Today it's a collection of industrial estates and densely populated patches of housing.

Egremont

Egremont developed as an affluent residential area in the early 19th century, and was named by one Captain Askew who built a house in the area in 1835 and named it after his Cumberland birthplace. Egremont Pier was built in 1827 and was the longest pier on Merseyside until it was damaged irreparably in 1946 when a coaster collided with it. Egremont also contains Wallasey Town Hall, which is an imposing edifice opened in 1916 and initially used as a war hospital. It's located overlooking the estuary and with its back to the town centre. This area of Egremont is now almost entirely housing, although there is a small shopping area on King Street which still shows some signs of its maritime history within its architecture.

Seacombe

Seacombe, the most south-easterly section of Wallasey, is best known for its Mersey Ferry terminal, with regular ferry boat departures to Pier Head in Liverpool and Woodside in Birkenhead. There is a commuter ferry service direct to Liverpool during peak hours, while for the rest of the day the ferries are geared to serving tourists with a circular cruise visiting Birkenhead Woodside ferry terminal as well. Seacombe is the last remaining of the three ferry terminals which used to connect the Borough of Wallasey, the others being Egremont Ferry and the New Brighton Ferry, which operated from its own pier, running parallel to the New Brighton pleasure pier. Seacombe Ferry is also the starting point of a seven mile unbroken promenade, mostly traffic-free, running alongside the River Mersey to Harrison Drive beyond New Brighton. Local landmarks are the church of St Paul which stands on its own traffic island and the ventilation tower for the Kingsway Tunnel with its mighty extraction fans. As with Poulton, the area developed with housing for workers in the docks and nearby industries, and much of the housing is council-owned or terraced. The Guinea Gap swimming baths are located between Seacombe and Egremont.

Wallasey Government

From Anglo-Saxon times Wallasey was part of the the Hundred of Wirral (also known as The Wapentake of Wirral) which was the ancient administrative area for the Wirral Peninsula. Its name is believed to have originated from the *Hundred of Wilaveston*, the historic name for Willaston, which was an important assembly point in the Wirral Hundred during the Middle Ages. The *ton* suffix in a place name normally indicates a previous use as a meeting location for officials. During its existence, the hundred was one of the Hundreds of Cheshire.

The term 'hundred' goes back to at least to the time of King Alfred. He divided the country into counties or shires and these in turn into hundreds, subdivided into tithings or towns. Historians have never agreed as to what is really meant by a 'hundred', but it seems likely that is has a military origin, i.e. the district furnishing a hundred warriors. Alternatively it may signify the area occupied by a hundred families or be a unit of a hundred hides of land.

Order was maintained for the Wirral by the appointments of local palatine offices called 'Sergeants' of the Peace' who were under the control of a 'Grand Sergeant'. The Hundred was 'perambulated' (inspected) by these sergeants who were assisted by staff known as 'bedells' who had knowledge of all offences against the peace. They had powers to arrest offenders, and in early days might instantly behead them, if caught in the act.

The earliest recorded history of court action was in 1309 when Thomas Ebba, of Poulton, attacked Matthew de Walley. Ebba was killed in the attack and de Walley was arrested and taken to Chester Castle. The Hundred Court found that de Walley had acted in self-defence and was released with a 40d fine.

Since 1100 the Wirral had been under Forest Laws as much of the region was forested. In 1347 many of the inhabitants were brought before the court for offences connected with the forest. Houses and mills built without licence were ordered to be pulled down, and enclosures made for agricultural purposes were thrown open.

One of the last Hundred Courts was on 3rd September, 1855, which were then held quarterly, and it sat at Tranmere Hotel. An action for damages for false imprisonment was brought by James McMahon of Liscard, a schoolmaster, against Elliot Hodson, a Birkenhead police detective.

With the increasing growth of population in Wallasey it was soon apparent that a change in the form of local government was required. On 8th May, 1845, the Wallasey Improvement Act was passed which authorised the appointment of twenty-one Commissioners, who were all local businessmen. The legislation included powers for "paving, lighting, watching, cleansing, and otherwise improving the Parish of Wallasey, in the County of Cheshire, and for establishing a Police, and also a Market, within the said Parish, and for other purposes". The Commissioners were elected for three years, one-third of their number retiring annually but being eligible for re-election. The Commissioners were empowered to construct common sewers and to drain the land for building purposes. Also powers were obtained to purchase the ferries. They met for the first time in a room above the stables of the Queens Arms Hotel, Liscard on 12th June, 1845.

The Commissioners apparently did not perform their obligations to the parish. The ferries were never purchased, no market was ever made and their provision for 'watching' consisted of only three police officers - a chief and two men. The most serious failure was the concern of neglect of public health within the parish. The whole country had already received a scare in the cholera epidemic of 1832-1833. Liverpool had suffered more than most but the cholera of 1832 had actually originated from Seacombe.

The main problem for the Commissioners was the 'Wallasey Pool', which was then a wide inlet open to the Mersey tidal estuary. At low water the smell of silt, mud and the inhabitants dumping refuse was quite revolting and nauseating. Matters were not improved with the development of Birkenhead Docks which necessitated the building of a wall across the mouth of the Pool and the damming up of the water behind it to make the Great Float. The situation was made even worse when the Dock Committee became bankrupt in 1847, leaving the area a marsh. With an increasing population and those left unemployed by the dock collapse it's not hard to understand the daunting task in public health for the Commissioners. In response to the situation the inhabitants of Seacombe sent a petition to the Board of Health in June, 1851.

An inquiry was held at Parry's Hotel, Seacombe on 31st July, 1851, by Mr Robert Rawlinson, Superintendent Inspector under the Public Health Act, 1848. The Inspector found that the problems of Seacombe, was also found in the rest of Wallasey. The sewers were urgently needed but were resisted because under the Wallasey Improvement Act, 1845, it stated that the owners of the property had to pay for any sewering but under the Public Health Act the soon to be elected Local Board would have the power to levy a sewer rate on tenants. The owner's reluctance in constructing sewers was heard at the Inquiry.

Further reports were also heard at the Inquiry including a report that there was no public lighting in the Parish and only a small private gasworks which only supplied Egremont Ferry. Also urgently needing attention was the housing conditions in the district. The worst was the area known as Mersey Street, which adjoined Seacombe Ferry, and was quite abominable. In fact the mortality rate of Poulton-cum-Seacombe was far greater than even in the worst district of Liverpool.

It was the Inspector's view that Wallasey was in a similar condition to that of Poulton-cum-Seacombe. The issue with Birkenhead Docks could not be solely held responsible for much of the trouble in public health. The Inspector went on to say that "if Wallasey Commissioners had put in force the powers of their Act as it now exists to their fullest extent, many nuisances complained of would have been abated. But apparently most of the clauses relating to sanitary were, have, up to this time, remained a dead letter".

The resulting Inquiry found the Commissioners being replaced under the Wallasey Order of 1852 by a Local Board of Health established under the Public Health Act, 1848.

On the 18th April, 1853 'The Public Health Act, 1853' ordered the Wallasey Local Board of fifteen persons should be elected to supersede the Commissioners. Six members were elected by Liscard, six by Poulton-cum-Seacombe and three to Wallasey. One of their first duties was to provide an adequate water supply for the district. Previously Poulton-cum-Seacombe was supplied with water from three wells. The first pump was situated at Somerville, second, a well by the road side at the junction of the Dock Road and Poulton Bridge Road and the third at Clough and Galan's Yard, on the north side and very near Wallasey Pool.

Before the sinking of the wells by the Commissioners for the public water supply, the tenants were dependent on private wells, one to several houses. The landlord had to supply each house with two large wooden butts for rain water. The Local Board obtained powers to construct waterworks in 1858, which resulted in the construction of a well and pump in Poulton (later to become the Gas works which closed in 1962) and a elevated tank at Mill Lane which was completed in 1861 and formally opened by Mr Tollemache, M.P. In 1883 the Committee was advised to construct a reservoir at New Brighton and brought into use in 1887 on Gorsehill Road (the Water Tower being constructed in 1905).

The Local Board took steps to acquire most of the land along the river and, in 1860, took over the Mersey Ferries. Other steps that the board took were to purchase the Liscard Hall estates in 1890 at a cost of 1/10d per square yard for the 37 acre land and mansion. Later a further 20 adjoining acre was acquired and opened to the public as Central Park.

The original offices of the Local Board were situated at the bottom of Church Street, Egremont, and these remained the headquarters after the Local Board was replaced by the Urban District Council in 1894 under the Local Government Act of that year. The district was divided into eight wards, New Brighton, Upper Brighton, Liscard, Egremont, North Seacombe, South Seacombe, Poulton and Wallasey. Three representatives were elected for each ward and the first chairman was Richard Steel of Zig Zag Hall.

In June, 1902 the Council attempted to increase its powers by securing authority to appoint a Mayor, Alderman and a Town Clerk as well as making by-laws and setting up a separate police force so an application was made for incorporation as a Borough. A petition was presented but was strongly opposed and incorporation was refused by the Privy Council. It was not until 1910 that Wallasey achieved Borough status, its charter being the first to be granted by King George V.

The wards were increased to ten, and the first meeting of the new Council met on 11th November, 1910. The Council, with a Liberal majority, consisted of 10 Alderman and 30 Councillors who invited Mr James Thomas Chester, though not actually a Town Councillor, as the boroughs first Mayor. The Chains of Office of the Mayor's and Mayoress being raised by public subscription. The Arms of Wallasey, incorporated in the Mayor's Chain, were granted by the College of Arms on 8th September, 1910. It carries the Wirral Horn in the right of the shield, with three wheat sheaf's representing Cheshire on the opposite side. A fully-rigged galleon in full sail underneath represented the town's maritime connections. The crest had a knight's helmet and trident dolphins. The motto and leaves completed the Coat of Arms. In heraldic language it reads:-

Or on the waves of the Sea a three-masted Ship in full sail proper, on a chief Azure, to the dexter three Garbs, two and one of the first, and to the sinister a Bugle-horn proper, stringed and garnished gold.

And for the crest, on a wreath of the colours, a Dolphin head downwards proper, entwining a Trident erect or Manting Or and azure.

Motto : *Audemus dum cavemus*
Translated - "We are bold whilst we are cautious"

County Borough status was granted on 1st April, 1914. A decision was made that a New Town Hall should be built and the area chosen was in Brighton Street on the site of North Meade House. The foundation stone of the New Town Hall was laid by King George V on 25th March, 1914. The building was used during the First World War as a military hospital and was not opened for municipal purposes until 3rd November, 1920. In 1918 Wallasey, previously in the Wirral Parliamentary Division, became a Parliamentary Borough, and the first member to be elected was the Conservative Dr. Bouverie Macdonald, a local well-known practitioner.

A Local Act in 1920 saw the number of wards increase to 14 and the Council to 14 Alderman and 42 Councillors. The Act gave further powers concerning health and also town improvements which included the construction of libraries, schools but most importantly the building of houses and roads.

On 1st April, 1928, the Parish of Moreton and part of the Parish of Bidston, were added to the Borough. The number of wards was increased from 14 to 16, the two new wards, Leasowe and Moreton, being represented by five members, two Councillors each and one Alderman; later an additional Councillor for Moreton was added. When Saughall Massie was added to the Borough by the County of Chester Review Order, 1933, an additional ward was created represented by one Councillor and at the same time an additional Alderman was appointed. The total number of Councillors for the Borough now stood at 64. In 1950 Moreton and Saughall Massie were amalgamated and the new Moreton and Saughall Massie ward and the Leasowe ward were then represented by three Councillors each; the number of wards was reduced to 16 but the Council remained the same.

With war looming the Council in early 1939 had appointed an Emergency Committee of three members with full power to act on behalf of the Council in time of war in all matters of civil defence. This power was later extended to include air-raid precautions. Other important war-time controls were food and fuel rationing. In September 1939 a Food Control Committee, consisting of fifteen members was appointed. The Town Clerk was appointed Food Control Officer. The Food Control Committee had various sub-committees, one of which dealt with British Restaurants and communal feeding. Two Restaurants were established to provide cheap meals to the public. One was located in Borough Road, Seacombe, and the other in Wallasey Road, Liscard. The Committee was also responsible for the reissuing of ration cards.

After the war the Local Authority implemented new Acts of Parliament which included the gas and electricity being transferred to the National Board (1948), institutional care of patients in hospitals has become the responsibility of the Ministry of Health acting through Liverpool Regional Hospital Boards of the Ministry of Health (National Health Service Act, 1948). An Act of Parliament in 1949 saw Housing Improvement grants.

In the General Election of 1945 the Conservatives decided that the Candidate would be Captain Ernest Marples (9 December 1907 – 6 July 1978), who stood against George Reakes and Labour's Tom Finlay Marples was returned to Westminster with a majority 3,810. Marples went on undefeated to represent the Borough as its M.P. until 1974. He was also Minister of Transport (14 October 1959 – 16 October 1964) in Harold MacMillan's government and introduced yellow lines, seat belts and parking meters.

The County Borough of Wallasey ended on 1st April 1974 when the Town became part of the Wirral Metropolitan District.

Mayors of Wallasey

1910/11 James Thomas Chester
1911/12 Dr. John Oldershaw C.B.E
1912/13 Francis Storey
1913/14 Thomas Valentine Burrows
1914/15 Benjamin Swanwick
1915/16 Sidney Stanley Dawson, M.Comm., F.C.A
1916/17 Edwin Peace, O.B.E
1917/18 Frank Fawcett Scott
1918/19 Walter Eastwood
1919/20 Edward Geoffrey Parkinson
1920/21 Charles Hewetson Nelson
1921/22 Augstine Quinn
1922/23 William Smithson Chantrell
1923/24 Alfred Henry Evans
1924/25 Robert Rawlinson
1925/26 John William Holdsworth
1926/27 James Urmson
1927/28 John McMillan, M.B, C.H.B
1928/29 Albert Wrigley, B.A
1929/30 John G. Storey
1930/31 Joseph Hughes
1931/32 David Percy Charlesworth, J.P
1932/33 Frederick Stanley Atkin
1933/34 Henry James Hall
1934/35 Samuel Panter Brick
1935/36 Frederick Henry Thornton, F.C.A
1936/37 George Leonard Reakes, J.P
1937/38 Alfred William Vicary Scoins
1938/39 Arthur Frank Pullen
1939/42 Percy Geden Davies
1943/45 John Pennington
1945/46 William Bruno Millard
1946/47 Bertie George King, J.P
1947/49 James Longworth Gill

1949/50 Robert Yates Knagg
1950/51 James Haywood Wensley, O.B.E,., J.P 1
1951/52 George Henry Young
1952/53 William Osborne Hannaford, J.P
1953/54 John Pennington Ashton, M.C., T.D
1954/55 William Hardy, F.S.M.C
1955/56 John Couper Low
1956/57 Bertram Brooker
1957/58 Henry Bedington
1958/59 Tom Fred Herbert Wilson
1959/60 Mark Edward Bogin
1960/61 Cyril George Edward Dingle. J.P
1961/62 John Stanley Kemp Morris
1962/63 Evan Glyn Roberts, J.P
1963/64 Alfred Ernest Martin
1964/65 Miriam Lyons, S.C.M., S.E.N., M.R.S.H
1965/66 Cecil George Tomkins, M.Inst., M., J.P
1966/67 Thomas Garnett
1967/68 Phoebe Bentzien
1968/69 George Raymond Holmes
1969/70 Sir Fred Harvey Hutty, B.Comm., J.P
1970/71 Walter Jones
1971/72 Harold Tom Kenham Morris, F.C.A
1972/73 John George Clarke, J.P
1973/74 Donald Buchanan Kennedy (Last Mayor)2

Wallasey Members of Parliament

1918/22 Dr Bouverie McDonald (Conservative Unionist)

1922/31 Sir Richard Chadwick (Conservative)

1931/42 Lt. Col. T.T.C Moore-Brabazon (Conservative)

---

1 The Rise & Progress of Wallasey - E.C Woods and P.C Brown
2 Almost An Island - Noel E Smith

1942/45 George L. Reakes (Independent)

1945/74 Ernest Marples (Conservative)

1974 Mrs Lynda Chalker (Conservative) 3

Freedom of Wallasey

1919 Viscount French of Ypres, P.C., G.C.B., O.M., B.C.L., G.C.V.D., K.C.M.G., LL.D.,

1920 Dr. John Oldershaw, C.B.E., M.D., J.P

1920 Alderman Francis Storey, J.P

1932 Alderman Walter Eastwood, J.P

1932 Alderman Edward Geoffrey Parkinson

1960 Cyril George Edward Dingle, J.P

1960 Alderman William Osborne Hannaford, J.P

1960 John Roberts, Esq., M.B.E., J.P

1973 The Rt. Hon. Ernest Marples, P.C., M.P

1973 Alderman John Pennington Ashton, C.B.E., M.C., T.D

1973 Alderman Philip Alfred Bannister

1973 Alderman Mrs Miriam Lyons, S.C.M., S.E.N., M.R.S.N

1973 Alderman Evan Glyn Roberts, J.P

1973 Arthur Graham Harrison, O.B.E., D.S.C 4

---

3 The Wirral Peninsula - Norman Ellison

Honorary Alderman
Alfred Ernest Martin

Freedom of Entry

624 (1st C L C A V) Crane Operating Squadron R.E (T.A) Wallasey"...Right, Privilege and Honour of marching through streets of Wallasey on all ceremonial occasions with bayonet fixed, drum bearing and colours flying". 5

Meeting Of The Wallasey Commissioners

Liverpool Mercury Friday, 8th May 1846

The usual monthly meeting of the Commissioners appointed under the Wallasey Improvement Act was held last evening. At the Queen's Arms, Liscard. Henry Winch, Esq., presided. The proceedings of the Improvement Committee were read in reference to the application for a grant of land at the stone quarry, in Magazines-road, for the purpose of building a school, made by the Rev. Mr. Tobin, and which had been referred back for consideration at a former meeting. The committee recommended, after further considering the subject, that the grant be on the terms formerly stated by them. Mr. Crump, seconded by Mr. Mann, moved the confirmation of the proceedings.6 Mr. North, at considerably length, urged upon the Board the justice of granting a site of land for the purpose of a school as it was the centre of a district where upwards of 280 children were growing up, deficient of all the means of instruction. He contended that the grant would be strictly legal – in fact, there would be quite as much

---

4 Wallasey Now & Then - Irene Birch. Wendy S Bennett, Paul E Davies and Sheila Hamilton

5 A Perambulation of the Hundred of Wirral - Harold Edgar Young

6 Liverpool Mercury Friday, 8th May 1846

legality in giving the site in question for a school as accepting the piece of land, which they had done, from Mr. Littledale, on which they proposed to build offices. Mr. Mawdesley objected to the grant, and considered the members of the Church who asked for it were adequate to carry out such an object as that they sought to obtain by their individual efforts. Mr. Fisher also opposed the grant, contending that the commissioners had no power, under the act if Parliament, to give land for any purpose, as they merely held it for the benefit of the freeholders. He moved, as an amendment, the confirmation of the proceedings of the Improvement Committee, except so much as related to the school and the grant of land; the motion was seconded by Mr. Parry. Mr. Halliday supported the grant, considering that education, above all other things, was the most valuable property which could be conferred on the community. The grant was supported by Mr. Mann, and after some remarks by other members, a division took place, when the amendment was carried by a majority of eleven to eight. The application for the grant of land was, consequently, rejected. – The proceedings of the Finance Committee were read and confirmed. – A motion was adopted to the effect that the Improvement Committee were to report on the property of appointing a person as foreman over the men employed in making the roads, at a salary not exceeding 27s per week. – Mr. Healey having drawn the attention of the commissioners to the practice of carrying away gravel from the shores of the river, it was referred to the Improvement Committee to consider the expediency of making application to the Commissioners of Woods and Forests, that the gravel on the sea side, within the jurisdiction of Wallasey, be reserved to the use of the authorities. The proceedings terminated shortly before nine o'clock.

Liverpool Mercury Friday, 6th November 1846

The usual monthly meeting of this body was held last evening, at the Queen's Arms Hotel, Liscard, Henry Winch, Esq., in the chair. The proceedings of the Finance Committee referred to a meeting which had been convened by the Birkenhead Dock Commissioners, relative to the construction of the sea wall on the north side of the pool, and the neccessity of raising funds from the landowners and others for carrying the work into execution. If a sufficient sum were not advanced for the purpose, it had been imtimated that the Dock Commissioners would apply to Parliament to confine their operations to the south side of the Pool. A meeting of the landowners is to be held at Wallasey, to consider the subject, and the Law clerk was instruxted to attend. Mr. Mann, seconded by Mr. Mawdsley, moved that the improvement of the road to Wallasey Village and Carrion Hill be postponed, which subject was referred to in the proceedings of the Improvement Committee. After some discussion the amendment was put and lost, and the proceedings were therefore confirmed. The proceedings of the Finanace Committee contained a recommendation that a rate of 1s. 3d. in the pound be laid in the ensuing year. Mr.Meadows, seconded by Mr. Edwards, moved that the rate be 9d. in the pound, and that the proceedings of the committee be confirmed, subject to the lateration. Mr. Atherton stated that the property of the township last yer was £31,161, abd this year £32,000; a rate of 1s. 3d. in the pound would produce £2000. which would be required for the current expenses and the improvements recommended vy the Improvement Committee.7 Mr. Halliday supported a rate of 1s; and, on a division, the proceedings of the Finance Committee were confirmed with such alteration. The Law clerk read copies of a correspondence which had passed vetween himself, Mr. Armistead, and Dr. Byrth, relative to the rent charge. It appeared that Mr. Armistead objected to the proposal of the Commissioners to leave the matter to the decision of counsel, but offered an annual [ayment in lieu of the rate, to settle the matter in an amicable manner. although not admitting his liability. The letters were referred to the Finaance Committee, with instructions to take such preceedings as they might deem nexessary. Mr. Meadow's brought forward a motion to the effect that the salary of Mr. West,

---

7 Liverpool Mercury Friday, 6th November 1846

the surveyor, namely, £125, should be given to him in full of all demands, and that he should not be allowed any extra charges. He objected a claim of £40 made by the surveyor on account of a survey made for water and gas. Several members considered the claim made by Mr. West as perfectly justifiable, as he had performed a service not within the scope of the act; it was, however, desirable that he should show hoe the money had been expended. Mr. Fisher thought the surveyor bound to perform whatever the commissioners required, except in special cases, where he might have to get extra aid. The discussion had not terminated when our reporter left the room, at half-past eight o'clock.

The Seven Schools of Wallasey

Education in Wallasey was extremely developed compared to many places in Wirral at the time. The first evidence of a school is the burial of a headmaster in St Hilary's in 1595. From this point we know that the children of Wallasey received some sort of education. Records show that sometime after; a separate school building was built on the site of St Hillary's Parish making it the first school in Wallasey.

After that a new second school was erected in Breck Road in 1799. The small school building was to educate the children incorporating a 6 day week for the scholars. As the population grew, so too did the amount of pupils attending the school. In 1834 records show that there were 83 pupils using this small school. It was soon decided that a new school house was required where the young children could be educated separately. Shortly after in 1840 a new third school house was built in Nelsons gutter and the infants transferred to this building for their education. This school remained in use until 1907 when it became surplus to requirement.

A fourth school was opened in 1854 to cope with the growing amount of pupils. This School was built in a small lane known as Back Lane. The school ran successfully for many years although it was plagued with building problems from the outset, ranging from structural deficiencies to poor lighting. Years later the name of Back Lane was changed to what we call today "St Georges Road".

In 1876 a fifth school was opened in Withens Lane in an area known as Flag Field. This was a name given locally due to the large flag stones which were sunk into the ground to allow easier movement and stop people from having to walk in mud during the winter months. The school costs exceeded a record £13,600 and were used as an Elementary School for both boys & girls of Wallasey Village.

In 1911 a sixth school was built, and the old school was demolished. The new school had many new amenities including playing fields and classroom equipment. But again as numbers began to grow, the board began to look for a new and bigger school to run.

In 1967 a seventh school was opened formally by H.R.H the Duchess of Kent and was known as the new "Wallasey Grammar School". And so at the end of the term the pupils left the School at Withens Lane and began their new term at the Grammar school which was built in Birkett Avenue on the newly created Leasowe Estate. The school was later named Henry Meoles Senior Comprehensive School.

Wallasey Town Hall

The image above is the original town hall of Wallasey that was situated on the corner of Church Street in Egremont.

28

Wallasey Town Hall was built to replace the old Town Hall and is a magnificent renaissance-style building in brick with Darley Dale stone cladding. The Foundation stone was laid into position by means of electricity, by King George V in 1914, while 9,000 school children sang in the choir.

The above image shows the town hall in the background whilst looking down Demesne Street.

Its nickname 'back-to-front' town hall arose as it was built to face the river and has a fine flight of steps leading up from the promenade. It was adapted as a military hospital in World War I and suffered a direct hit in World War II. Surmounted by a 7ft copper urn the town hall stands 180ft above promenade level and the BBC sometimes used it for television shows, wrestling and snooker matches. Wallasey became part of the Metropolitan Borough of Wirral in 1974 and council meetings are still held there.

Wallasey Properties for Sale

Here is a guide to the price's of housing to buy and let in days gone by as advertised in the local paper.

Liverpool Mercury Thursday, May 18th 1899

Properties to Let & Buy

Apartment to be let

Egremont – 3 Serpentine Road – Super APARTMENTS, with or without partial board, for Gentleman dining in town; moderate terms.

Egremont – Comfortable APARTMENTS; suit two gentlemen or married couple. Terms moderate – Apply 19 Pool Road.

Egremont – Front APRTMENTS: would suit gentleman; good cooking and attendance; bath, &c. – 6, Blenheim Road, facing Mariners' Home, off Promenade (five minutes from ferry).

Egremont –Front Sitting Room and Bedroom, bath, piano and every home comfort; near to tram and ferry; 10s per week. – 12 Brompton Avenue, Egremont.

Egremont – 40, Claredon Road – SITTING ROOM and single or Double Bedded Room; near ferry and bus.
Egremont – Comfortable BED and SITTING ROOM (bath, hot and cold water); near ferry, no other lodgers or children; terms moderate – 34, Wright Street.

Egremont – APARTMENTS for two or three Gentlemen in well furnished house; terms moderate. – 60 Falkland Road.

Egremont – Comfortable Front APARTMENTS, close to both ferries and promenade; bath, piano; terms moderate – 37, Littledale Road.

Liscard – 4, Sheen Road, Seabank Road. – A Gentleman desired to join another in Sitting Room; separate bedroom; baths; close to promenade.

Near Promenade and Egremont Ferry. – One or two BEDROOMS, with or without partial Board; no children – 47, Rudgrave Square.

To be let – Unfurnished Houses

Egremont – 59 Charlotte Road, two sitting, three bedrooms, bath, w.c; beautiful; rent £19

Egremont – 4, Ramle Terrace. Rice Lane, containing two

entertaining and five bedrooms, &c.; good garden; rent £2 15s. per month clear. Key next door. – W.E. Nelson. 22 Lord Street. Telephone 5876.

Egremont – 19, Wensley Avenue; two sitting and four bedrooms, bath, w.c., hot and cold water; rent £2 7s 8d. per month clear. Key next door. W.E. Nelson. 22 Lord Street. Telephone 5876.

Liscard – 6, Cecil Road – Newly decorated, six roomed HOUSE; large yard, few minutes from ferry: key at No. 2. – Apply J.Marsh and Co. 9 Union Court, Castle Street, Liverpool. Telephone 6808.

Liscard – 8, Lancaster Avenue, containing two kitchens; three bedrooms, parlour, bath, and w.c; rent 7s. 6d. week clear; key at No. 5. -- J. Bridgeford and Co. 22 Lord Street. Tel. 7080.
Liscard – 1, Marion Villas, Burns Avenue, Semi-detached House (close to tram route); two sitting and five bedrooms; rent £23. Key next door. -- W.E. Nelson. 22 Lord Street. Telephone 5876.

Liscard – 17 and 19 Massey Park – Excellent HOUSES, newly decorated; eight apartments, bath, &c.; £20 clear. Keys at 21. – Apply Fisher and Co. Garston.

Liscard – Parkfield Drive and Mill Lane – Cheapest HOUSES in the locality; each contains four bedrooms, bathroom, hot and cold water, two parlours, kitchen, and scullery, and good yard; rent only £2 3s. 4d per month clear of all taxes.

Liscard – 76 Seaview Road, Liscard, containing two sitting and four bedrooms, and usual conveniences; large garden at back; rent £28 - W.E. Nelson. 22 Lord Street. Telephone 5876.

New Brighton – 3, Mount Pleasant Road. £30 per annum.

New Brighton – No. 1 Mount Road, Upper Brighton. Semi-detached; drawing, dining, and breakfast rooms; five bedrooms; kitchens on ground floor; washing kitchen, larder, wine cellar, butler's pantry, bath, w.c, hot and cold water; gardens back and front; rent £45. Key at 25, Mount Road – N.B. – Has splendid and uninterrupted views over Wallasey; the Welsh mountains, and the Great Orme's Head. – Apply to John Hughes, 14. Tower Buildings, Old Churchyard.

New Brighton – 53, Meadow Street. Rent £20.

New Brighton – St. George's Mount – "WOODCOTE'; three entertaining rooms, seven bedrooms, &c; sheltered and healthy situation; pleasant view front and back. Apply next door.

New Brighton – No. 1, Pickering Road; contains breakfast room, two parlours, five bedrooms, kitchen, and several pantries; rent £40. – Apply to W. And J. Venmore, 200, Scotland Road, Liverpool.

New Brighton – 4, Prescott Street, - Large SHOP, with excellent windows, suitable for grocers, draper's, or other business; surrounded by increasing residential houses; good opening for a branch establishment; house attached. Key at No. 8 – W.E. Nelson, 22 Lord S Treet. Telephone 5876.

Seacombe – 4, The Grove, Somerville, Semi-detached HOUSE (ten minutes walk from ferry); two entertaining and four bed rooms; rent £23 per annum. Key next door – W.E. Nelson, 22 Lord Street. Telephone 5878.

Seacombe – 46, Kenilworth Road, Rent £2 16s. 8d
Seacombe – 48, Kenilworth Road, Rent £2 16s. 8d

Seacombe – 65, Poulton Road – Conveniently situated. House to be let: rent £27.

Seacombe – 17, Rappart Road; parlour, kitchens, three bedrooms, bath, hot and cold water; rent £1.9s; monthly clear – E.A. Kenyon, 13 Massey Park, Liscard.

Wallasey – Pretty new HOUSES, Keswick Road; seven rooms and small conservatory; £30 per annum; five minutes from railway station and gold links. – Voughan, 13 Leasowe Avenue, Wallasey.

Wallasey – (near Station, Shore and Gold Links). – To be Let 1 and 9, Moreton Grove; four bedrooms, bath, hot and cold, &c.; two entertaining rooms; kitchen, scullery, &c; rent £25.

Wallasey – 5, Wallacre Road – Capital Family House, five minutes from station, containing two entertaining rooms, two kitchens, five bedrooms, bath, lavatory, &c., and fitted with all modern conveniences; garden back and front; rent £30 per annum – Apply J. Bridgeford and Co. 22 Lord Street. Tel. 7080.

To be let – Business Premises

Liscard Village – Good Blacksmith Shop. Rent low. – Wensley and Parle, 17a South Castle Street.

Seacombe – 154 Brighton Street, Seacombe, to be let; rent £45; fixtures and electric fittings extra – Apply Bell Williams, Son, and Wireman, 40, North John Street, Liverpool.

Seacombe – St. Paul's Road, No. 116 – First class SHOP, suitable for butcher, fishmonger, &c.; rent £30. –J.Stanley, 23, South Castle Street, Liverpool.

Seacombe – To be let, FRUIT and FLORIST'S: splendid opening for greengrocery business; Fixtures cheap – Apply 13, Poulton Road, Seacombe.8

---

8 Liverpool Mercury Thursday, May 18th 1899

Wallasey Local Board of Health

Liverpool Mercury Friday, 7th March 1856

The monthly meeting of this board was held last evening, at the Public Offices, Egremont, Mr. Pooley in the chair; and the other members present were Messrs Penny, Hill, Neville, Wilson, Roberts, Odell, and W.R. Coulborn.

A special meeting of the board was held on the 14th ult., at which it was agreed to apply to the General Board of Health for leave to borrow the sum of £3000 for constructing Trafalgar Road, King Street and Brighton Street.

The minutes of the works and health committee were read, and, on the motion of Mr. Pooley, were confirmed. – In answer to Mr. Odell, the chairman stated that all openings into the main sewers from the dwelling houses were to be made at the expense of the landlords of the property.

The proceedings of the finance, watch, and bye-law committee, which comprised nothing worthy of record, were read, and, on the motion of Mr. Hill, were confirmed. – The clerk read a letter from Mr. Thomas Scambler, superintendent of police, tendering his resignation, after serving in the capacity for 15 years. – A question was asked whether there was a member if the force who was suitable to fill the situation, but the board did not appear to think that a competent superintendent could be raised from the ranks of the Wallasey police force. – Mr. Odell observed that it might be gratifying for the officers who held subordinate situations to know that if their conduct, knowledge, and experience were such as to qualify them for promotion to a superior situation, the board would do so; but he regretted to say he did not think there was one of their present officers who was fit to be promoted to so responsible a situation as superintendent. – After a short conversation, the board resolved to advertise for a superintendent in the place of Mr. Scambler.

The Law-clerk read a petition to be presented to the House of Commons against the Liverpool and Birkenhead Dock Bill. The principal opposition to the bill was grounded on the fact that the parish of Wallasey was not properly represented in the proposed measure. – A short conversation ensued, in which the chairman remarked that the petition did great credit to the law-clerk, as it embraced all the points which affected the board, and which could not fail to attract the attention of the legislature. – The petition was adopted, and the seal of the board was affixed thereto.

The Law-clerk read an amended description of the properties in connection with the New Brighton, Egremont, and Seacombe ferries to be rated to the general district rate. The new rate had been objected to by Mr. Coulborn, and it appeared he had appealed to the Court of Queen Bench. – Mr Hill moved, pro forma, the adoption of the "amended description," observing that the question between Mr. Coulborn and the board was going to be raised in a friendly kind of way; there was nothing unpleasant about it. They merely wished to know whether Mr. Coulborn's view of the case or that of the board was correct. – Mr Coulborn said that the "amendment" was quite in order; be only objected to it for the purpose if guarding himself. – The proposition was agreed to.

A letter was read from Mr. John Hewitt, superintendent of the Liverpool fire brigade, offering to supply that board with a fire-engine similar to the one he had just constructed for the Birkenhead Commissioners. – The letter was referred.[9]

---

[9] Liverpool Mercury Friday, 7th March 1856

Some routine business, including some appeals against the rates, followed, and the board adjourned.

Liverpool Mercury Friday, 4th August 1871

The monthly meeting of this board was held yesterday, at the public offices, Egremont, the members present being the Rev. W.C. Greene (in the chair), Messrs. Littledale, Hughes, Mason, Davies, Skinner, Cowan, Wensley, Isherwood, Bowdler, Couldwell and Layland.

THE WALLASEY TRAMWAYS BILL:

The Chairman said that a day or two ago a paragraph in a Liverpool newspaper to the affect that the Wallasey Tramways Bill had been postponed til next year. This, however, was a mistake. The Metropolitan Tramway Bill had been postponed till next session, but all the other bills (including the Wallasey bill), which had been joined into one as a separate bill, had already passed the committee of the House of Lords, and would no doubt, be passed this session. The chairman added that if the laying down of the tramways in Wallasey was not begun this year, it would be commenced early next year.

THE RIVER APPROACHES:

The Chairman next returned to the settlement of the long vexed question of the river approaches. The board, he said, had gained advantages which they never expected. They had incurred considerable expense in their opposition to the Mersey Dock Bill, but if they had not stirred themselves in the matter they would have been left in the lurch.
Mr. Couldwell inquired what the expense would be.
Mr. Ishwerwood – Perhaps £1000
The Chairman thought the board might now rest and be satisfied. The services rendered by Mr. Laird, M.P., in the matter, had been very valuable, and he had no hesitation in saying that it was owing to the indefatigable exertions of that gentleman, both in Parliament and

*out of it, that a scheme had been carried which would be highly beneficial to all concerned. He moved the following resolution :-
"That the thanks of the board be given to Mr. J. Laird, M.P., for the valuable service rendered by him in the negotiations relating to the river approaches on the Liverpool side of the Mersey; and that in the opinion of this board it's chiefly owing to the ability and energy of Mr. Laird that a question so intimately affecting the interests of all the ferries, and consequently of the owners of property and ratepayers on the Cheshire side, has, after a suspense of more than 20 years, been satisfactory settled."
Mr. Littledale seconded the resolution, and endorsed all that had been said by the chairman respecting the services of Mr. Laird. He also spoke highly of the services of Mr. Greene and Mr. Simpson, solicitor, in the matter.*

The resolution was carried unanimously.

HEALTH COMMITTEE - THE SANITARY STATE OF SEACOMBE

*It appeared from the registrar's return that the number of death in the parish during the past month was 32, including 4 from smallpox, 1 from typhoid, 1 from scarlatina, and 3 from measles; the number for the corresponding period last year being 14, including 1 from scarlatina and 2 from diarrhoea.
Mr. Davies moved the conformation of the proceedings of the committee.
Mr. Bowdler objected to a recommendation to licence a slaughter house belonging to Mr. John Lee, butcher, behind the Stanley Arms, Seacombe, on the ground that the premises were in a densely populated district.
The Chairman referred to some observations made by Mr. Couldwell, at a late meeting of the committee, respecting the sanitary state of Seacombe. On going home it struck him that an inquiry should be made into the state of Seacombe, and accordingly, in company with Mr. Lea, surveyor to the board, and Mr. McPherson,*

medical officer of the Wallasey Dispensary, he went on Tuesday morning and inspected some of the worst places at Seacombe. From what he then saw he was bound to state that Mr. Couldwell had not at all exaggerated the state of things at Seacombe. He now solemnly and publicly declared that the state of things at Seacombe was discreditable, not only to the board, but to their officials and all concerned. He blamed the owners of property, who had crowded as many dwellings as possible on the smallest possible space. In fact, the wonder in his mind was not that scarlatina and smallpox visited Seacombe, but having got there, that those diseases should ever leave the place.10 He also attributed the state of things at Seacombe to the filthy habits of some of the inhabitants; but this state of things had been much aggravated by the neglect of the board and their officials. He was prepared to take his share of the responsibility, for he admitted that when he was a member of the committee they were very lax in the performance of their duty. It struck him that there was a great want of inspection. He was told there was a theoretical emptying of the middens, but he was informed that some of them were not emptied for six months. Other places were preparing for a visit of cholera, but he believed that if the diseases visited Seacombe it would be some time before it left. He confined his remarks to certain portions of Seacombe; he did not believe the parish generally to be unhealthy. He was afraid that Mr. Davies, the chairman of the committee, had seen these nuisances through the eyes of Mr. Lea, their surveyor, and that Mr. Lea had seen them through the eyes of the officials under him, and consequently nothing had been done. He concluded by offering to meet the committee with the view of suggesting a remedy of the state of things at Seacombe.

Mr Bowdler said he had intended to make an inspection of Seacombe, but having heard that the chairman was going round he refrained from doing so. He had seen a portion of the district, and he did not think they could find a parallel case in the worst districts of

---

10 Liverpool Mercury Friday, 4th August 1871

Liverpool. The courts were constructed in such a manner that a breath of wind could not get into them, unless there was a complete hurricane.

Mr. Davies said that if the chairman had intimated to him that he intended to make an inspection of Seacombe he would have been glad to accompany him. There was no doubt the sanitary arrangements at Seacombe were very bad, but he did not think blame ought to be attributed to the board of their offices. Their men went daily into the courts and alleys to clean them. He considered that a great number of these nuisances were the result of the filthy habits of the people, and it was almost impossible to keep clean the places where they lived.

Mr. Cowan remarked that some gentlemen who complained of nuisances permitted greater nuisances on their own premises. For instance, there was a smoky chimney at Mr. Bowdler's works, and another smoky chimney at Liscard. (Laughter)

Mr. Lea (the surveyor), in answer to Mr. Skinner, said he had received no complaints of the neglect at Seacombe.

Mr. Couldwell said people would not take the trouble of sending complaints to the board, and therefore he considered it the duty of Mr. Lea to go to Seacombe and see whether these nuisances existed or not.

After some further conversation, the proceedings were confirmed, it being understood that the chairman would meet the committee to consider what was to be done. The recommendation about the slaughter was referred back.

FERRY COMMITTEE

From the ferry accounts it appeared that the receipts last month were £3890 1s. 10d., against £4459 10s. 6d. The receipts from the 1st January to the 31st July, this year, were £18,302 15s. 5d., against £18,136 in the corresponding period of last year. The working *expenses during the latter period were – This year @ Working expenses, £9486; interest and sinking fund, £4490. Last year : Working expenses £12,336 8s. 10d., interest and sinking fun, £4491 1s. 9d.*

THE IMPROVEMENT OF SEACOMBE FERRY

Mr. Mason moved the confirmation of the proceedings of the ferry committees, which included the following resolution :- That it's desirable to carry into effect as early as possible the scheme for the improvement of Seacombe Ferry, approved by the board on the 4th of May last; and, with that view, that it be recommended that the manager be instructed to prepare the necessary specification and detailed drawings, in order that tenders for the execution of the work may be advertised for so soon as the sanction of Admiral Evans is obtained.

Mr. Mason said it was not in the power of the board to go at present into the large scheme of improved approaches at Seacombe, and after giving the matter every consideration it had been decided to adopt a plan which in its carrying out would not exceed £3000.
Mr. Davies moved, and Mr. Couldwell seconded, that the recommendation be referred back to the ferry committee.
Mr. Mason, in reply to Mr. Couldwell, said the expense would come out of the revenue of the board.

Mr. Couldwell contended that the board had no power to pay for the work out of revenue. If they spent one penny out of the revenue the item would be not only objected to before the auditor, but a protest would be sent to the Government. The people of Seacombe were not going to do with an expenditure on the ferry of only £3000.

Mr. Littledale – Where are you to get more?

Mr. Couldwell said the money should be provided in proper form, by calling a public meeting. The Seacombe people were determined not to be put off with £3000, unless the members of the board paid it out of their own pockets.

Mr. Skinner and Mr. Cowan spoke in favour of the resolution of the committee.

After some further conversation, the resolution to spend £3000 at Seacombe was agreed to; but, at the request of the ferry manager an amendment was carried that an engineer should be employed to prepare the plans and specifications.

FINANCE COMMITTEE

On the recommendation of this committee a sum of 100 guineas was voted to Mr. Roberts, the district auditor, for auditing the accounts of the board.

This was the whole of the business, and the board adjourned.

Wallasey and the Jubilee

Liverpool Mercury Monday, 25th July 1887

Jubilee Demonstration at Wallasey

Owing to the prevalence of measles amongst many of the children attending the elementary schools of Wallasey, the committee who had the management of the Jubilee celebration very properly determined not to hold the demonstration on the 21st ultimo, but to postpone it until a later date.

The epidemic of measles having now passed away, the celebration took place on Saturday last, and afforded much enjoyment and pleasure to the large number of juveniles who were privileged to participate in it. Some week ago more than one public meeting was held to devise the best means of celebrating her Majesty's Jubilee, and it was resolved that the demonstration should take the form of a treat to the children attending the elementary schools of the parish. To defray the expense the sum of £150 was subscribed, and with the money the committee were not only enabled to provide a substantial tea for the juveniles, but to present each child with a neat mug, or cup, bearing the likeness of the Queen, as a souvenir of the interesting event.

The children assembled at their respective schools about two o'clock, and accompanied by their teachers and the various ministers of religion, marched to the large field known as the Old Wallasey Grammar School ground, which they reached shortly before three o'clock. The weather was beautifully fine, and there was a great gathering of spectators. No fewer than 4200 children assembled, and as each school exhibited a profusion of small flags and banners, the sight was a very pretty one.

The following schools were represented:- Seacombe: St. Paul's, St. Joseph's Roman Catholic, Mission House, Wesleyan and Egremont. New Brighton: St. Peter and St. Paul's Roman Catholic, St. James (Egerton Street), St. James (Magazine Lane), and Rake Lane. Wallasey and Liscard: Wallasey Boys', Wallasey Girls, Poulton, St. Mary's. Amongst the gentlemen present were Mr. W.Chambres, chairman of the committee; Mr. W. Secretary; Mr. F.J.Harrison, honorary treasurer; Rev. W.E.B. Gunn, the Rev.Dr.Muir, the Rev. Canon Firth, the Rev. Canon Maraden, the Rev. A.E.P. Grey, the Rev. J.H.D. Cochrane, the Rev. Mr. Pinhorn, the Rev. J.F. Howson, the Rev. R.J. Weatherhead, the Rev. C.J. Foster, the Rev. Father Stanton, the Rev. R. Peart, the Rev. E.Stockdale,; Messrs. G.H. Peers, T.R. Bulley, W.T. Jacob, G.W. Fisher, R.J. Francis, W.B. Marshall, F. Pooley, &c.

With the children were five or six bands of music, and the procession on the field were headed by the New Brighton battery of the 1st Cheshire and Carnarvonshire Artillery Volunteers, under the command of Captain Parker and Lieutenant Nolid, After the juveniles had been marshalled on the ground, Mr W. Chambres delivered a short address, in which he congratulated all present upon having the opportunity to assemble to do honour to one whom God had spared to reign over the country for 50 years, and who during that time had discharged every duty as a Queen, as a wife, and as a mother, in a manner that had won the approbation of the nation. He did not wish to detain the large assembly, but he would again congratulate them on the fineness of the weather, and it was their earnest wish that God would spare her majesty for many years to occupy the high position she now held, and that she would continue to discharge all the duties appertaining to the Throne with the same zeal and fidelity that had marked her previous career. Enthusiastic cheers followed, and the juveniles sang the National Anthem and two hymns in capital style, the playing of the bands adding greatly to the general affect. Preceded by the volunteers, the children then "marched past" in good order, and, leaving the field, proceeded along Penkett Road to Manor Road. Here the procession separated, and the juveniles marched to their respective schools, where they were treated to tea and other refreshment on the most liberal scale. Sports and different amusements concluded the juvenile Jubilee demonstration in the parish of Wallasey. 11

---

11 Liverpool Mercury Monday, 25th July 1887

Liscard Castle

The building known as Liscard Castle once stood in the area which is today known as Castle Road and Turret Road, from which the street names are derived. The old house was built in 1815 and named Marine Villa. The building takes its nick name of "Liscard Castle" from its castle like appearance of its architecture. The house sported several turrets and thick walls, with intricate detailing such as shields and stone animals and crests. John Marsden was a resident of Marine Villa for many years and from his name the building was also given several other nick names such as; "Marsden Castle" and "Marsden Folly". In addition, the road we know today as Sea View; was originally called "Marsden's Lane", and this was named after Mr Marsden himself.

Liscard Castle, Liscard

Many years after the death of Mr Marsden, the building was separated into 3 residencies. They were called "The Castle, The Tower and The Turret". As time went by the building fell into a poor state of repair and became a victim of neglect. The large building was eventually pulled down in the spring of 1902. The stone lions from the building were said to have been taken from the site and disappeared for decades before finally reappearing on Dr Lyburn's house in Manor Road. The lion then apparently went missing never to be found a short time after.

Liscard Hall

A successful Liverpool merchant known as Sir John Tobin built Liscard Hall in 1835 on a plot of land originally owned by the Prior of Birkenhead. One of the fields that was bought was known as "Moorhey Field" and the other was called "Middle Moorhey". The land was purchased from F.R.Price, Esq, and the large project of building the Hall was undertaken. After several years the large hall was completed, at which time Sir John name it "Moor Heys House" after the fields which it was built upon. The building was later renamed "Liscard Hall" and fortunately for us this brilliant display of19th century neo-classical architecture still sits proudly within central park, dominating its skyline. The hall consists of five bays by six bays, with pillared porch and a pediment roof. Anarticle in the New Brighton Walrus also contains the following information: Sir John Tobin also had a fishing lodge at the very edge of the river, at a spot called Codling Gap. Opposite here he moored his yacht, which he used to cross the river in preference to using the ferryboats. Lady Tobin always kept a telescope in a room at the Hall, the window of which commanded a view of the river, so that when it was stormy she could watch the boat crossing, and seeing her husband's safe arrival, be relieved of her anxiety at the earliest possible moment.

After the death of Sir John Tobin, Liscard Hall was passed down to his son in law Mr Harold Littledale who later died in 1889. A little known fact about the strange past of the hall is that Harold's son, wanted to marry his cousin (Sir John Tobin's grand-daughter), which was legal at the time; however his father objected and he soon became a recluse living at the Hall. He also died in 1889 shortly after his father and is buried in St Hillary's graveyard.

Death of Sir John Tobin

Liverpool Mercury (2nd Edition) Friday, 28th February 1851

We learn with regret that Sir John Tobin, Knight, died at his residence, last night, at Liscard Hall. The deceased was upwards of eighty years of age.12

Liverpool Mercury Monday, 4th March 1851

As we announced in our second edition of Friday, Sir John Tobin died at his residence, in Liscard, on Thursday night, in the eighty-ninth year of his age. For many years Sir John had been connected

---

12 Liverpool Mercury (2nd Edition) Friday, 28th February 1851

48

with the mercantile interests of Liverpool, and stood very high in the commercial world, as an enterprising merchant and an honourable man. The Isle of Man was Sir John's native place, and in his earlier years he went to sea. During the wars of Napoleon he commanded on his own account a privateer. He was one of the first to enter upon the African palm oil trade – a traffic which he superseded the slave trade. He next turned his attention to steam navigation, at a time when it was gradually rising into importance, and built and equipped at his own expense the largest steamer which had ever been launched into the Mersey. This fine vessel, which was called the Liverpool, made several trips to New York, and was then sold to the Oriental Steam Navigation Company. Sir John Tobin was one of the first to appreciate the capabilities of the Cheshire shore as a place of dock accommodation, and took an active part, along with Mr. Laird, in the purchase of the Wallasey estate. He was Mayor of the town in 1820, when George the Fourth ascended the throne, and received the honour of Knighthood. The widow of Sir John survives him. He leaves four children – the Rev. John Tobin, the incumbent of Egremont, Mrs. Cockshott, Mrs. Col.Reddie, and Mrs. Harold Littledale.13

After Harold Littledale died the Hall and grounds were purchased by the Wallasey Local Board (Now Wirral Council) and opened to the public for the first time. The grounds were quickly refurbished and became known as Central Park.

---

13 Liverpool Mercury Monday, 4th March 1851

For a while after, the building was used as an art college for the borough which was received with great interest. However the number of students enrolling dropped sharply during World War II. The Home Guard HQ shared the accommodation and some of its members were induced to become students at the school. The Art College closed in 1982 at which time it was leased to a local company until 2003 at which time it was retaken by the Council. In 2003 a council document revealed that the Hall required approximately £285,000 worth of work to bring it up to a required standard.

Sadly on the 7th July 2008 due to frequent access by vandals to the old manor house, a fire was started that swept through the building engulfing it in flames and seriously damaging the structure. The follow day the building was knocked down and became another part of Wallasey's quickly disappearing history.

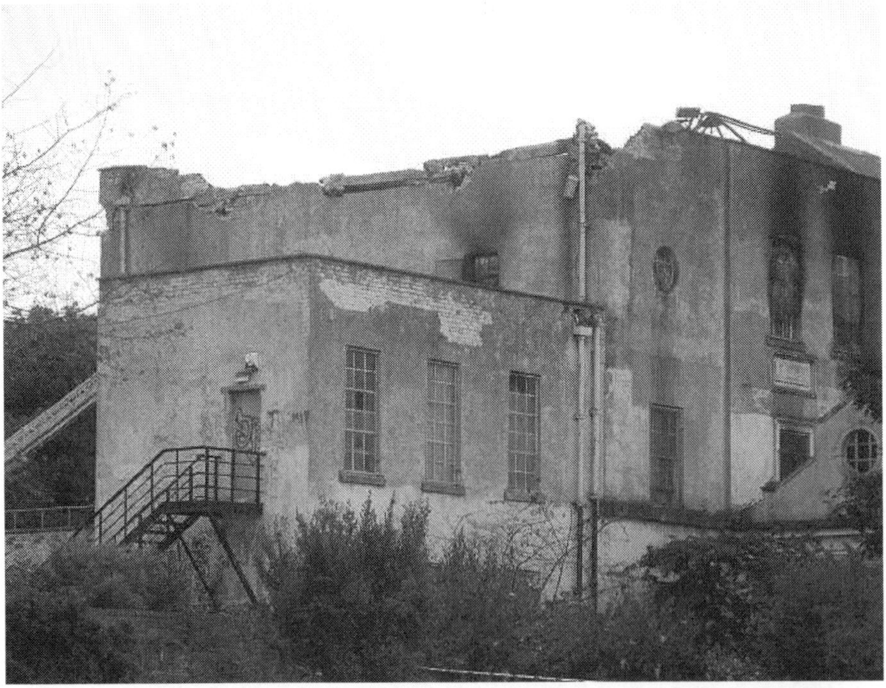

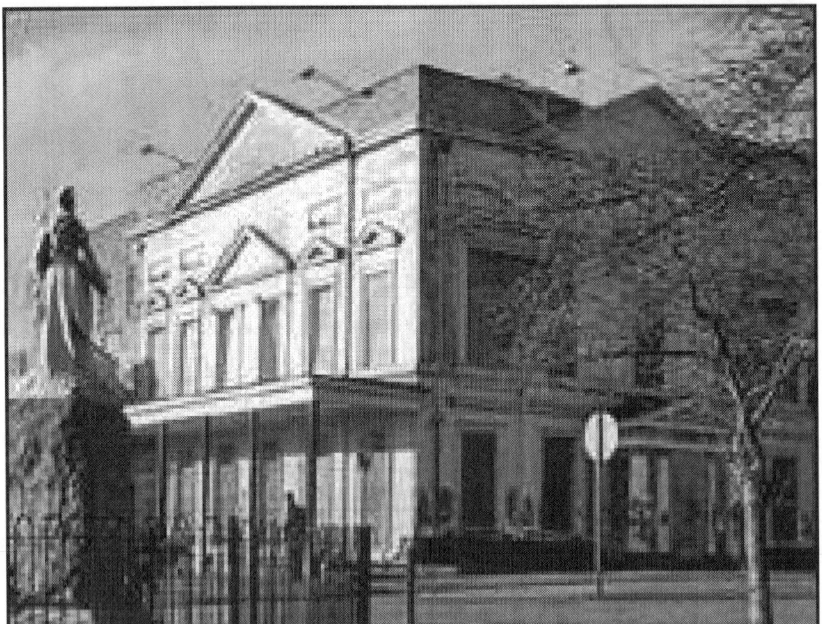

BBC News Tuesday, 8 July 2008

Historic hall to be knocked down

An historic Wirral building is being demolished after it was badly damaged by a fire.

The blaze swept through the Grade II Listed Liscard Hall, in Wallasey, overnight on Sunday.

Wirral Council said structural engineers examined the building after the fire and decided it was unsafe and would have to be demolished.

The hall, in Central Park, was built in about 1840 as a home for Sir John Tobin, a Liverpool merchant.

Up to eight fire engines were sent to Liscard Hall on Sunday night to tackle the fire, which caused the hall's roof to partially collapse.

On Tuesday, a Wirral Council spokesman said: "Following Sunday night's fire which caused extensive damage to Liscard Hall, structural engineers have decided that the building has been made unsafe and will therefore have to be demolished."

Security guards are being placed at the site around the clock to prevent any vandalism at the site.

"While the council remains deeply saddened by the fire, we remain committed to putting the site to good public use and will bring forward proposals in the near future," the spokesman added.[14]

---

[14] BBC News Tuesday, 8 July 2008

St Johns Church

St John's Church is situated next to Central Park on Liscard Road. It's quite a unique church which stands out from others with its large stone columns and Grecian architecture. The church dates back to 1832 when its voluminous rooms would welcome up to nearly 2000 parishioners at a single time. In addition it also boasts a record of having the largest unsupported ceiling on the Wirral. The church was erected at the request of Sir John Tobin and was built from locally quarried materials from the Newlands Drive Quarry.

Liscard House

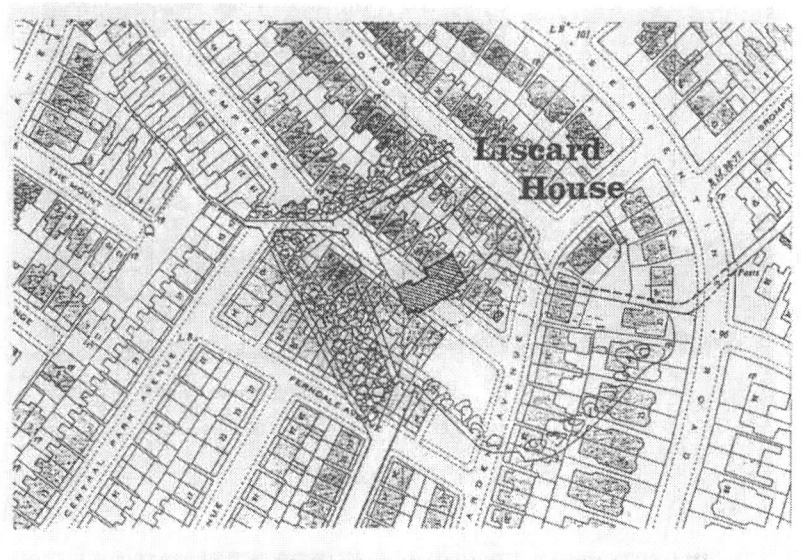

SITE OF "LISCARD HOUSE" IN 1875 IN RELATION TO HOUSES IN 1926

Opposite Liscard Hall, on the east side of Liscard Road, stood 'Liscard House', approached through gates, known as 'Tobin Gates', and along a carriage-drive the site of which is now occupied by Chatsworth Avenue. The house was situated at what is now the junction of Eaton Avenue and Ferndale Avenue, and was built about 1833 by Sir John Tobin for his son, the Revd. John Tobin, M.A, the first incumbent of St. John's Church, Egremont. St. John's Church was erected at the same time on 7,000 square yards of land given by Sir John Tobin, who also contributed at least 1,000 towards the cost. The Rev. John Tobin, who was only 24 at the time of his appointment to St. John's had previously been a curate at Burnley. His wife was a local girl, Emily Ann Arnaud, and a portion, if not all, of the 'North Meade' estate, on which the Town Hall now stands, formed part of his Marriage Settlement until 1845, when it was sold to Misses Hannah, Cicely and Mary Leyland, who conducted a boarding-school there for some years.

The Rev. Tobin, a member of the Liverpool Committee for the Relief of Widows and Orphans of Clergymen, was a man of ample proportions, and the story goes that on one occasion he had crossed the river when there were a number of trippers from Lancashire on board. In those days the gangway planks, were without handrails, and were not too secure, and the Revd. Tobin overheard one of the strangers about to land say to his companion, "Wait a minute and let the fat old chap go first, it it bears him, it will be safe for us".

The Revd. Tobin remained at Liscard Hall until 1862, when he resigned and moved to the South of England. He finally died at Caversham, Oxford, in 1874, at the age of 65. For some years 'Liscard House' was occupied by Mr Joseph Donnell, a Corn Merchant, and a later tenant was Mr John Cattle, who in 1886 purchased the old Grosvenor Brewery in Borough Road, Seacombe. By 1898 Chatsworth Avenue had been constructed, but the house was still standing, although it had been empty for three years. It was demolished soon afterwards.

Highfield House

Highfield House was first built about 1850 by Thomas Peers, a Cotton Broker, as a private residence. It was eventually purchased by the Corporation in 1919 from the Reece family whose house it had finally become and in order to cater for new arrivals in the town 'Highfield' was converted into Wallasey's first Maternity Hospital and opened in 1921.

In its term as a private residence it was the home of several families at various times. Its first owner, Thomas Peers, died on the middle 1850's, and by 1860 the house was occupied by a Mr Charles Shaw, who once took the whole of the scholars from the national School in Liscard Road to Eastham for the day, the first treat that anybody in the parish could recall. he was followed by the Twiname family, and later by another Cotton Broker, William Peers on this occasion. Thomas Gorman, a Wholesale Provision Merchant, who is commemorated by a large cross in front of St. Albans Church, purchased the property in 1876, and sold it in 1889 to Captain Alexander McGachen, a Master Mariner, who spent six years there before disposing of the estate to Mr Samuel reece, of dairy fame. It was on the death of Mr Reece's widow that the house and grounds were acquired by the Corporation. The house was damaged beyond repair in the last war air-raids, and was subsequently demolished.

North meade House

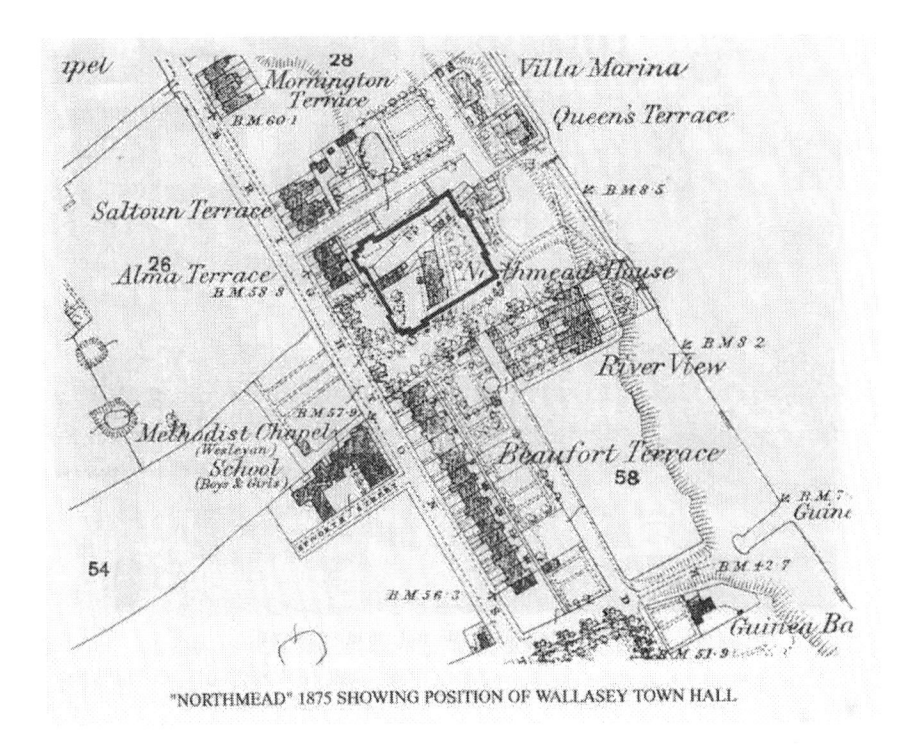

"NORTHMEAD" 1875 SHOWING POSITION OF WALLASEY TOWN HALL

North Meade was large mansion which stood in Brighton Street, with grounds running down to the seawall. It appears to have consisted of two separate units of accommodation, probably because a bungalow was built in the grounds to cope with the situation where an irate father would refuse his sons admission to the house proper if they arrived home after a certain hour at night. The property originally formed part of the Marriage Settlement of the Revd. John Tobin, son of Sir John Tobin, of Liscard Hall, and first incumbent of St. John's Church, Egremont, but was sold by the Trustees of the Settlement in 1845 to three sisters, Hannah, Cicely and Mary Leyland, who established a boarding school there. By 1863 all three sisters had died, and the property passed to a fourth sister, Ellen, who sold it in 1867 to a Mr George Hulse, a turtle merchant in a large way of business in Liverpool.

There were various tenants over the years, notably John Joyce, Ship-owner, Justice of the Peace, and member of the Local Board, who lived at the house in the late 1880's prior to his removal to 'Seabank House', but by 1893 the Grosvenor Ladies' Academy was in occupation. George Hulse had died in 1871, but his Trustees retained possession of the property until 1898, when they sold the two houses and 9,623 square yards of land to Councillor John Kiernan, an Amusement Caterer, who proposed to build a theatre on the site. The Council, however, had other plans and made him a good offer the following year, with the result that he sold out to them for £6,400 plus a cancellation fee, and built the Irving Theatre instead, in what is now Borough Road. The site of the theatre was previously occupied by 'Hope House', a charming little residence in its own ground, also owned by the Hulse family, and much of the stone for the theatre came from the old St. George's Church in Lord Street, Liverpool, which was being demolished at that time. After using 'North Meade' as a depot for some years, the Council offices being nearby at the bottom of Church Street, demolished the buildings, and in 1914 King George V laid the foundation-stone of the New Town Hall in their place.

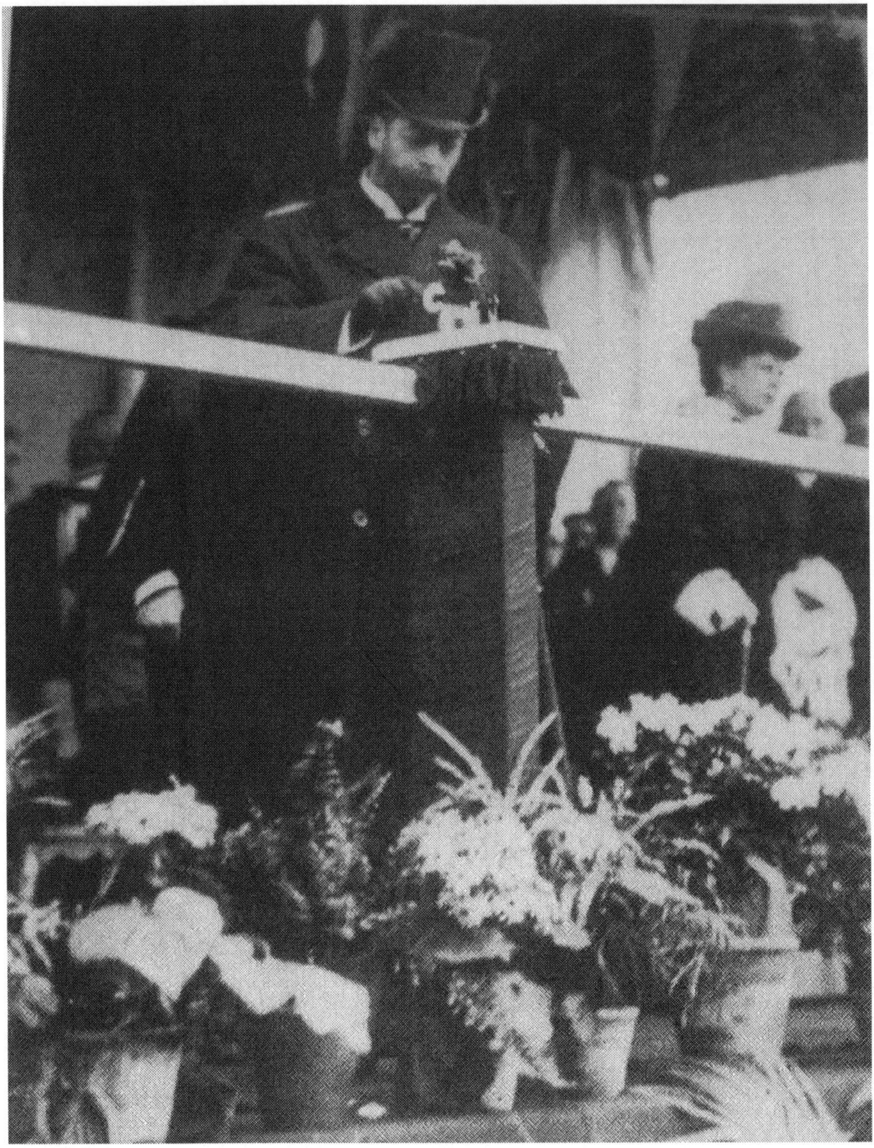

Wallasey Old Dwellings

There were many old dwellings scattered around Wallasey, some of which still exist, but many of which have been long since demolished. Some of the oldest residential buildings recorded in Wallasey village were that of:

Willow Cottage which was built in 1737 from local stone and had been whitewashed several times giving it a distinct look. The old building stood on a crooked angle with its side almost to the road. The date stone as always bore the date, and the also the initials of "R.I.O.M." I am not sure as to whether this was the owner of the building, or the architect; but little else is recorded of the property except for the overwhelming size of a large tree in the front garden not shown in the picture above.

Laburnum Cottage was another local cottage which was named after the Laburnum tree in the garden. Again this small edifice was also built from local stone. It's believed to have been constructed around 1815 and owned by Thomas Sparks but has long since been demolished.

Liscard Manor House

'Liscard Manor House', which stood on the foot of Manor Lane in extensive grounds, and according to the date on the ship bell which used to hang there, was probably built around 1790. The owner in those days, and also Lord of the Manor, was John Hough, whose father, Charles Hough, had inherited the estate under the will of his cousin, Anne Meols, sole survivor of the Meols family of Wallasey Old Hall, which until it was demolished in 1864 stood just below St. Hilary's Church. John Hough died in 1797, and four years later the estate and all manorial rights were purchased from his Executors by John Penkett for the sum of just over £2,500. Penkett, a well known Liverpool merchant, was also agent to the gunpowder magazines at Liscard, a lucrative post when you consider that every ship that left the port in those days was armed. He lived in Duke Street, Liverpool, and used the Manor House, which until 1841 was known as 'Sea Bank', as a summer residence.

When John Penkett died in 1838 he left the house to his daughter, Mary Anne, who had married her cousin, John D. Maddock, in 1820, and was subsequently known as the Lady of the Manor until she died in 1888. Among her gifts were the stone for St. Hilary's Church from her quarry at the top of Mount Pleasant Road, and the land and £800 for the erection of St. Mary's Church in Withens Church. During the course of her life, Mrs Maddock appears to have had six children, two sons and four daughters. The eldest son, John Penkett Maddock, was born at 'Sea Bank Cottage' in 1825 and was baptised at St. Hilary's Church, but he only survived one year, and was buried at St. George's Church in Liverpool. The youngest boy, William Worthington Maddock, was born at 'Sea Bank', later the Manor House, in 1826. He was baptised at St. Thomas Church Liverpool, and became an Ensign in Her Majesty's 98th Regiment in 1846. He was posted to India, but two years later, when returning to England as a result of ill health, he died on board the P & O Steam Packet 'Haddington', and was later buried at St. Hilary's Churchyard. Anna, the eldest daughter, born in 1822, married Timothy Bristow Hughes, a member of a local family, and they lived at 'Sea Bank Cottage' for a number of years. She died in 1865 at the age of 43, followed four years later by her 18 year old daughter, Lucy, but Mr Bristow Hughes himself, who served for four years as Churchwarden at St. Hilary's, lived to be 76, dying in 1892 and joining his wife and daughter in the churchyard.

Of the three remaining girls, Margaret Elizabeth was born at Number 105 Duke Street, Liverpool, in 1823. Emily Frances was born at 'Sea Bank' in 1831 and Clara Mary Anne, the youngest, was born in 1834, also at 'Sea Bank'. She was married at St. James' Church, Paddington, London, in 1857 to William Savage Crawley, son of a Gloucestershire parson, but while a tombstone in St. Hilary's churchyard records that he died in 1892 at the age of 68, there is no mention of his wife, presumably buried elsewhere.

As previously mentioned, the name of the house was changed from 'Sea Bank' to 'Liscard Manor House' in 1841, and 'Sea Bank' was given to the house standing at the corner of Manor Lane and the promenade, consisting of two cottages made into one. About 1850 Mrs. Maddock had deserted the Manor House for 'Sea Bank', and in

1856 the Manor House estate, then tenanted by Mr John Naylor, a partner in Leyland's Bank, was offered at auction but apparently a sale did not materialise. It would seem that Mrs. Maddock may have been becoming financially embarrassed, as in 1857 she borrowed £10,000 on the security on part of the land and in 1897 the loan was increased to £20.000. In addition, she owed her Solicitors upward of £10,000, and it was evitable that the disposal of the property would have to be put in hand before very long.

In 1882, part of the grounds, was sold for the erection of the 'Homes Of the Aged Mariners', and in 1890, after Mrs. Maddock's death, the Trustees of her Will and her mortgagees entered into an Agreement for the sale of further portions of the estate to a Mr. David Beano Rappart, a Land Agent, for £18,000. He in turn, sold to the Liscard Manor Estate & Co Ltd for a similar sum, and within a few years the Drives running off Sea Bank Road began to make their first appearance. The Manor House itself remained in the occupation of various tenants, the last resident being a Mr. Davidson, who went there in 1902.

For some years a school was conducted in one of the rooms, but when Mr. Davidson moved to Birkenhead in 1935, the house was converted into an infirmary for the Mariner's Homes, and was finally demolished in 1937.

Clifton Hall

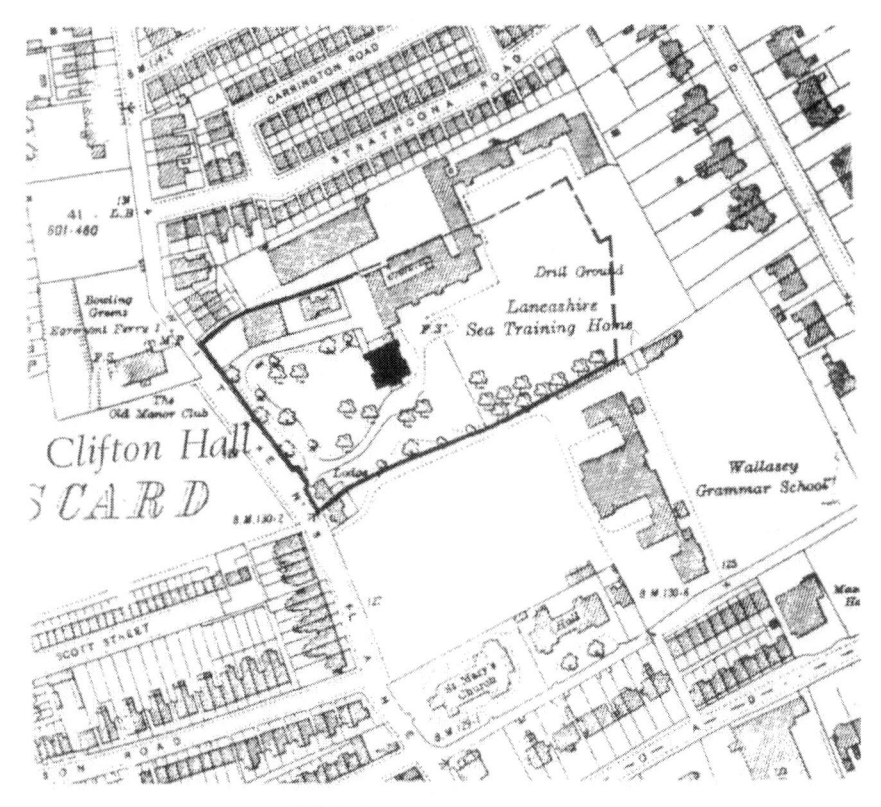

SITE OF "CLIFTON HALL" IN 1926

'Clifton Hall' was quite imposing. Built in stone, two storey's high, the ground floor was emphasised by strong horizontal lines in the stone whilst the upper floor was finished in a tighter joint. The front elevation faced south away from Withens Lane and was accentuated by a protecting porch with composite fluted columns. The front was five bays wide with tall single windows, and the parapet above the bays was higher over the end and centre sections and finished in an overhanging coping giving it the look of an Egyptian temple. At the rear of the hall to the north was a large conservatory. The entrance to the grounds was via a pair of double iron gates set in stone columns with single gates on either side. Beside the gates was a small lodge which lasted longer than the hall. The drive went in a circular route to the hall and around the grounds terminating by a coach house and stable and nearby on the north boundary was an orchard with greenhouse.

The earliest reference to the property was in March, 1840, when Thomas Chadwick mortgaged a field known as the 'Hippicar' to a Mr Joseph Reece to secure a loan of £100. In April, 1841, he borrowed a further £100 from the same source, and two years later borrowed yet another £300 on the security of the land, on this occasion executing a mortgage in favour of Joseph Reece and a Mr G.H. Crump, an Attorney, who was at that time was living in 'Pool Cottage' in Poulton Road, and who married as his second wife one of the daughters of Mrs. Maddock of 'Liscard Manor House'.

In August, 1843 Chadwick and his mortgages sold the 'Hippicar' to John Taylor, a Corn Broker on the point of retiring, for £1,526, and the following year Mr. Taylor built the house. Having duly retired he died in 1851, and in 1864, following on the death of his widow at Scarborough in 1860, the house passed to his nephew, a Mr. F.T Payne, under the terms of the Will.

In the meantime, there had been a variety of tenants, one of whom was Mr Edward Oliver, a Merchant, who was a resident from 1855 to 1857. Mr. Oliver was followed at 'Clifton Hall' by Peter Wright, Clerk of the Peace of Liverpool, who was reputed to employ a negro as a manservant, but in 1865 we find that a Mr. Hugh Dixon, a Merchant and Ship-owner, one of whose daughters married the Revd. R.B Billinge, a curate at St. Hilary's Church. Mr Dixon died in 1868, aged 48, being buried in St. Hilary's Churchyard, and by 1875 a Mr. Carvill, also a Ship-owner, had taken over. However, in 1869 Mr. Payne, the owner, had sold the property for £4,500 to Samuel Smith, a Cotton Broker who had previously been living at 'The Woodlands', now part of Vale Park and apparently did not move into 'Clifton Hall' until about 1876.

Samuel Smith was born at the small village of Roberton, Borgue, Kirkcudbrightshire, in 1836, the son of a gentleman farmer. Showing considerable scholastic ability at an early age, he was originally destined for the Church, but changed his mind and in 1854 came south to Liverpool, where he too apprenticeship with Logan & Co, Cotton Brokers. Ten years later he went into partnership with Mr Edwards to found the firm of Smith, Edwards & Co, a venture in which he was later joined by his two brothers, James and Anthony. He was also a partner in the Liverpool offices of James Finlay & Co, Merchants of Glasgow.

Owing to the American Civil War, cotton was virtually unobtainable from the United States, with the result that the firm turned to Egypt and India for its supplies, and it was then that Smith developed a love for India which was to last all his life. In 1878 he became a Town councillor in Liverpool, representing the Castle Street Ward, and four years later, having raised his political sights, he was elected Member of Parliament for Liverpool in the Liberal interest, defeating a well known citizen in the person of Sir Arthur Forwood. Three years later, however, there was another Election, with a heavy swing to the Tories, and Mr. Smith was unseated for the next two years. In 1886 he was elected to represent the Flint Boroughs, and some time later became a Privy Councillor. He had left 'Clifton Hall' in 1883 for Princess Park, Liverpool, where he set up house at 'Carleton', South Gate, and identified himself with the National Society for the Prevention to Cruelty to Children, which he helped to establish. It's said that he aimed to devote two-thirds of his income to charity, and that this cost him between £8,000 and £10,000 annually.

In 1893 Mr Smith's wife, a Mrs Melville Christieson, of Biggar, Lanarkshire, died, to be followed five years later by his only son, John Gordon Smith, a partner in the firm and Secretary of the Navy League, who fell a victim to typhoid fever. His father erected the Gordon Smith institute for Seamen in his memory, at a cost of £7,000, and thereafter spent most of his time abroad. It was while he was attending the Indian National Conference at Calcutta in 1906 that news of his sudden death was received in Liverpool, and cast a gloom over the business community. He is commemorated by a granite memorial erected in 1909 at the Lodge Lane entrance at Sefton Park, at a cost of £1,850 and unveiled by the then Lord Mayor of the City, and by a stained glass window in Egremont Presbyterian Church, as it was known then.

When Samuel Smith moved to Liverpool in 1883, his Trustees sold the 'Clifton Hall' estate for £4,500 to Captain John Herron, Master Mariner, Ship-owner, Justice of the Peace, Member of the Local Board, and Chairman of the Ferries Committee, who named one of their ferry boats after him. Captain Herron first saw the light of day in Ireland in 1820, probably at a small village called Kircubbin, on the shores of Strangford Lough. At the early age of 13 he was apprenticed to a Liverpool ship-owner, and obtained his Master's Ticket when barely out of his teens. In 1850 he married a Miss Jane Carson at St. Thomas Church, Walton-on-the-Hill, and she followed the not unusual practice of those days of accompanying him to sea, as it's on record that in 1856 one of their son's was born on board the sailing ship 'Lord Raglan', of which Captain Herron was then in command. About that time the Captain was engaged in carrying troops to the Crimea and later to India at the time of the Great Mutiny, in fact on one occasion he witnessed the execution of some of the mutineers, who were blown from the muzzles of the guns.

His seafaring days came to an end in the 1860s when he was made Marine Superintendant of the fleet of Mr S.R Graves, a well known Liverpool owner, also Irish born, but when that gentlemen decided to stand for Parliament and sold his ships, Captain Herron himself became the owner, first in partnership with his brother under the name William and John Herron and later to John Herron & Co, with his son-in-law, Captain Isaiah Weaver, of 'Mount Pleasant House', Wallasey, as one of his partners. Although Mrs Heron presented her husband with eight children, the marriage was not without tragedy in as much as five of the children, two sons and three daughters, predeceased their parents, one of the daughters Mary, the first born, being lost at sea in 1899 with her husband and two children, when one of their father's sailing ships, the 'Lord Raglan', presumable named after his earlier command, left San Francisco for Queenstown with a cargo of wheat and vanished without trace.

Mrs Herron died in April 1897, and barely a month later, at the age of 77, her husband succumbed to an attack of pneumonia, said to have been caught while attending the funeral of a friend, Mr H.A Bailey, in St. Hilary's Churchyard, He was buried in Flaybrick Cemetery on 28th May, 1897, six ferrymen acting as pall-bearers.

During his lifetime Captain Herron took an active part in local affairs, being Chairman of the Wallasey Local Board in 1892, Chairman of the Liscard Branch of the Wirral Liberal Association, a Governor of Wallasey Grammar School, and an official of Egerton Presbyterian Church. Although his private benefactions were said to overshadow his public gifts, he did, in fact, present the band stand in Central Park to the town, and gave £600 to the Jubilee Fund for the erection of Victoria Central Hospital, in memory of his wife.

In 1901 Captain Herron's son John, who was his Executor, sold the house and approximately five acres of land to the Navy League for £6,100. The Navy League was an organisation started in 1895-6 to take poor young boys of good character off the streets and train them for the Royal Navy or the Merchant Navy. Navy League Homes were set up in various places including Wallasey on the 'Clifton Hall Estate'. The foundation stone was laid on October 18th 1902 by Lord Strathcona and Mount Royal. By 1903 additional buildings for training and living were opened for use. The Captain Superintendant lived in 'Clifton Hall' itself.

The Boys were full time boarders for up to two years receiving training in seamanship and allied interests, which would fit them for life at sea. Local cinemas gave them privileged rates for some performances and Church Parade was a regular event accompanied by their band. Due to the economic recession and various other difficulties the Homes did not survive the Second World War. Money was scarce, the school leaving age was raised, entry requirements in the Services were of a higher standard and the Homes could just not compete with other facilities and the costs of modernisation. The land and the buildings of 'Clifton Hall' covering a total of 36,608 square yards were sold to the Local Authority for

£28,500 on October 13th 1948, for the purpose of forming an Adult Education Centre.

Very sadly 'Clifton Hall' was demolished in the early 1950's, dry rot being the reason for this decision plus the cost of restoration. The Navy League quarters were left untouched and new teaching accommodations were built which formed what became known as the North Wirral College of Technology. In 1982 Wirral Metropolitan College, which included Withens Lane College, Birkenhead and Carlett Park, were created. In June 1996 it was announced that Withens Lane College was to close. In 1997 the college closed.

Home Croft

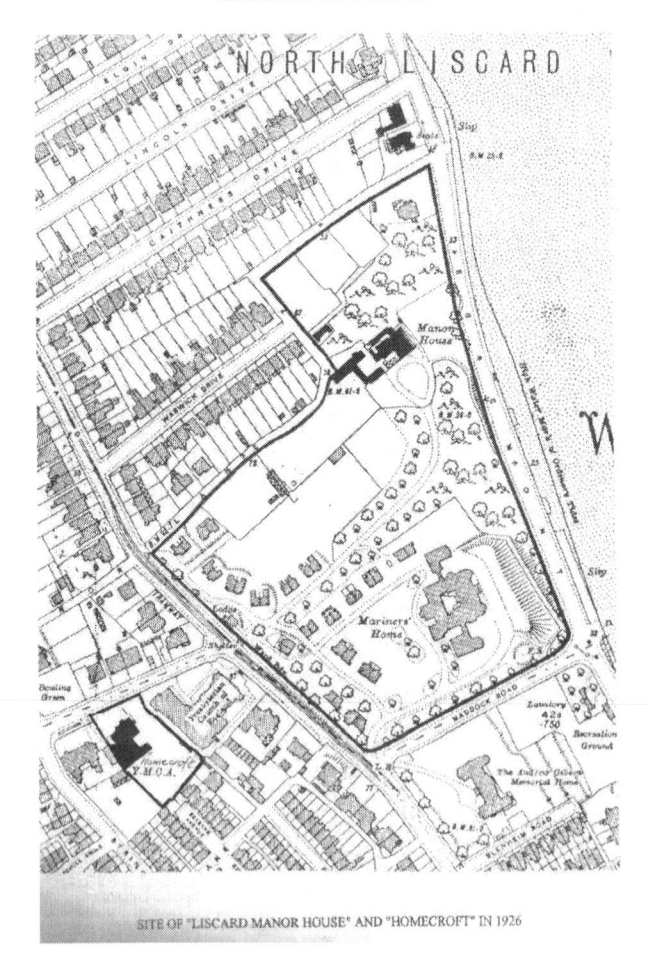

SITE OF "LISCARD MANOR HOUSE" AND "HOMECROFT" IN 1926

'Home Croft' dates back from 1848, when it was built by Henry Pooley on land purchased from the 'Liscard Manor House' the previous year. Mr Pooley, if for nothing else, was famous for his weighing machines, which was produced at his Albion Foundry in Manchester and Liverpool and were to be found at one time in every railway station in the country. One of the first members of the Wallasey Local Board on its formation in 1853, and its Chairman for 5 years, he was a zealous worker in the public interest, particularly with regard to the Ferries and the provision of an adequate water supply for the district. Not only did his firm build the Water Tower in Mill Lane in the 1860's, but he also presented a number of drinking fountains for the parish.

In 1858, Mr Pooley, an ardent Wesleyan laid the foundation stone of Seacombe Wesleyan Church, now demolished, and obviously did not neglect his other duties, as his 12th child was born shortly after 'Home Croft' was built! There were 5 boys and 7 girls, one of whom did not survive childhood, and as each girl was married her father built a house for her.

Declining appointments as Justice of the Peace on account of deafness, Mr Pooley retired from business in 1873 and died in 1878. The widow of the belated Mr Pooley left 'Home Croft' for Penkett Road and twenty years later the house was purchased by the YMCA Association. For 112 years the Wallasey YMCA served the local community but due to cuts to local authority funding it was announced it would close on 30th September 2011. Currently the building is vacant and it's future uncertain.

Birds House

The "Bird House" is the oldest known dwelling in Wallasey and even Wirral. An old farmer's house made from probably local sandstone and erected in 1621 according to the date stone.

This house has now been vacated by its elderly owner. It has been extended quite a bit in its 400 year life and buttresses erected on the outside walls to strengthen them.

Nelsons Gutter

Nelsons Gutter or the "Nelly" contained several historically valued buildings, including Sam Salisbury's cottage which was a long white washed cottage with thatched roof. The cottage sustained a direct hit in 1941 from a German bomb which completely obliterated it and caused severe damaged to Carlyle cottage next door. Another house close by known as Buxton house was also hit during the war by an incendiary bomb and subsequently burnt down during the raid. (More information can be found elsewhere in the book)

Heath Bank

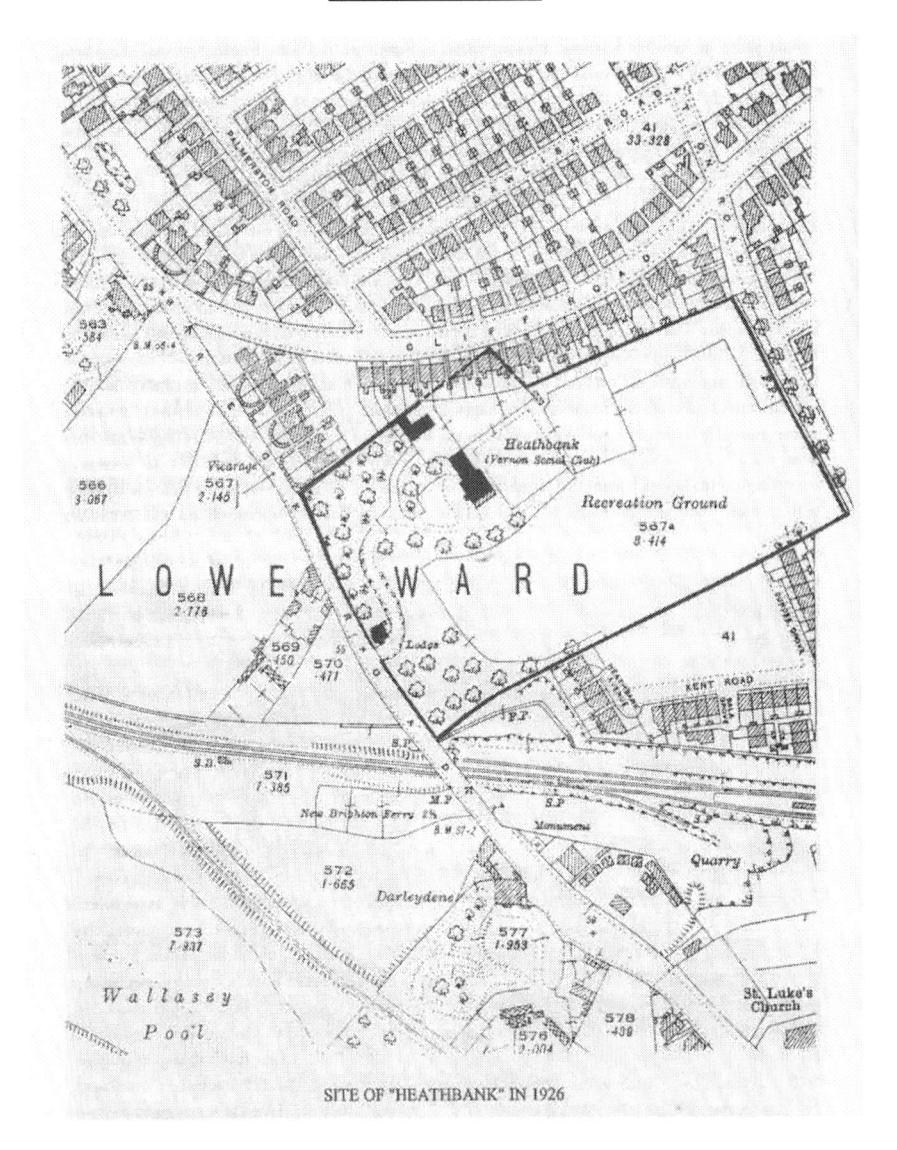

SITE OF "HEATHBANK" IN 1926

In Breck Road, there once stood an imposing mansion known as 'Heath Bank'. The history of the house dates back to January, 1829, when one John Wilson, Merchant, Ship-owner and partner in the firm of Wilson & Cort, of 27 Exchange Alley North, Liverpool, purchased two fields known as 'Boods Hey' and 'The Croft', on the east side of what was then Poulton and Wallasey Lane, at a cost of £1,000. These fields measured, respectively, 7 acres 1 rood 39 perches and 1 acre 1 rood 38 perches, and the vendors were the Revd. Sir Phillip Grey-

Egerton and Phillip de Malpas. Egerton was a member of a family which had owned land in Wallasey for well over a hundred years, together with Sir John Tobin. Of Oak Hill, Liverpool, and later 'Liscard Hall', who earlier had made considerable purchases of land in the neighbourhood. For reasons which have not emerged, the name of Thomas Ogilvy, a well-known Merchant living in the district, also appeared in the transaction. He was a partner in the prominent Liverpool firm of Ogilvy, Gillanders & co., and in 1839 was to be found living at 'Seafield', Wallasey, better known to present day resident as 'Elleray Park'. There was no further mention of him, and he presumably either died or left the district, but as a matter of interest, the Registers at St. Hilary's Church contain the names of five of his children who were baptized their between the years 1833 and 1839.

Construction of the house appears to have been undertaken soon after the purchase of the land, and it would seem that the work must have been completed by 1834, for in that year, possibly to finance the cost; John Wilson mortgaged the property to a Mr John Rigby to secure a loan of £4,000. Rather less than 2 years later the loan was repaid, but in 1844 Wilson sold the estate to Mr John Ripley, of Canning Street, Liverpool, a member of a well-known local family. The consideration on this occasion was £6,500, and Ripley, who according to the census returns was a bachelor, occupied the house until 1866, when he died and was buried in St. Hilary's Churchyard, a brass plate and two lights in the North Transept of the Church perpetuating his memory.

Apart from the fact that Mr. Ripley was appointed a Trustee of the Wallasey Free School in 1852, and was a member of the Committee of the old Infirmary in Brownlow Hill, Liverpool, not very much information regarding him has come to light, but it possible that he was related to Harold Littledale, son-in-law of Sir John Tobin, as they are buried side-by-side in the Churchyard, in identical graveyards. The grave of John Wilson, the builder of the house, is also buried in the Churchyard, when he was buried in 1867, having during his stay at 'Heath Bank' served for two years as

Churchwarden. John Ripley's coachman, incidentally, was Thomas George, father of Tom and Will George, one of whom, if not both, played for Wallasey Cricket Club as far back as 1869.

Following John Ripley's death, his Trustees sold the property for £7,000 to Peter Wright, Attorney, partner in the legal firm of Wright, Ewer and Wright (better known in modern times as Wright, Becket and Pennington) and Clerk of the Peace of Liverpool, the equivalent of Town Clerk. He immediately mortgaged the estate to two members of the family, A.T & G.E Wright, also Attorneys, for the full amount if the purchase-money, and this mortgage was still in existence six years later, when the property changed hands once more, the purchaser on this occasion being John McInnes, a Scot who had left the country of his birth as a young man, and having patented a special anti-fouling composition for ships' bottoms, had proceeded to make a good deal of money. He remained in residence at 'Heath Bank' until his death in December, 1896, when he, too, found a last resting place at St. Hilary's. He has laid up considerable treasure on earth, as his Will was proved for £165,500, but in his lifetime, although he was said to be somewhat eccentric, he was known for his benefactions, particularly to the Victoria Central Hospital, which although the foundation-stone was not laid until after his death, was nevertheless the subject of bazaars and other fund-raising efforts in the preceding years. He did, in fact, give the one-and-a-half acre site on which the Hospital and the Wallasey Dispensary formerly stood. He was also associated in the foundation of the Seacombe Cottage Hospital, and presented the McInnes Cottages to the Homes for Aged Mariners at Egremont.

Mrs McInnes, the widow, died in December, 1900, and in 1902 the property was acquired by Captain Isaiah Weaver, a partner in John Herron & Co., Ship owner's, and then living at Mount Pleasant House, Mount Pleasant Road, Wallasey. The purchase cost him £4,375, but there is no evidence that he ever moved into the house, and it must be assumed that the transaction represented an investment on his part. This is supported by the fact that in 1905 he granted a five-year-lease to a Mr Thomas Wilson, a Shipping Butcher, at an annual rental of £130, but the lease does not appear to have been renewed, and it has not so far been possible to discover the identity of any later tenants. Captain Weaver died intestate in 1911, and the property passed to his surviving son and heir-at-law, Frederick William Herron Weaver, who in 1912 sold off 85 yards of the land to Wallasey Corporation, to facilitate the construction of Cliff Road, which now forms the northern boundary of the estate. In 1920 Mr Weaver, who had moved out of the area, disposed of the house and remaining grounds to the Vernon Trustees, for use as a sports-ground for the employees of William Vernon and Sons, part of Spillers Ltd. Early in 1972 proposals were being made to sell the entire estate, and outline planning permission was, in fact, granted for the erection of something like 105 houses, but there was opposition in various quarters, and efforts were made to continue the estate in its existing. There were successful for a time, but some years later the house was demolished, and the builders took over.

Manor Lodge

In 1844 John Penkett, Lord of the Manor of Liscard sold a piece of land at the corner of Manor Road and Withens Lane to Robert Sinclair, at a price of £456. The house was subsequently known as 'Manor Lodge' had been built on the land by 1850, and appears to have passed into the hands of Mr Sinclair's four daughters. Later the property was sold to a Mr Henry Cram, a Ship-owner, but by 1870 a Ladies' School, conducted by the Misses De Watteau and Allison, was in occupation. Miss Allison appears to have continued the school single-handed by 1875 before moving on elsewhere.

In 1880 Captain Benjamin Gleadell, a Master Mariner, was in residence at the house. He was noteworthy as much as a young boy he ran away to sea and rose to become Master of the White Star liner "Germanic" and at a later date, Commodore of the White Star Line itself and finally President. He died at sea in 1885 at the age of 59, and his grave is to be found at St. Hilary's Churchyard. One of his daughters married Francis Johnston, head of Robert Gilchrist & Co, one time well known Liverpool ship owner's. Ten years previously, in 1878, Johnston, whose father, incidentally, founded the old Oakdale Mission in Seacombe, had been a passenger on the Wallasey ferry-boat "Gem" when she was in collision in mid-river with the Brocklebank ship "Bowfell" in dense fog. Several lives were lost, and Johnston, although rescued, lost his hearing. While living in Wallasey, he and his wife attended Egremont Presbyterian Church, but in 1920 they moved to 'Merida', Noctorum, where he died in 1929. After Captain Gleadell's death his widow, Maria Gleadell, continued to live at 'Manor Lodge' until her own death in 1915, when she too was buried in the family grave, together with two sons and a daughter, both boys having predeceased their mother.

Following on Mrs Gleadell's death, the house was occupied by a Mrs Weathrope for a time, but in 1930 the property had been converted into the 'William Fletcher Rogers Home for Elderly Ladies, and, continued such until it was completely demolished in an air-raid during the last war, and some eighteen of the residents were killed.

Buxton House

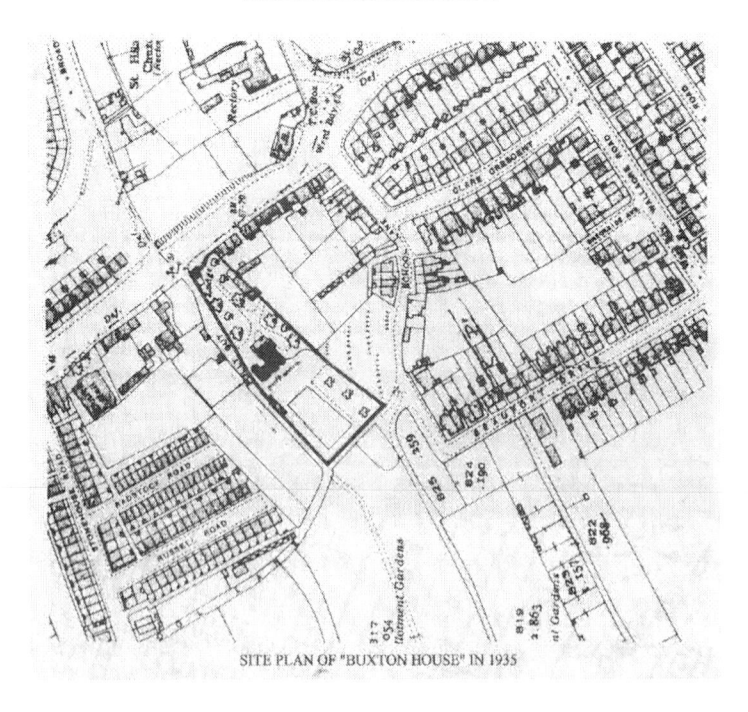

SITE PLAN OF "BUXTON HOUSE" IN 1935

Buxton House' once stood in Wallasey Village, just past the Parish Hall, and on the corner of what used to be known as Smithy Lane, where the entrance gate-posts are still to be seen. The title-deeds indicate that in 1849 a Mr Thomas Peers, Merchant purchased the estate, on which an earlier house then stood, from the Trustees of the Wills of Lady Elizabeth Murray and of Mrs K Backhouse, for £1,000. These two ladies were the daughters of Richard Kent, Merchant, of Liverpool, and they had a brother, Joseph, who at some date had changed his name by deed-poll to Green on inheriting the Poulton Lancelyn Estates in Bebington.

By 1856, Thomas Peers, who also appears to have been the owner of Highfield House, later incorporated in the Maternity Hospital in Mill Lane, Wallasey, had died, and his Executors sold the Buxton Villa estate, as it was then known, to Messrs Kershaw, who fifteen months later resold the property to Robert Isaac, a well-known Liverpool wholesale and retails fishmonger, for £900. Isaac demolished the existing residence and erected a new house, on which he conferred the name of 'Buxton House'. Death overtook him after a few years' stay there, and in 1867 his devises and mortgages disposed of the property to Edward Billington, a Tea and Coffee Broker, for £2,800. A well-liked man, he remained in residence for many years, but by 1900 he and his widow had both passed away, and in 1907 Mr James increased the size of the estate by adding to it the disused St Hilary's Girls' School, which he purchased from the Rector and Wardens for £600, but in the meantime the house had been let to the Lamb family, Timber Merchants, who were in business in Liverpool for many years. After they left, the property stood empty for some years, and finally, in 1915, Mr James sold out to a Mr A.W Willmer. a well-known Cotton Broker, and Mr F.W Heape, at a price of £6,000.

The next tenant of note was Mr A Bruce Wallis, who was the Managing Director of Blackler's Stores, and he brought life to the building until 1923, when he departed for Warren Drive. The house was later converted into flats, and in 1930 Wallasey Corporation purchased the estate from Messrs Willmer and Heape for £8,000. In 1932, a Mr Frederick Hall, described as a Secretary, became the sole occupant, his name appearing in the Directory for the last time in 1941. At that time the house sustained severe damage by enemy action and later by fire, demolition becoming inevitable

Zig Zag Hall

SITE OF "ZIG ZAG" IN 1926

'Zig Zag Hall' in its early days, was in fact known as 'Zig Zag House'. Originally a farmhouse, it took its name from Zig Zag Lane, which wandered down from Rake Lane to the river, and in 1834 Thomas Lowry, then aged about 65, was to be found in residence there. Some years previously he had become principal of the firm of Lowry, Roscoe and Wardell, an offshoot of an earlier firm of bankers and colliery proprietors, in which William Roscoe, the famous man-of-letters, was a partner. In addition, Thomas Lowry owned a brewery in Cunliffe Street, Liverpool, where he resided at the time, and was also connected with the Liverpool Gas Light Company. of which he was Treasurer in 1821. The firm dissolved in 1827, and Thomas Lowry, who had moved first to High Seacombe and later to Rupert Hill, Everton, contented himself with his Brewery. His wife died in 1830, and on 24th March 1831, two of his daughters were married, Elizabeth, the elder, to William Mann, and Ann, the younger, to James Stringer.

In 1832 Thomas Lowry had apparently given up the brewery and joined his two sons-in-laws in the firm of Lowry, Stringer and Mann, at that time Merchants, and later Steam Sawmill Owners and Salt Proprietors, with premises in Seel Street, Liverpool. His own son died in 1833, and four years later he retired from business, the firm becoming Stringer and Mann. He was joined at 'Zig Zag House' in 1839 by his son-in-law, William Mann, and died a year or two later, but William Mann, who in addition to his other commitments was Deputy Chairman of the Liverpool Ship-owners' Association, was to occupy the house until his own death in 1864. On the cover of a large prayer-book in St. Hilary's Church his name, jointly with that of Richard Bateson, of 'Newland House', Wallasey, another mansion that has vanished into the limbo of the forgotten, appears as a Churchwarden in 1850. The records reveal that he served for three consecutive years in that capacity. It's also recorded that when the old St. Hilary's Church was burnt down in 1857, he was a member of the committee formed to legislate for the rebuilding of the Church, and contributed £150 towards to cost of the replacement.

William and Elizabeth Mann had seven children, three boys and four girls. The boys followed various occupations, Lowry Mann, the eldest, born in 1834, spending much but not all of his life in Wallasey, and participating to a considerable extent in the life of the community. The second son, however, who was born in 1839 and given his father's name of William, was to be found studying at Hamburg University when in his nineteenth year, but his stay there came to an end when he was called home on the account of the illness of his father. After the father's death William departed for New Zealand, where he obtained employment with a Surveyor, but soon decided that he wanted cattle. On the advice of a Catholic Priest he went to Australia, where he teamed up with some "Sheep men", travelling up the country with them and being left on occasion to care for single-handed for large numbers of sheep despite the presence of bands of savage blacks roaming in the area. His next move was to India to join his elder brother, Lowry, who had left Wallasey temporarily and gone there to found a coffee plantation. William was then beset with chills and fever, causing him to return to England, but the desire to travel re-asserted itself and a year or so later he left for South America. In Argentina he found work with cattlemen, which occupied him for the next two years, at the end of which he went to Virginia, where his other brother, Arthur Joynson Mann, had purchased a property which he called 'Mannsfield' and occupied with his wife Marion and their two young daughters. After Arthur's death, at the early age of 42, Marion, his wife, returned to her native Ireland, and William bought 'Mannsfield', living there with two Englishmen for a year, at the end of which he returned to England to visit his mother, who was still living at 'Zig Zag House'. There he met Eleanor Atkinson, who was tutoring two sons of one of his sisters, and after three months married her at Bunbury Church, thereafter returning with her to 'Mannsfield'. His death occurred in 1910 but his descendants still occupy the property.

Of William Mann's four daughters, at least three made good marriages. Two of them, Elizabeth in 1857 and Adah in 1864, found husbands in the persons of two brothers, Ford North and Henry North, sons of John North of 'Stonebark', Warren Drive. Ford North, at the time of his wedding a barrister-at-law, was destined to become the Hon. Sir Ford North, a Judge in the Chancery Court, but his brother Henry, who was in business as an Insurance Broker had the misfortune to lose his wife after five years of married life. Her tombstone in St. Hilary's Churchyard records that she died in 1869, at the early age of 31.

In 1865 the third daughter, Anne, who had been born at 'Zig Zag House' twenty-three years earlier, married the Revd. John Graham, a curate at St. Hilary's at the time, and son of the reigning Bishop of Chester, who performed the marriage ceremony. There were two sons of this last marriage, but on the death of her husband Anne married again, on this occasion her bridegroom being Robert Slatter, by whom she had a further son.

Ellen Mann, the youngest of the four girls, did not marry. She was something of an artist, and the picture of 'Zig Zag House', painted in the late 1870's is still in the possession of the family in America.

William Mann's widow, Elizabeth, passed away in 1873, and her death marked the end of the family's direct connection with the house, as in 1874 Captain John Herron, the ship-owners, became the occupant, remaining there for two or three years before moving on to Manor Road, and finally, to 'Clifton Hall' in Withens Lane. 'Zig Zag House' was purchased in 1881, by Mr T. H Sheen, who rebuilt the house and renamed it 'Zig Zag Hall'. He was followed in 1880 by Richard Steel, Cotton Broker and first Chairman of the Wallasey Urban District Council on its formation in 1894. He had the reputation of being rather forthright, and on one occasion, when having made some somewhat libellous remarks about another member, Mr A.T Wright, a well known Solicitor, at one of the meetings, he found a Writ on his breakfast-table the next morning, and was forced to make a tactical withdrawal. On another occasion, in 1906, he sued John Joyce, the ship-owner, for slander over the case of a Corporation employee who had been dismissed for embezzlement. The action was heard at St. George's Hall and a excited a good deal of local interest, but after hearing the evidence the jury found in favour of Joyce.

After Mr Steel's death in 1910, his widow remained at the house until the mid 1920's, when it was demolished and Steel Avenue and Sheen Road constructed on the site.

The Monkey House Toilets, Liscard

The Monkey House, built in 1904, was a pagoda-like shelter house with glass windows, which was situated on a small island in the centre of the cross roads ,opposite what was the Bank Of Liverpool, which later became Martin's Bank and then as we know it today, Barclays Bank. Inside were wooden seats where folk would gather to chat and look out through the windows. It was a meeting place for friends. It got its name from the fact that people were always staring out of the windows, like monkeys in their house. Underneath the Monkey House were the public toilets.

Seaview Road

Seaview Road, running from Liscard Village / Wallasey Road to the junction of Mount Pleasant Road and Hose Side Road, was originally known as Marsden Lane (named after John Astley Marsden who lived at Liscard Castle) but the road was actually named after a house that once stood where Harvey Road is today.

In the 1930s the shops in Sea View (two words in those days) Road were, from the Wellington Hotel, Haigh's the fish and chip shop, Mrs Hitchlock tobacconist, Bill Morton, the grocer, which later became Rediffusion the radio cable people. There were no televisions at that time. Subscribers to the company were supplied with a speaker and the programmes were relayed to people's homes by means of cable. The main receiving station was in Birkenhead. There was the tailor, Mr Feintuch, who was on the opposite corner of Silverlea Avenue. Next door was the opticians run by Mr Harris. At a later date, Mr Hayes took over the business. He was a keen photographer and was the founder member of the Wallasey Amateur Photographic Society in 1904. At No.27 was Bill Molyneux, the butcher, and next to Whalley Chandlers was Irving Little, the paint people, and on the corner of Merton Road was Foster's, the greengrocers.

Fred Foster started the business in the arcade in Borough Road in about 1890. His brother, Charles, was also a greengrocer. Charles came from Lincolnshire and decided to come to Birkenhead with the idea of setting up some kind of business. He came across a chap who had a large amount of tomatoes which had been wet with sea-water as the cargo was being shipped to Birkenhead Docks; he sold them cheaply to Charles who then sold them from a garage at the back of Robb's Store in Grange Road. He sold the lot and decided to set up as a greengrocer in 1889 at 183 Grange Road and did well. He also opened another shop in the Old Chester Road. Fred's business in the arcade suffered bomb damage and was burnt down during the Second World War, but opened another one at the top of Borough Road opposite the Embassy. The business was carried on by his son, Frank, who opened the Seaview Road branch and then followed that with one at Moreton. There was also a shop in Liscard Road. Charles' son, Basil, was working for his father in Birkenhead in 1950 but decided to work for his Uncle in Wallasey. Increasing competition from Supermarkets soon saw the Foster's greengrocers close by the turn of the 21st Century.

There use to be a drinking fountain just by Merton Road in about 1874 and there was another one in the middle of the road at the bottom of Manor Road and Liscard Village. The one is Seaview Road was made in the shape of a shell. Other shopkeepers in the road in the 1930s included Walter Burrows, the grocer, Thackwray's furniture store and Bill Parry, the pork butcher. The Health Store was at No.43 for many years and John Wilde was the baker. Rene's Cafe opened in the late 1960's and continues to this day.

Liscard Palace cinema opened on 25th November, 1911 and Claude Adams was the manager in the 1930s. The best seats cost 1s. 0d. and 3d in the front stalls. On the other side of the entrance were two shops and the upper portion of the front elevation had arched windows and fancy plaster work. The cinema closed down in 1959 due to poor attendances. It became Lennon's Supermarket for some time then Gateway Supermarket. Today it's the Shoe market.

No.57 was originally a private dwelling where Alfred Johnson., M.D resided. Later Dr. C Thompson, M.B., B.Ch. B.A.O also resided at the address. The premises were converted into a shop and Mr Cohen opened a furniture store. Another popular furniture store was Mr. Steggles' British Furniture land or the British Furnishing Company at No.61. Edward Ellison established a tea shop at No.73 and was there for a number of years.

Coker's were the well-known florists in Seaview Road. They had their shop at N.67 and were the leading florists in the town after the Second World War. Their nursery was next to the Belvidere Playing Fields. Between Burns Avenue and Massey Park were a selection of houses and shops which were all demolished by 1982 and various car showrooms and car mechanics are there today including Stanleys public house.

On the other side of the road from Liscard Village there were the premises of Mr. Gibbon, the carriage proprietor, which was demolished in the 1920s to make way for the Capitol Picture House and the Capital buildings. The cinema was opened on Saturday, 4th September, 1926. Admission prices ranged from 6d. to 1 Shilling. 2d and the cinema could hold 1,390 people. It closed own in 1974 and went over to Bingo. Today it's an empty shell. There was a glass canopy outside the entrance with Barclay's Bank one side and Marriot's Ice Cream Parlour on the other. Later the shop went over to selling sweets and chocolates as well as cigarettes.

Lavell's were the connectionist's at No.2 in the mid 1950s. Mr. J.W. Horn, the gents' outfitter, opened a double shop at Nos.4 and 6 next to the Ice Cream Parlour. In the pre-Second World War years and right up to the 1970s, they sold a fine selection of men's wear, including a wide variety of shirts and hats. They also supplied school uniforms. Today it's the William Hill Betting Shop. Mr. R.A Strother opened a branch of his musical business at No.8 and Heavysege, the wine and spirit merchants were at No.12 as well as at No.50.

Ben Stroude took over the drapers (T.Evans and Son) at No.14. Mr Henry Grundy had a fancy goods and gift shop at No.16. He lived at 42 Serpentine Road, and his daughter was a well-known actress of the 1920's under the name of Betty Balfour (1903-1977). Betty played 'Squibbs Hopkins' in the *Squibbs*' series which were popular comedies and also appeared in a film directed by Alfred Hitchcock called 'Champagne' which was released in 1928. Betty was often considered as the "English Mary Pickford". Grundy's shop was later taken over by Robert Knagg and Son.

Robert Yates Knagg was Mayor of Wallasey in 1949/50. Harry Holt had the chemist in the 1930s and continued after the war. Coffee Roast Bistro opened in the 1950s and has recently closed (September 2010) and at No.24 was Thomas the fruiterer.

In the 1930s Bethels's were the cabinet makers and furniture suppliers. Dickson's the cycle shop, Mr. Lewis the jeweller, and Max Novick was the tailor at No.44. Madam Black is where the ladies went to have their hair waved and set. Heavysege and Company were the wine merchants who went lower down the road to No.12. Two buildings that no longer exist are No.48 and No.50 which were demolished in the early 1980s to make way for the car park entrance. The last two businesses to reside here was Nelson Ladies Fashions and Mister Douglas, the ladies hairdressers.

Egerton Grove

Egerton Grove comprised of three 16th Century cottages that stood on the corner of Egerton Grove and was opposite the General Post Office. It was a long and low thatched building made of sandstone and whitewashed. At some time the roof to the left-hand cottage had been changed to slate. The right hand cottage was particularly distinctive for the wide border of seashell decoration embedded in plaster around the end window opening. The cottages were demolished in 1924 and Hebron Hall was built on the site. Egerton Grove was so named for the large number of trees growing both sides of the little road.

Liscard Village

The first mention of the settlement known today as Liscard was around 1260ad, and is recorded as being called "Lisnekarke". The name derives from the Welsh words "Llys" and "Carreg", with roughly translates into fort at height". In the past the name has been spelt with several variations including Liscak in 1260, Lisecair in 1277, Lysenker in 1295 and Lyscart in the 14th Century.

Like the rest of the area most of the residents from the earlier time would have been fisherman, farmers and sea traders. The population was extremely small due to the harshness of the environment. Liscard used to be a bitter inhospitable place consisting of muddy fields, dirt tracks and heavy set sand dunes with marshland outskirts. Liscard, like most of the other Boroughs; received its population boom in the mid 19th Century which can be confirmed by many of its historical buildings left around the area.

In the late 1800s and early 1900s there were a great number of horses within the town and so consequently this meant animal food was in great demand. Fred Cheshire sold hay and straw and his business was taken over by Alf Beynon. At one time Alf was a Coal Merchant. Another member of the family was at No.23 - John Benyon, the florist and nurseryman. At No. 17, Bob Dugdale had a milk-house in Miss Curtis' old shop. Bill Albones was the cobbler. Next to the garage were Joshua Mills and Sons, the painters. They were also plumbers and did a lot of work all over Liscard and other parts of the town. Mrs Eva Nichol was a 'wardrobe dealer' and William Gibbon lived at 'Inglefield' with Stephen Gibbons at No. 1. There used to be a butcher named Jack Fellows along here at No. 11, and Tom Peers had greengrocers.

Gibson's stables were at the end of the road and were established in 1860. Today the site is now derelict though at one time was the Capitol Cinema. Gibson's had a large yard, stables and carriage buildings. They hired out horses for the Fire Brigade. They were carriage proprietors and they were often hired for weddings and funerals. They were soon to move with the times and went over to motor vehicles. Mr Gibson moved down the road to No.25 and had a fine, large garage. Mr Harold Gibson was at No.23. In front of their forecourt were large iron gates which were kept closed and only opened to allow the cars to go in and out. As the years went by, the firm became part of the John W. Griffith and Son, the leading wedding and funeral directors in the town. The buildings were later demolished to make way for rebuilding.

One of the most popular shops in Liscard Village was 'Ellison Brothers' at No.15. They then took over Nos.13 to 17. The business was started by Harry and his brother in King Street, long before the First World War. The local plumbers persuaded him to stock their needs and soon Ellison's were to sell cast-iron toilet cisterns bearing their name on the sides. They moved to Liscard in the early 1930s and soon became the leading shop for wallpaper and paints, selling a large selection of colours in allsorts finishes and brands. They opened new premises in Oxton Road and Conway Street, as well as keeping the one in King Street (although they had moved to new premises) and Heswall. Eventually the business was taken over by a Yorkshire company who called their shops 'Decca Mecca' and a few years later they in turn were taken over by 'Fads' and the old building was demolished to make for a modern D.I.Y store. Today Tesco Metro occupies the site.

Wallasey Road

Wallasey Road, running from Liscard Town Centre to St. Hilary Brow, was originally known as 'Liscard and Wallasey Road'.

Looking at shops in the post war years of the late 1940s from the Liscard end began with Burton Montague Ltd, the tailors, George Lunt & Sons, the bakers, who have traded in Liscard since the 1920s. Next door, on the corner of Conway Street, was the pawnbrokers, Isaac Bellwood, who took over from Crane's Pawnbrokers after the First World War. Behind the Merseyside and North Wales Electricity Board showrooms was a children's playground sited off St. Alban's Terrace. At No. 19 was the City Funeral Furnishers run by Samuel Pritchard & Sons. Thomas Tickle was the ladies outfitters at No. 21 and Thelma's Cafe was next door. On the corner of St. Alban's Road was the 'Castle Hotel;' where Mrs Edith McQuone was the landlady. The public house was often called 'The Garden Inn' on account of the little gardens that were close by.

On the opposite corner of St. Alban's Road was Lobster's Pet Cafe which later became the Nat West Bank. For many years Percy Bailey had a shop at No.37 and was continued on by Mrs Clarrisa Bailey as a stationery business. The Catholics could buy Missal or a set of Rosary Beads at the shop. Other shops included Kwong Tong Laundry, which in the 1930s was Soo Wong Laundry and next door was Frank Gibson, the grocer, who extended the shop to No.53.

'The Boot Inn' existed in Elizabethan times. Originally it was a small whitewashed cottage, which stood on the rough road leading to Wallasey Village. This was knocked down and a two-storey building was erected in its place. Mr. Stephen was the landlord at one time and Bill Cash had the public house during the First World War, then George Wildgoose took over licence in the 1920s.

With the increase of traffic the road formed a sort of bottle-neck and the local authority suggested road widening and so a new 'Boot Inn' was built and in 1925 the old one was demolished.

There were a few more shops along Wallasey Road to Torrington Road and Belvidere Road junction which included Crompton & Jones Estate Agents and Challoner's Tobacconist. In the 1920s Joe Collins, the Liverpool Billiard Champion, had the Wallasey Billiard Saloon, at 93a, which was approached down a side entry. There were nine tables and many good players use to visit the saloon from time to time to play matches.

Further along the road was Wood's the Butcher, and among other shops was Mr. Thomas, the chemist (later Mr. Ambrose and Irwin's the grocers on the corner of Torrington Road where Mr. Arthur Grosvenor was the manager.

On the right hand side of the road, starting at the old 'Wellington Hotel', the original public house was built in the 1800's and was a popular meeting place for the locals. It had an "L" shaped bar and Harry Liversage was the landlord in the post war years after the Second World War. Due to road widening a plot next to the Wellington Pub on the Seaview Road side was purchased as the site for a replacement, the foundations of which were laid in June 1936. The new hotel and Coronation Buildings were built in 1937. Originally there was a single-storey thatched cottage next to the public house, followed by a two-storey cottage.

Continuing along Wallasey Road we have Marks & Spencers who had been located in Liscard Road but were bombed in the 1941 Wallasey Blitz so moved temporarily to No. 9-10. Jim Kent established his auction rooms after the Second World War at 14 and 15 Wallasey Road. There was also a social club in Wallasey Road which was above the shops and known as 'Coronation Social Club' and it was active in the 1930's.

In 1919 the town agreed there should be a market but it was some years before it was built. The site chosen was once occupied by 'Clairville Cottage'. The new building took the name of 'Central Market'. In the front of the Market in the 1920s was the showroom Rymers, which was later taken over by Sonia's gown shop. Central Market Garage was owned by Mr. Huggin's. The Market used to be covered on the inside where there were roughly about 20 stalls selling mainly a wide selection of produce. The stalls could be moved away and boards, like pallets, were laid flat on the floor for skaters to skate on. The wheels of the skaters were wooden. A rail was attached to the edge to stop the skaters running into the spectators. The Market was demolished by the early 1960s and new shops were built in its place. No. 40 to No. 52 were built by 1966 and No.54 to No. 60 were built soon after.

On the corner of Moseley Avenue stood Black's, the men's outfitters, which closed for business only recently after serving the community for more than half a century. There was a well-known grocery business at No. 68 and 70 called Monteith's. William Monteith then moved to a commanding position on the corner of Liscard Road and Wallasey Road, opposite the old 'Monkey House' shelter and had the largest grocery shop in Liscard. Previously the site had been occupied by Ellis Jones' mill. It was called Victoria Steam Mills. When the grocers finally closed down the property was taken over by Montague Burton, the tailors. The old premises at No.68 and 70 was taken over by Hugh Charlton, another grocer who remained for many years. Mr Boughey established his estate agency at No. 72 and the firm continues to this day. Bert Handy had a fine men's outfitters in the 1930's and continued after the Second World War at No. 104. He sold fine shirts and hats as well as supplying farms with their clothing needs. Leicester Stationery and Artists needs etc., were established in the 1930's at No. 106.

On the other side of Belvidere Road was a number of shops including William Brown's hardware business. Other shops included Miss Flynn's millinery (later Mrs. England's) John Crail, the baker in the 1920s and later to become Robert Plant's grocers. The Co-operative Society opened a large branch in this row of shops some years later.

The Breck

The Breck is a large feature of Wallasey village which cannot be passed by un-noticed. The Breck rises to around 180 feet at its peak as was a large open common for the people of the township. In 1845 Sir John Tobin of Liscard Hall purchased the land and worked the rocks as a quarry. The largest and most sheer rock face is known locally as Grannies Rock. The Breck was an old playground for the older people of Wallasey and many people would climb or attempt to climb the rock face. In recent years this has stopped as many of the foot holes and grips have eroded which is the only method of being able to climb up the face.

The top ground of the Breck is a relatively flat area which had been used as a bed for the large crane to sit on whilst it lifted materials from inside the quarry. This part of the rock face was much more difficult to climb and has resulted in several injuries and reported deaths. In Noel E Smiths book "Sand Stone & Mortar" he mentions that a young boy in 1927 attempted to jump from the top and parachute down using an umbrella. Needless to say the poor lad did not survive.

Before the massive onset of housing after WW2 the view from the Breck would have been that of large opened field with sporadic towns and villages dotted around the landscape. The Breck Footpath, behind the elevated houses on Breck Road next to the Ship Inn, was one of the main access routes to the Breck and Wallasey Mill. The Breck was once very extensive but by 1814 it was enclosed due to the encroachment of houses and the open land. As mentioned, stone from here built Leasowe Road. The contractor cut the road through the rock from St. Hilary's Brow to gain access as this was the nearest quarry.

Wallasey Village Brow

Wallasey Village brow is one of the highest points in Wallasey today and had several notable buildings on it. The Brow has changed dramatically over the years. At one time it was a very steep hill used only for horse and cart and only wide enough to fit one down. At the bottom of the hill, stood an old inn that was known as the "Sebastopol Inn". It's believed that the inn was named after the victory in the Crimean War.

The Old School House

The old school house was sold to local family man Penrose James who rented it to a local building company J.M Evans & Co. Within years

Mr James had sold the building off and it was occupied by local man, Mr Harry Morgan who ran it as the local Smithy. There were 2 other blacksmiths in the village already, the first being in Folly Lane close by, which was named Ledshams Forge and another on St Hilary's brow run by the same family. Below is a postcard that shows the old school building being used as a Blacksmiths in 1924.

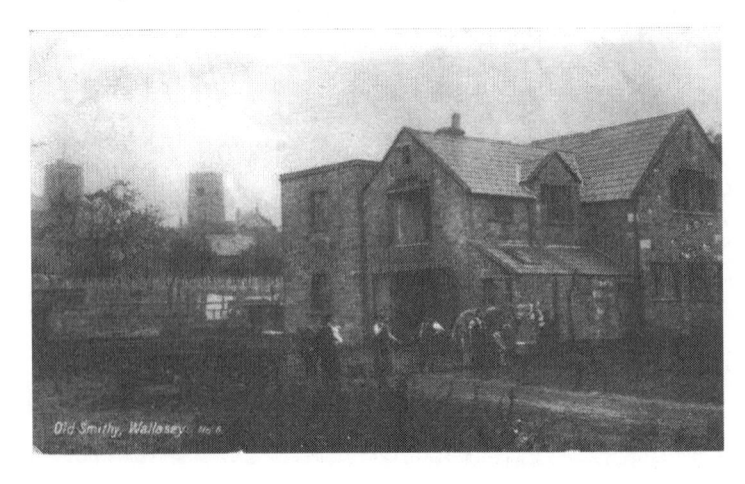

Darley Dene

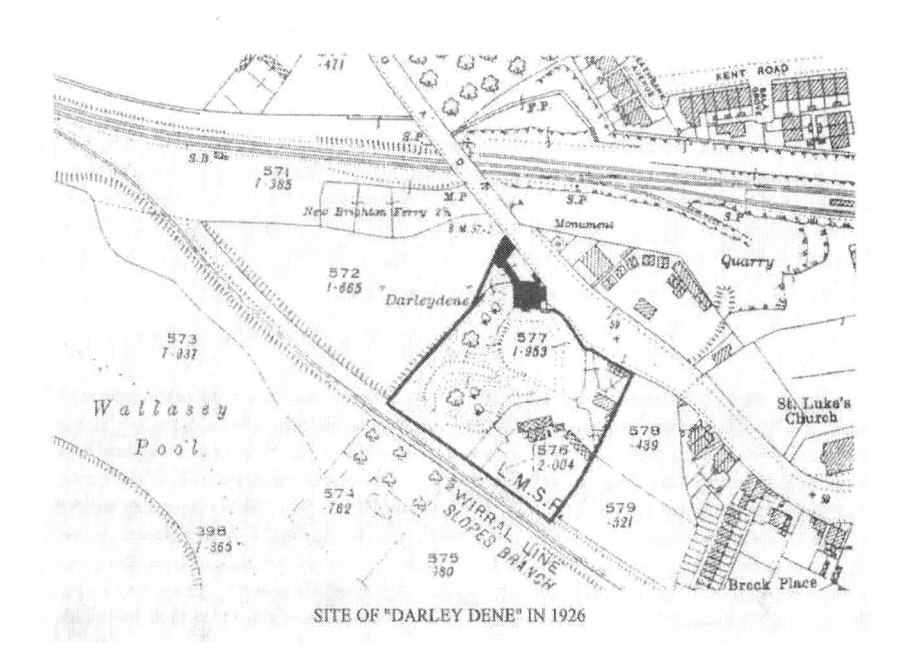

SITE OF "DARLEY DENE" IN 1926

It's stated in "The Rise and Progress of Wallasey" that 'Darley Dene' was built and occupied by Mr Thomas Monk, of the firm of Monk & Newell, Contractors, who were responsible for the construction of the Great Float Docks and the Seacombe Ferry Approaches of 1876, and in whose honour Monk Road and Newell Road were named. They also lowered St Hilary's Brow by eight feet at the top, to reduce the gradient. While it's perfectly true that Mr Monk lived at 'The Slopes', as the house was then called, from 1878 until the late 1880's, his name does not figure in a schedule of deeds in the possession of the Mersey Docks and Harbour Company, and it would this appear that he was a tenant only. It seems that we ha veto go considerably further back to find the origin of the building, and the earliest reference so far discovered, is a deed of Lease and Release of land, dated 1833, by Richard Smith, presumably Lord of the Manor of Poulton, and another to Sir John Tobin, who was known to be purchasing large quantities of land in the area as a speculation. In 1847 a Conveyance of the land was executed by William Shand, Merchant, of Springwood, Allerton, and Sir John Tobin to Mr John Bewley, an Accountant then living at 'Rose Cottage', Liscard and having his office at No.1 Brunswick Street, Liverpool. In 1845, Mr Bewley is shown as being in residence at 'The Slopes', and the inference is that the house was built at that time. It's said, with what truth is not known, that an astronomer was present during the construction, to ensure that the foundations were set North, South, East and West.

With one break, Mr Bewley continued at 'The Slopes' until the early 1870's, presumably until his death, and the house was then let to a Lt. Col. Clay, of the firm of Clay, Inman & Co. Iron Merchants, whose partner was Mr F.B Salmon, who lived for a time at Poulton Manor House. By 1878 the Lt.Col had moved to Birkenhead, and it was then that Mr Monk made his appearance. Following his departure there was two short-term tenants, but in 1895 Mrs D'Arcy Blackburn arrived on the scene, and was granted a lease of the property by the Trustees of John Bewley, deceased. She renamed the house 'Darley Dene', and later that year was joined by her uncle, Col. J.B Chantrell, who had lost his wife within the previous twelve months, and his son, William Smithson Chantrell, who subsequently entered local politics and attained the rank of Alderman. In 1896, John Bewley Jr., son of the original John Bewley, the builder of the house, died at Oxton, and this presumably decided the Trustees of his father's estate to dispose of the property. Mr R.C. de Grey Vyner, who already owned a good deal of land in the vicinity, was to dispose of the property. The Vyner family residences were Studly Royal at Ripon, and Gautby Hall in Lincolnshire, and those names are commemorated by various roads in the area - Ripon Road and Studley Road in Wallasey, and Gautby Road in Birkenhead. Mrs D'Arcy Blackburn had previously been a member of St. Hilary's congregation but transferred to St. Luke's, Poulton, when that church was opened for worship in 1900. She died in 1920, and in the same year Mr Vyner sold 172 acres of land in the area, including 'Darley Dene', to the Mersey Docks and Harbour Board. Alderman Chantrell, who appears to have taken over the lease of the property in 1909, remained in residence as the Board's tenant until his own death in November, 1938, and the following March the Trustees of his estates gave notice of termination of the tenancy. At the outbreak of war the Army took over, and it was in a heavy air-raid on the 12th March, 1941, that the house received a mortal blow, involving the deaths of seventeen soldiers. After later use for Civil Defence purposes, the demolition of the property was completed in 1959, and so passed one of the best-known of the old Wallasey mansions.

St Hilary's Church

Twenty three Monarchs and forty seven Rectors have come and gone since the first small church dedicated to St Hilary was erected in the 12th Century. Since then there have been six church buildings, the present one has been with us since 1859 occupying a position above the level of the old tower which was part of the fourth (1530) and fifth church buildings.

Until 1833 St Hilary's was the only Anglican Parish church in Wallasey. The building at that time was dilapidated and the size of a small village church. It was now overtaken by the building of new churches each with its own independent Parish. St John's Egremont (1833) with seating for 1,800 and its own burial ground, followed by St Pauls Seacombe (1847) then St James New Brighton (1856) and St Marys Liscard (1885) and others followed. All this was due to the Victorian population explosion and consequently massive house building.

109

Clearly when the leading church in Wallasey was left standing both by size and condition by these new parish churches something needed to be done. Fortunately, the answer lay in the fire which with the exception of the tower the church building was completely burnt down. The cause! Well, the overheated boiler after complaints from the congregation at the lack of heat during services was the most likely possibility. The fact that the horse drawn fire engine had to come from Birkenhead did not help, but the insurance did.

This report was printed in the Liverpool Daily Post Feb 2nd 1857:

The Parish Church of Wallasey, an ancient edifice, was utterly destroyed by fire yesterday forenoon. We have made enquiries respecting the catastrophe, and the following is the result. It appears that yesterday morning, so early as 2 o'clock, an inhabitant of the village, on looking through his bedroom window, discovered smoke and flame issuing from the church, and immediately communicated the fact to the rector, the Rev P Haggit. The Rector and several of the parishioners proceeded at once to the spot, and found that the flames were breaking through the windows, and the fire presented an alarming aspect. A messenger was dispatched for the Birkenhead Fire Brigade and engine that being the nearest from which effectual assistance could be had in such an emergency. In the meantime the flames spread rapidly, the persons present being unable to do anything towards arresting their progress.

From every window the fire burst forth, and burnt with such brilliancy as to be visible from a distance of several miles. In a brief period the roof fell in, shortly afterwards the fire brigade from Birkenhead arrived at half past three, but even then any efforts they could make were inoperative from the want of a supply of water. After some time water was obtained and the engine got into play, but it was then too late to make any effectual efforts towards arresting the progress of the fire. The body of the church was completely gutted and presented nothing but a heap of smouldering ruins.[15] *The register books and some documents of value connected with the church were the only things saved from the conflagration. The organ created a few years ago, and which cost three hundred guineas, was totally consumed, also a handsome font, presented to the church by Mr Chambers. The church contained a set of six bells, which fell with a tremendous crash during the progress of the fire. Only two of the bells remain entire, the remainder being broken to pieces. The church underwent very extensive improvements a year or two ago,*

---

15 Liverpool Daily Post Feb 2nd 1857

and a large sum of money was expended. A new roof was added, and the organ and the font previously alluded to were introduced at the same time. As to the origin of the fire there is little doubt. The fires connected with the flues for heating the building were lighted as usual about eight on Saturday evening, and it's supposed that some of the flues, becoming overheated, had ignited the flooring, and thus led to the fatal results which followed.

The loss is covered by insurance in the Sun Fire office to the extent of about £2000. The church was one of the oldest ecclesiastical edifices in the neighbourhood. The tower bears the date of 1530, although the church itself was rebuilt about 100 years ago. The ruins constitute an interesting sight; and during the whole of yesterday crowds went to view the desolation.

Liverpool Mercury Tuesday, 3rd February 1857

Destruction of Wallasey Church by Fire

On Sunday morning the ancient church of Wallasey, so well known to all who make occasional excursions to the Cheshire side of the Mersey, was totally destroyed by fire. The particulars of the catastrophe, so far as we have been able to learn, are as follows :- About two o'clock on Sunday morning an inhabitant of the village, on looking through his bed room window, discovered smoke and flames issuing from the church, and immediately communicated the fact to the rector, the Rev. F. Haggit. The rector and several of the parishioners proceeded at once to the spot, and found that their worst fears were realised. The flames were breaking through the windows, and the fire presented an alarming aspect. A messenger was dispatched for the Birkenhead fire brigade and engine, that being the nearest place from which any effectual assistance could be had in such an emergency. In the meantime the flames spread rapidly, the persons present being unable to do anything towards arresting their progress. From every window the fire burst forth, and burnt with such brilliancy as to be visible from a distance of several miles. In a very short time the roof of the body of the edifice fell in, and then it became evident that the building must very soon be utterly destroyed. The fire brigade from Birkenhead arrived about half-past three, but even then any efforts they could make were inoperative from the want of a supply of water. After some time water was obtained and the engine got into play, but it was then too late to make any effectual efforts towards arresting the progress of the devouring element. The whole of the body of the church was completely gutted, and presented nothing but a heap of smouldering ruins. The tower remains standing, this portion if the edifice having to extent been preserved by the effects of the fire brigade. The register books and some documents of value connected with the church were the only things saved from the conflagration. The handsome organ, which was erected a few years ago, and which cost three hundred guineas, was totally consumed, also a handsome font, presented to the church by Mr. Chambers. The church contained a set of six bells, which fell with a tremendous crash during the progress of the fire. Only two of the bells remain entire, the remainder being broken to pieces. The church underwent very extensive improvements a year or two ago, and a large sum of money was expended.16 As for the origin of the fire, little doubt is entertained. The fires connected with the flues for heating the building were lighted as usual about eight on Saturday evening. This was the ordinary practice on that the church might be sufficiently warmed when the congregation assembled the following morning for

---

16 Liverpool Mercury Tuesday, 3rd February 1857

divine service. It's supposed that some of the flues, becoming overheated, had ignited the flooring, and thus led to the results which followed. The loss is covered by insurance un the Sun Fire Office to the extent of £2000, but this, it's considered, will fall far short of the actual damage which has resulted from the conflagration. The church was one of the oldest ecclesiastical edifices in the neighbourhood. The tower bears the date of 1530, although the church itself was re-built about 100 years ago. During the day the ruins were visited by a large number of gentry on the Cheshire side, among whom we noticed Mr. D. Neilson, Mr. J.C. Ewart, M.P., Mr. Commissioner Parry, Mr. T.S. Raffles, etc., etc.

In 1859 the present church was consecrated. It had gas lighting until 1912. A small addition was added in 1923. Later the original pews were removed and chairs installed together with movable rear screens making a useful space narthex.

The Organ was built in 1861 by Henry Willis to the design of W. T. Best, who was the organist at St George's Hall, Liverpool. He was also the organist at this church for 3 years. The organ had two manuals.

Around 1903 the instrument was entirely reconstructed as a three manual organ of 39 stops and 15 couplers. In 1924 the organ was moved to the North choir aisle above the vestry. The rebuilt organ was designed by George Dixon and built by Rushworth and Dreaper. The organ was completely refurbished in 2010/11.St Hilary's and the Tudor Tower is a listed building. Each year, along with other Merseyside listed buildings; this church is open for inspection by the public with displays of its long history.

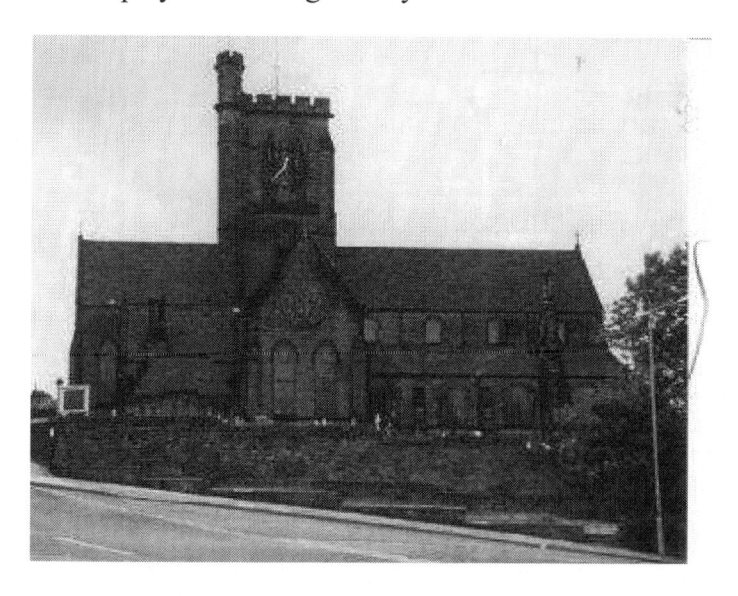

St Hilary's Brow

The two pictures give an insight into how St Hilary's brow looked between the years of 1900-05. The picture below contains a very strange looking edifice which stood just on the bottom of the Brow, near the Sebastopol Inn just at the crossing of Breck Road.

The old building was destroyed in 1930 to allow the road to be widened and was a casualty of a population boom like so many other buildings in Wallasey Village. Also in the picture to the right of the house, there was a small pathway, which lead up to the old Wallasey Mill.

Pictures of Breck Road, date unknown.

Old Wallasey Mill

The old Wallasey Mill stood on Breck Road just behind the old school house from 1765 until 1887, when it was deemed unfit for use.

A large house called Millthwaite was built on the site of the old mill and prospered for many years before finally being torn down to make way for flats which were named Millthwaite Court. Nothing remains of the old mill or the site except for the small pathway which once lead the millers up to their place of work.

Wallasey Model Farm

17 Picture, painted by C. H. Scott

The Model Farm in Liscard was owned by Harold Littledale, the son-in-law of Sir John Tobin. He was a well-known merchant in Liverpool and created the farm as a sort of hobby, rather than a business. The farm building stood in Mill Lane, while the farmhouse still stands in what is now Rullerton Road on the corner of Eldow Road. It dates from 1841 and had small fine diamond-shaped panes of glass in the windows.

The farm had all the latest machinery for up-to-date farming, for threshing wheat, dividing and grinding. It could also crush animal foods as well as mix food and churn butter. The buildings were very well-ventilated, the dairy being constructed with double walls so as to exclude the hot weather in summer. The machinery was operated by a powerful steam engine. There was also a place for smoking hams. Many farmers from far and wide came to see the Model Farm to study its methods and see the modern technology. The farm covered some 440 acres, as far as Wallasey Golf Links, as it's today, where the sheep were farmed. The Piggeries were near what is now Marlowe Road.

Wallasey Mill Pond

There was a pond close to the farm off Mill Lane, where the farm labourer's lived in the small cottages. There was a small island in the middle of the pond with a few trees growing and covered in grass. The Bailiff had his own house by the cottages. After Harold Littledale's death in 1889, the estate was purchased by the Council and some of the land was transformed into parts of Central Park.

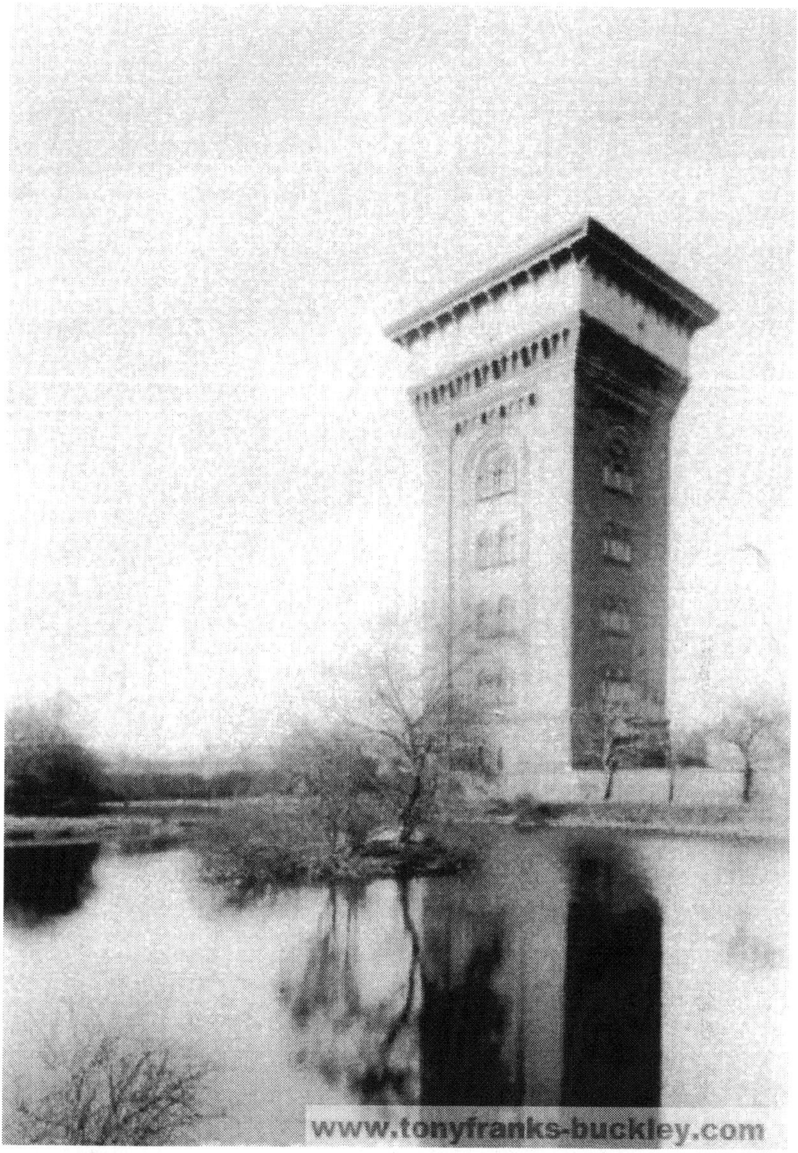
www.tonyfranks-buckley.com

Wallasey Village

Looking at Wallasey Village during the 1920s we begin at the top of School Lane, with No.1 being at one time a public house called 'Ring of Bells' where John Robinson was the landlord. Joe Coventry also had it at one time. In the early 1900's it was converted into a house and a shop. Mr. Jack Jones ran a small business which was later carried on by his wife. Mr and Mrs. Harold Kemp came to live in the house part. Their son, Herbert, became a member of the Wallasey Silver Band as a boy and was a member for many years.. Harold Kemp was an electrician. The small, slated house had a shop window on one side of the building with the name "J.Jones" written above. Over the door was an advert for "Players Please" (cigarettes) and further adverts were at the side of the shop window for "Wild's Gold Flake" and "Will's Capstan Navy Cut". Another sign for "Craven A" cigarettes appeared under the window.

George Cross lived at No.11 and it was later the home of Mrs. Fowler. Next door was Tom Fowler, the shoe maker. Stanley Strong, the dairyman was along here, where the welders (Fells and Grant) set up business. Mrs. Campbell lived at No.21, where Bob Williams used to live. Fred Voss was a market Gardener at No.25. His family may of owned a farm in Liscard. Bill Clooney was the cobbler at No.29. He was a small gentleman with an artificial leg, having lost it in the First World War. His cosy little shop was heated by an oil lamp and was converted from a "two up and two down" terraced house. On the wall was a glass case in which he proudly displayed his war medals.

Mrs. Francis Billington lived in 'Buxton House'. Tom Broster came to live at No.53 and next door to Jack Lidget was the home of the Halewood family at No.51, David Halewood was a market gardener. His father used to be the Water Inspector. Their cottage was between Live Farm and Buxton House. Not only was he the water inspector, but he was the Sergeant-in-Charge of the local fire volunteer fire brigade. he had six men in his charge who were dressed in blue uniforms and who wore brass helmets. They had to pull a red-painted handcart. Often the gorse would catch alight in the hot weather and they would be called out to deal with it.

Stonehouse Road gets its name from the large old house called "Stonehouse" which stood opposite the Black Horse. It was built in 1693 and was demolished in 1895. John Robinson lived there at one time.

In the 1930s we had Doug Tate (greengrocers), Mrs. Holroy's chip shop and Harry Ellison, the wallpaper and paint business, opened a branch at No.73. Ted Williams was the verger at St. Hilary's Church. He lived at No.93 Wallasey Village and Jim Cartan did quite a lot of bricklaying in the village. He lived next door, which later became Walton's chemist, who had crossed from the other side of the road. The Co-operative grocery was on the corner of Lycett Road and Mr. Bee was the fruiterer and florist, Herbert Triplett opened as a fishmonger. Lunts the bakers and the dressmaker, Mrs. Jones, and Mr. Peter Grant was the ironmonger on the corner. Lawton's farm was at the top of Leasowe Road which became the site of Roberts, the butchers. Bill Lawton was a farmer until about 1902. There used to a lamp post in the middle of Leasowe Road, with a horse-trough in the base. At a later date the trough was removed and a public drinking bollard was put there in its place. Mrs. Swindells took over Broome's confectionery shop at No.113 and the popular grocer was Owen McEneany, the property being known as 'Avondale'. The British and Argentine Meat Company was No.117 (later Dewhursts) and Sam Ledsham had the fruit shop next door. Mr. Howard gave up the fish and chip shop and Mr. Fell opened a furniture store in the premises. Coombes had boot repairers and there was MacFisheries next to the chip shop (Fred Cundle). Bill Spark used to live at No.125, Ted Ledder had a shop and Bill Humphreys was the manager of the fishmongers (Neptune Fish Marts). Mr. Moody used to have this shop. He was a boot and shoe dealer.

The 'Stone Cottages' were built around about 1840/1850, and are near the top of Marlwood Avenue. These are the 'two up and two down' type and are the last of such cottages in the village. There are three in number. In No.2 was Joe Howard and later his daughter, Mary, lived there. Harold Pemberton, the printer, lived next door. In the end house was Ted Ledder, who had his shop in the village at No.133. Joe Hazelhurst came to live No.1. He was a member of the Wallasey Silver Band.

P.L. Edwards was the draper on the corner of Beechwood Avenue. The sold boots and shoes in the early days. Then they sold school uniforms. Harry Hocking had the stationers who had opened in Mr. Atkinson's old shop on the opposite side of the road. Mr. Rogers had the chemists shop until Walter Quayle bought the business. They were qualified in optics and also sold wine and spirits. He was also a photographic chemist and Mr. Quayle Jr. was a keen amateur photographer. Anthony Quayle, the famous actor, was a relative of Mr. Quayle.

Next door was the butchers. The Robinsons were the decorators and plumbers in the village. George Webster was the market gardener and Fred Webster before him. Bill Rogers had also been a market gardener, as had Ted Webster in the 1890's. George York was the grocer. He had been the manager of Tranton's grocery business. The tobacconists was run by Mrs. Povall. Then there was the market gardener which was run by another well-known village family, the Sparks. Tom Sparks and his sons were very hard workers. By the garage was the builders, Tate, Pumford and Doughty, who built many houses in Wallasey. Mrs. String was landlord at 'The Farmers Arms'. There were three little cottages known as 'Mersey Cottages' In the 1930's, Arthur Watson lived at No.1, Arthur Broster in the next cottage and Frank Little at No.3. Henry Webster lived at 'Mersey House'. He was the market gardener. Miss Bamber ran a small cafe by the cinema and Mrs. Walsin had the confectioners. William Fowler was later at N0.227. The old "Cosy Cosmo" (the Coliseum picture-house) opened on Whit Monday, 1913. In those days it was a pretty little picture-house, being decorated in blue, white and gold with matching carpets. Harry Manchester was manager in 1935. In 1941 the building received a direct hit and had to be demolished. It was rebuilt in 1951 and appropriately renamed as "Phoenix". After a considerable life it closed on 6th July, 1983 and was demolished. It is now the site of sheltered housing.

Joe Wragg, the police officer, lived in Wirral villas in the 1890's. The old Presbyterian Hall became the Central Hall for the Plymouth Brethren. The 'Mission Hall Cottages' were close by and Jim Courtney lived in one of them. He worked for the railway as a signalman. Martha Joynson used to live in one of the cottages in the 1800's.

Phil Maddocks was the barber and Mrs. Morris was the confectioner on the corner of Green Lane. Bob Kelly was the grocer on the other side. He had been taken over from John Jones. His cafe was at 259, 261 and 275 and was known as 'Village Cafe'. They had a large room for whist drives and parties. Bill Holmes was the butcher and Jim Walton was the fruiterer at No.267, who had Dan Darragh's old shop.

Bert Leigh had the outfitters, and Mary Spencer was the fruiterers. Boult Brothers were the ironmongers and Bob Kelly had his shop, along with Mr. Rogers. who had a grocers shop next door to Irwin's grocers on the corner of Bidston Avenue. Storey's drapery was in the old outfitters and Mr. Samuel Morgan was the jeweller. The post office was on this side of the road and Mrs. Roberts was in charge. Mr. Walter Spriging was the pharmacist. Barber and Company were next to the Bank of Liverpool and Martins. The bank opened on 15th November, 1909, and Mr. Roberts was the manager in the 1920s. The Station-master's house stood on the corner of the approach to the station and Bob Jones was the station-master. He lived in 'Station House'. It used to have a small garden in front but, due to road widening, was removed. Frank Bennion was the Station-master in the 1920's, also Albert Mack was Station-master in 1936.

On the right-hand side of Wallasey Village, we have the 'Cheshire Cheese' public house which, although rebuilt, dates back to the 1600's. The present building was erected in 1885 and, not long after this date, Ted Bryant was the landlord. During the First World War, Robert Davies was the licensee and Bill Bryan was there in the 1920's. Years ago they served home-brewed ale and one could get bread, dairy and milk cheese there. Just past the public house there was a field which was known as the "Old Field" where the lads built their bonfire to celebrate Guy Fawkes Night. Opposite the field was a tin shed where the fire engine was kept. On the corner of Folly Lane was a house and shop which was run by Mrs Campbell. She sold sweets and tobacco. Later there was a laundry along here and Bill Hall had confectioners in what was Mrs. Ledsham's old shop. There was a smithy on the corner of Folly Lane. On the corner of Perrin Road there was Welton's chemists and Arthur Kersley was the upholster at No.52. Tramton's the grocers were there, as was Mrs. Davies the tailor. Mrs. Luxton had the chandlers next to the Black Horse, James Westcott had the inn during the 1850's and when he died his wife, Hannah, continued on and then David Burrowman took charge. Jim Lawton was landlord in the 1890's and a few years later Alf Peers was the popular host. The old inn had been built in 1722 and was demolished in 1931. Lucy Gilbert kept the little 'Cabin'sweet shop in the village. Alf Hughes lived in the 'Black Horse Cottages'. Mrs. Ada Williams lived in 'The Cottage' and Frank Rowe was the fruiterer at No. 88. Marshall Ramsbottom used to have the 'Dairy Farm there at one time.

Miss. Norman was the draper, and Jane Hamilton had the post office and grocers, which was eventually taken over by Mr. Howard and, in turn, his two daughters took over the post office. It had ceased to be a grocers, it have been changed to a stationers. Mr. Arthur Capper was the dentist, who was in practice on Tuesdays and Thursday between 3.00pm and 7.00pm. There was another dentist who also practised with Mr. Capper whose name was Mr. Middleton.

Mr. William Hayes was the optologist in the same building. Mrs. Maude Peachey had a confectioners at No. 94 and George Strong had his dairy lower down the road.Next door was the home of the local midwife, Mrs. McFall. The Williams brothers were grocers and next door was a wine shop. Above was the local Conservative Club. Mr. Tom Linton was the manager of the London Joint City and Midland Bank for some years, and on the other corner of St. John's Road was Hamilton's Bakery. Miss. Tessa Brew as the manageress. Mr. Hamilton's son, Herbert 'Duke', was a footballer and he played for Tranmere Rovers, Everton (1926) and Preston North End. The family lived in St. John's Road. Harold Nichols was the barber and Mr. Moody did the boot repairing. William Sparks and Sons were the dairymen at No.144 and Mrs. Hardwich was a draper. Fred Clough worked on the market gardens and the district nurse lived next door. Everybody knew Nurse Mary Bishop. Tom Cooil, the saddle maker was by the grocers and Charlie Garner was a fruiterer. Bryon and Francis were the poultry dealers. Jim Webster had 'Pear Tree Farm'. It got its name from a large pear tree that grew in the garden. At one time the cottage was called 'The Poplars'.

Alice Webster looked after the farm at one time. They had a field by Sandy Lane which was for grazing. The farm was by 'Big Yard' which ran between the village and St. George's Road. There were a number of small houses in the 'yard' and among the people that lived there was Ernie Hazelhurst, the market gardener, Arthur Rome, the painter and Harold Rogers, who worked at the reservoir. There were also piggeries and greenhouses which were later owned by George Jackson. The authorities decided to widen the road and the farmhouse had to be knocked down in 1961. Next to the farm was a boot repairer. 'Willow Cottage' stood at right angles to the main road. The whitewashed cottage was demolished for road widening in March 1946. It had been built in 1737 and only the house-plate remains. It is kept at Earlston Library and has the initials 'R.I.O.M.' In the 1930s it was known as 'Willow Nurseries', where the Jones family lived in the cottage from 1903. They brought up seven children there. Herbert Jones was a gardener and jobber. He was also a florist and sold bedding plants.

At No. 146 was the furniture maker, Charles Dalrymple. He had knocked a number of small building into one. The tunnel had to walk through a sort of tunnel-like passage to see the products on show. Tables, chairs, sideboards, etc., were all made of oak and other timbers which were all nicely stained and polished. The site is now part of St. Mary's College grounds. John Baker (confectioner) and Arthur Cornwell (hardware) were in this part of the village. Robert Webster lived at No.160 and he was a market gardener. George Shaw kept the 'Traveller's Rest' public house. Dick Goodwin and Ted Farnworth were previous landlords. It closed in 1939. The College grounds now occupy the site. Thomas Sparks lived 'Laburnum Cottage', which had been built in 1816. This fine sandstone cottage had to be demolished for road widening. Mr. Sparks died on 10th April, 1932. His son married Miss. Povall from the Village. The cottage carried the initials TSA which stood for Thomas Senior and Maybe Anne. There were two other sons, who lived in Marlwood Road. The cottage stood where St. Mary's College grounds are. Eric Barker, a policeman, lived at No.90 and George Nelson lived in the next house. George Strong was next door-but-one to the policeman. It was then called 'Holly Cottage'.

'Mason's Cottages' were at the bottom of Sandy Lane. One or two had been made into small shops. They were demolished to make way for the tramlines in 1910/1911. Mrs. Cunningham lived by the Presbyterian Church and her husband used to be a market gardener. Next to the church was 'Dean's Cottages'. At No.222 was Mr Cuthbert, the seed merchant. George Dean, the market gardener, lived in the row, as well as a couple of other gardeners. Another row of cottages were called 'Kendrick's Cottages' and the Lighthouse Inn was in the care of Mrs Jones. Sarah Kendrick was the landlady at one time. It was once two cottages and said to have been established in about 1718. The local fishermen used to gather here for a chat and a drink of ale. The old building was knocked down in 1966 on completion of the new public house.

'Billy's Gowns' the fashion shop was run by Miss Windsor and Miss. Jenson. Horn's, the outfitters, were next to Harry Smith's hardware shop and Mr. Jones was the butcher. Mr. Mumford, the photographer, used to have his shop and studio in this part of the village in about 1915. After the war he thought he might do better in New Brighton so he moved to Victoria Road. Jack Skirrow was the fruiterer at No. 264 and the ladies fashion shop was owned by Sergeant and Newell. Farther along the main road was the stationers and newsagents who have been known for years as the 'Criterion Bazaar Company'. These shops were in the Grove Arcade. At the end of the row of shops was Reece's Cafe. They had several branches throughout Merseyside. Mrs. Reece once lived at 'Highfield' in Mill Lane. Reece's had another cafe in Harrison Drive, which was a wooden building on supports, which catered for the number of crowds going to the beach. Above the shops was the 'Grove Hotel', which opened in 1909 as a temperance hotel. In 1920 it cost 5s. 0d. for entrance to the ballroom to enjoy dancing to the music of Arthur Gregson. In the 1950's it became the Melody Inn Club. This block of shops had been extended in the early 1900's. The Grove Cafe used to be at the end of the row at about that time and they put on some very nice luncheons, dinners and afternoon teas. In the 1950's the upstairs was transformed into the Melody Inn Club until it was badly damaged by fire in the 1960's.

Thomas Suckley was the steward of the Grove Golf Club and he lived in 'Summer Cottage'. The Post Office was, at one time, at No.171 and Miss. Kemp lived next door. Madge Kemp was a market gardener and had her land in Grove Road, running to St. George's Road. The work was too heavy for one, so she asked Sammy Lovell for help. Madge later went to live in Green Lane.

'The Springs' is at the very end of the village and was the home of the solicitor, Albert Wright. It was built in 1840. It is thought that one of the fireplaces in the house came from the old 'Great Eastern' iron ship and the wooden paneling in the lounge was once a racing box which was connected with the old Wallasey Races. The porch of this sandstone house seems to have been added at a later date as the name 'Springs' above is somewhat hidden. It is thought that the house may have once been a school house.

Harrison Park & Drive

Harrison Park was presented to the public in 1896 by the Harrison family which was received with much gratitude amongst the local populace. Harrison drive opened shortly after in 1901 and stretched right down to the shore line, where there was a bathing station complete with a cafeteria and changing rooms. The drive suffered from many teething problems in the early days mainly arising from sand blowing across it, sometimes leaving it barely recognisable.

A New Park for Wallasey

Liverpool Mercury Wednesday, 8th January 1890

Local Government Board Inquiry

At the Public Offices, Egremont, yesterday, Major-General C.Phipps Carey, R.E., held an inquiry on behalf of the Local Government Board into the application of the Wallasey Local Board to borrow £25,000 for the purchase of land to be used as a public, and £350 for works of sewerage. Besides a very large attendance of the public, the following members of the Wallasey Local Board were also present :- Messrs T. Dean, G.H. Peers, R. McGeoch, J. Davies and W. Evans. Mr. Danger (solicitor to the local board) supported the application on behalf of the local board, and Mr. A.T. Wright appeared on behalf of owners of land and for the New Brighton Ratepayers' Association. opposing the application.

Mr. Danger said that the estate which the board wished to convert into a public park consisted of 50 acres. upon which the Liscard Hall, with washhouses, cottages. stables, and vineries, with two entrance lodges, stood. About 22 acres was arable and meadow land, and it had a long frontage along the Liscard Road and on the north end of the Mill Lane. On the west side, and behind the Liscard Hall, there existed what was now termed the recreation ground, which was presented to the parish by a gentleman, well known in the district about four or five years ago. These grounds were, however, not freely used, in consequence of the difficulty of access. The proposed park could be purchased for £23,000, at the rate £460 per acre. The contract had been entered into, subject to the Local Government Board, giving their sanction to the borrowing of £25,000 for the purchase and other expenses. The board had taken the feeling of the ratepayers on this matter by means of a vote in answer to the question which was addressed by circular to every ratepayer, "Are you in favour or not of the acquisition by the Wallasey Local Board of the Liscard Hall estate for the recreation and games". The result of this inquiry was 2799 votes in favour of the proposed scheme and 575 against.[18]

---

18 Liverpool Mercury Wednesday, 8th January 1890

Mr. Vickess (clerk to the board) having explained the financial position of the board, Mr. Heap (chairman of the board) said that he considered the board should acquire the park, as its financial position quite justified the expenditure necessary to do so. (Hear, hear).

Major Chambres, Messrs. James Smith, Henry Wall, F.Johnson, W.G.Holland, G.H.Peers. R.McGeoch all spoke in favour of the scheme, and remarked on the advantage which the poor of the district would derive from the park, and the benefit the inhabitants generally would receive from it.

Mr.G.H.Ball opposed the application. In doing so he said that the scheme itself of constructing a park was most desirable for public health and improvements if all kinds were, no doubt, of great advantage to the district; but what they had to consider was whether they could afford to expend on this park. So far as the scheme itself was concerned, it was feasible and reasonable of they would limit the park to something like 23 acres; but 50 acres made it too large to sustain. (Cries of "no, no"). He referred to the park at Stanley, which he said, was over 100 acres in extent; but a portion was sold off for building purposes. so that it was limited to an acre of something like 90 acres. To maintain that 90 acres an expenditure of something like £1100 or £1200 per annum was necessary, and yet the park was in a deplorable condition (A voice : "More shame to the Liverpool Corporation"). It had been stated that the annual charge for the purpose of the proposed park would not exceed 1⅞d. in the pound, but that was the cost of the land only, and nothing whatever was charged for maintenance. The £2000 which had recently been borrowed was calculated to provide something like £100 a year towards the expenses of maintaining the park. As to the canvass among the ratepayers, no reliance whatever could be placed upon it. A large proportion of the persons who had signed were not ratepayers, and the ratepayers themselves had been derived as to the actual cost. It was not true that the whole of the opposition had come *from New Brighton - it had come from Wallasey. (A voice : "It has come from yourself alone." Laughter).*

Mr.W.Colbourne also opposed the movement, remarking that the park would not be an advantage to the whole of the district (Hear, hear).

The Rev. J.H.D.Cochran, on behalf of the working people, strongly advocated the utility of the proposed park. He had worked in a crowded parish of Liverpool, but in no part of Liverpool were the poor people so densely crowded together as in the village of Liscard. He thought, like the rich, the poor people should have a garden and recreation ground wherein they could enjoy their leisure, and to be any use that park or garden must be within half a mile of the people. (Hear, hear).

Mr. M.T.Graveson maintained that a park would develop the property in the neighbourhood. If the land fell into the hands of the builders, as most assuredly it would do, there would be a large wilderness of streets and the rural character of the district would be completely changed, and the property which would be built on the site would almost ruin the good property in the neighbourhood. He contended that the park would prove one of the greatest blessings to the district. (Hear, hear).

Mr. J.M. Hawkins spoke of the depreciation in the value of property as having now stopped, and that the board had acquired the park at a reasonable rate when the value of property was greatly depreciated. Mr. Ball did not represent the feeling of the board - (Hear, hear) - and he doubted whether any scheme had come before the Local Government Board with a greater preponderance in its favour, both in the board and amongst the outside ratepayers. (Hear, hear). He referred to the great increase in the ferry receipts - over £4000. This would entirely cover the cost without an increase in the rates, and in a few years they would have cleared off a debt for which 6d. in the pound was now being paid by the ratepayers. The policy of the board was to acquire the park when it could be acquired, but to leave the laying out until the time when more funds were available. The proposal of the board was not to spend a large amount in maintenance, but to acquire the park and leave any larger expenditure in laying it out until a further period. (Hear, hear).

Mr. Brooks, a ratepayer in Liscard, said that out of 1600 people he had visited between Seacombe and New Brighton, only 25 were directly in opposition to the proposal.

Mr. Peers also supported the scheme.

Mr. Wright then called a number of ratepayers and property owners, who gave their views in opposition to the scheme. The feeling expressed by these witnesses was that the park was totally unnecessary for the welfare of the neighbourhood, and that the financial condition of the board was not such as to justify so large an expenditure simply for the purpose of amusement and recreation. Some of them were in favour of a modified scheme.

At the conclusion of the evidence Mr. Wright, in reviewing the various arguments addressed in opposition, remarked that the board was in debt to such an extent that they ought not to be allowed to increase it. Already it amounted to about £16 per head of the population as compared with £6 in Liverpool. The site was not central for the whole district, although it was central for Seacombe and Liscard, but these townships were not alone going to pay for the park.

Mr. Danger having addressed the meeting, the commissioner signified his intention of reporting the results of the inquiry to the Local Government Board.

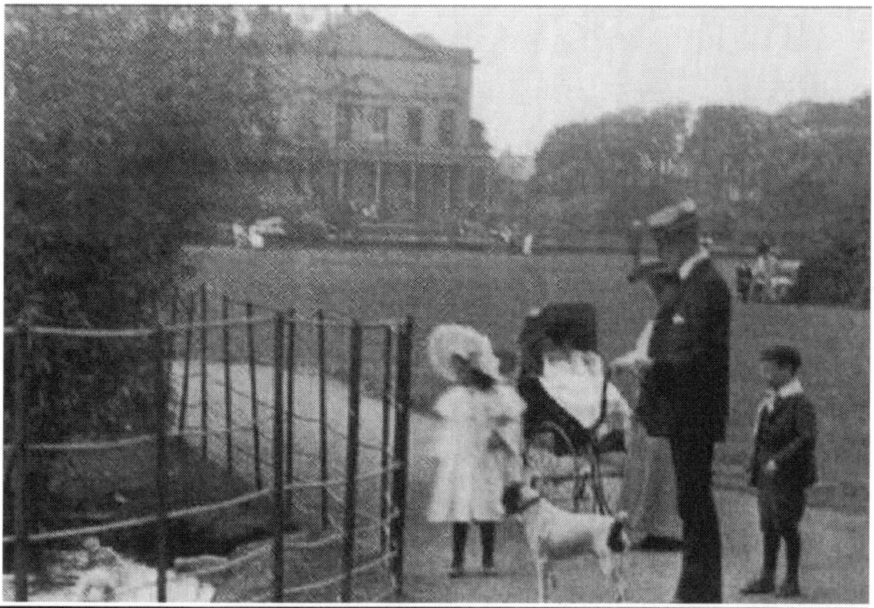

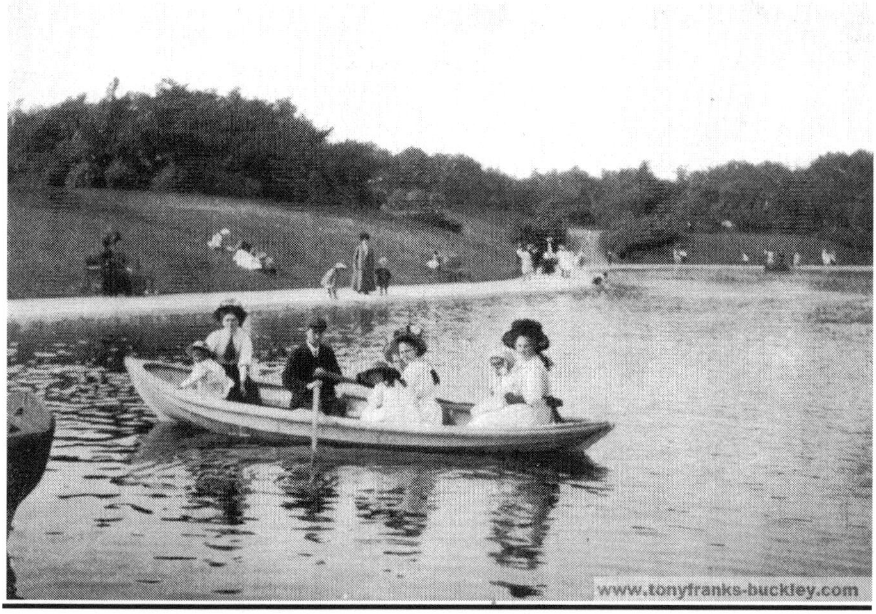
www.tonyfranks-buckley.com

New Brighton Vale Park

In 1830 the area of land now occupied by Vale Park was formerly an estate called Liscard Vale, this being the origin of the park's name. The estate was later divided, with the second estate being named The Woodlands, now recalled by Woodland Drive, the Road situated at the park's Western boundary. In 1898, at a cost of £7,750, both estates were purchased by Wallasey Urban District Council, with the intention of providing a 'lung' or breathing space for an increasing population. The combined grounds opened as Vale Park on 20th May 1899.

Vale House built c1830 was originally a family home possibly belonging to a Cotton broker and was later extended. The family of Charles Holland, a Liverpool businessman and Wirral JP, lived here for over 50 years. Charles Holland travelled widely, returning with Botanical specimens and many of the trees now gracing the park were planted by his gardeners. For much of the 20th century Vale House accommodated the park staff, though it lay disused for some years the Friends of Vale Park encouraged the council to restore it. It opened as a community centre in 1993.

VALE PARK, NEW BRIGHTON.

William Grinsell Burston was the first Head Gardener of Vale Park, though his title was Curator, perhaps reflecting the knowledge and expertise of someone in this position at the end of 19th century. He came to Liscard Vale as Head Gardener in 1890. When the estate was taken over by the council; 'W.G' (as he was always known) stayed on and became Curator to the new Vale Park. Most of the laying out of the park, arranging the flower beds and paths, etc was undertaken by him. He was considered to be an expert Botanist, and spent many hours sorting seeds and discussing rare plants with specialists from Liverpool museum. W.G. died at Vale Park House in 1918.

Ernest Burston, W.G's youngest son worked as a Vale Park gardener between 1918 and 1946 living with his wife in Vale House which had been converted into two flats following his father's death. In 1926 a Doric-columned bandstand was constructed and played host to brass band concerts as it continues to do so to this day.

Vale Park, showing New Band Stand, New Brighton

The park eventually passed into the hands of Wirral Borough Council and has seen some restoration over the years, mainly due to the efforts of The Friends of Vale Park. A successful application for funding in 1999 enabled restorative work to the Bandstand to be undertaken. Works included; waterproof treatment to the dome roof and rainwater channels, refurbishment of performers changing facility, re-laying of staging, exterior painting and re-cladding to the rear elevation to improve security of the structure.

During 1999 funding was also sought to replace the entire perimeter fencing of the bandstand site to both better secure and define the space as a performance/events area. This work coincided with the parks centenary celebrations, the date of which is commemorated in steelwork topping the gate entrance into the area.

The park is still open to visitors and Vale House now sports a tea room which offers a relaxing view across the flower gardens which each year are beautifully presented.

Earlston House

SITE OF EARLSTON HOUSE 1926

Earlston House, now part of the Central Library, was originally a private residence. Initially the house belonged to John Ashley Marsden, of Liscard Castle, but its origins are a little obscure. An older house incorporated in it to some extent is shown on early maps as Old Liscard Manor House but that title appears to have been transferred in 1841 to the residence then known as 'Sea Bank', at the foot of Manor Lane. It was probably then that the name of the house was changed to 'Rose Mount', possibly by George Grant, who in the year mentioned moved here from his existing residence in Rodney Street, Liverpool.

Mr Grant, a magistrate, was a member of the firm of John Gladstone & Co., Merchants, of Castle Street and Union Court, Liverpool, and was thus a partner of Sir John Gladstone, Baronet, Member of Parliament, and father of William Ewart Gladstone, later Prime Minister. Sir John was a founder-member of the Athenaeum in Liverpool, and as far back as 1814, shortly after the Honourable East India Company's monopoly had been broken, he and George Grant despatched the first ship, the 'Kingsmill', from Liverpool to India, the round voyage being completed fifteen months later.

On the 7th and 8th January, 1838, Merseyside was struck by a tremendous hurricane, and as a result many ships were in difficulty. At least two, the 'Pennsylvania' and 'The Lockwood's', were driven ashore near Leasowe with great loss of life, some of the crew and passengers of the former being buried in St. Hilary's Churchyard. Great hardship was caused to the dependants, and the occurrence resulted in the immediate formation of the Liverpool Shipwreck and Humane Society. George Grant, who was then Chairman of the West India Association, and numbered among his other activities membership of the Liverpool Committee for the Relief of the Widows and Orphans and Clergymen, and the Vice-Presidency of the Liverpool Friendly Society, later the Liverpool Savings Bank, served on the permanent committee of the Shipwreck Society from its inception until 1860.

In 1855, however, he left 'Rose Mount' for Gambier Terrace, Liverpool, and was succeeded by Thomas Addison, of Horsfall & Addison , Stockbrokers, who had previously been living in Mount Road. After two years at 'Rose Mount' Mr Addison departed for 'Gorselands', a large house standing at the corner of Albion Street and Atherton Street, and 'Rose Mount' was then purchased by Robert Bell, a Tea Merchant, from the Executors of J.A Marsden, deceased. He was joined in 1860 by his son-in-law and partner, Lowry Mann, eldest son of William Mann of 'Zig Zag House'. In those days the grounds of the house, roughly 23 acres in extent, stretched as far as Seaview Road, and there must have been a pleasant outlook for the rear windows. Lowry Mann, like his father before him, had served a term as Churchwarden at St. Hilary's, and he frequently lent the lower field to the Sunday school for its annual "Treat".

It was about this time that the name was changed to 'Earlston House', a title which held well throughout the rest of its life as a private house. Robert Bell, who had continued to live at the house, died in 1878, and in 1883 Lowry Mann sold the estate to the Trustees of Anthony Gordon Smith for occupation by Mr Smith, a partner in the cotton broking firm of Smith, Edwards & Co., who were reputed to have made a lot of money at the time of the American Civil War. On Mr Smith's death in 1898, at the early age of 48, the property was purchased by the Corporation from his Executors for £20,000, and the Library was opened the following year. Thanks to a grant of £9,000 from the Carnegie Trust in 1908, the present extension was built and brought into use in 1911. The old house lost a wing in an air-raid in the last war, and the present staff car park now occupies the site.

Lowry Mann did not survive his departure from 'Earlston House' for very long, as he died in 1887 at the age of 52, and lies in St. Hilary's Churchyard with his wife who had followed him in 1890, and their only child, a daughter, Mary Margaret who had married and died in Bridgnorth, aged 45, in 1905.

Breck Hey House

SITE OF BRECK HEY IN 1911

Opposite the Central Library, in the days before the present Kirkway was cut through, there was an earlier Kirkway. It ran between Mount Pleasant Road and Earlston Road, adjacent to what later became a hockey ground of the High School, and later an extension of the School itself, then, as it today, new housing. At the Earlston Road end of the footpath, on the opposite corner to Kirk Cottages, stood stables belonging to a large house, fronting on to Mount Pleasant Road, opposite Mount Road, and known as 'Breck Hey'. Records show that in 1832 the site was part of land owned by John Ashley Marsden, of 'Liscard Castle', and that the house must have been erected within the next few years, as it was known to have been occupied by Palgrave Simpson, a well known Solicitor, who came from London in the 1850's to join the firm known as Simpson, North, Harley & Co.

Mr Simpson, having spent ten years in Wallasey, moved to Liverpool, and the estate was then sold by the Trustees of J.A Marsden, deceased, to Edward Hodgson Harrison, partner in Whitaker, Whitefield & Co., Brokers of Liverpool, a Director of the old Bank of Liverpool, Deputy Chairman of the London & Lancashire Fire Insurance Company, and a brother of Thomas and James Harrison, the ship owner's, the latter of whom was also a Wallasey resident. The purchase price was £3,589, and in 1870 Mr Harrison added to the estate by acquiring the Mill Field adjacent to the property, at a cost of £900, thus bringing the total area to something over four acres.

In 1884, Edward Harrison, who does not appear to have participated in the running of his brothers' ships, although he was a shareholder, sold the entire property to T.Raffles Bully, a Cotton Broker, for £4,000, and moved to Eastham. Where he had built for him large mansion known as 'Plymyard', and where he finally died in 1907 at the age of 82. Mr Bulley, who as a partner in S.M Bulley & Son, the well known Liverpool Cotton Broker and Merchants, was a man of considerable wealth, was nevertheless a Socialist who believed in assisting the under-dog, and life in the family home was not over-luxurious as a result, his four daughters being brought up to appreciate the value of money. Apart from the fact that he became a Wallasey Alderman, he was a brother of the founder of Ness Gardens, and was associated with him in the formation of Bees Limited, the seeds men.

In 1909 Alderman Bulley sold 6,471 square yards of land, part of 'Breck Hey' estate, to Cheshire County Council for £1,500 in connection with the establishment of the hockey ground mentioned earlier, and following his death in 1921 his Executors sold the house and the remaining land to Wallasey Corporation in 1923, for £5,000. In 1925 the present Kirkway was cut through, and the land on either side was sold to builders for the erection of the semi-detached houses which are there today. 'Breck Hey' itself was demolished at the same time. According to a niece of Alderman Bulley, the house was yellow-washed, and contained among other things a billiard room where plays could be staged. She remembered the large family parties at Christmas and other similar times, and mentioned that in those days, with belching chimneys and ship's funnels, it used to be said that one got black with soot just by walking in the 'Breck Hey' garden. Another lady has stated that she could remember visiting 'Breck Hey' when she was a child, and for a treat being allowed to go into the greenhouses to water the aspidistras!

The Mount

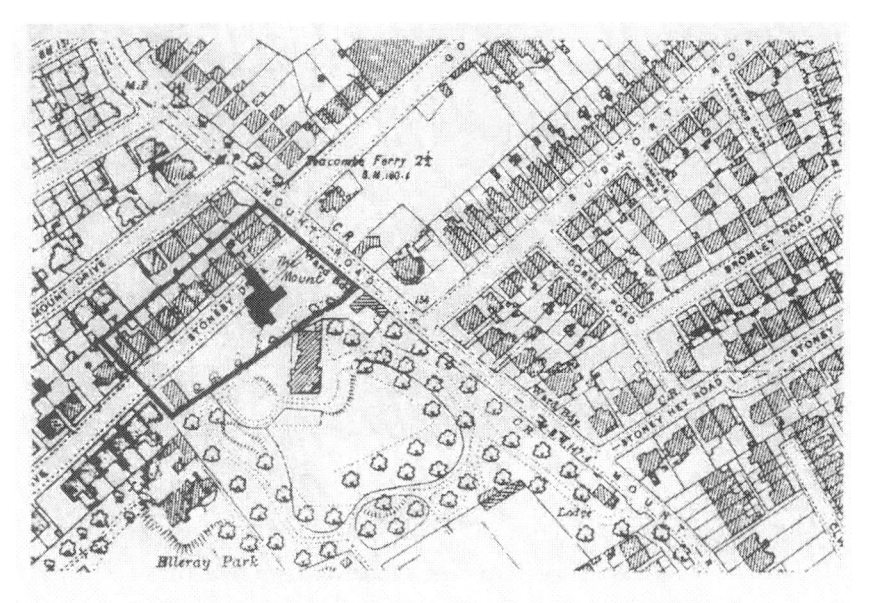

SITE OF "THE MOUNT" IN 1899 IN RELATION TO HOUSES IN 1926

Adjacent to 'Sudworth House', with access from Mount Road, stood another well-known house, called 'The Mount'. It's origin is obscure, but judging from the 1841 map it was owned by Thomas Sudworth, the probable builder of 'Sudworth House'. Mrs Sudworth, presumably then a widow, is shown in residence in 1843, but by 1849 she had been succeeded by Thomas Addison, a partner in Horsfall and Addison, Stockbrokers, of Liverpool. On his removal to 'Rose Mount', Earlston Road in 1855, Mr Addison was followed at 'The Mount' by Joseph Glynn Bateson, a partner with his father, Richard Bateson, of 'The Woodlands', New Brighton, and later of 'Newland House', Wallasey Road, in the cotton-broking firm of Richard Bateson & Sons.

Joseph Bateson had previously lived at 'Liscard Lodge', a large house standing in its own grounds in what is now Stoney Hey Road, and his stay at 'The Mount' lasted until 1868, when he gave way to Mr Francis D Lowndes, Registrar of what later became the Liverpool County Court, and a partner in the firm of what is now Lowndes & Co., Solicitors, who are still in practice in Liverpool. He had previously lived in Sandown Park, Wavertree, a fashionable area in those days, and in 1856 had married Dorothy Jane Livesey, daughter of James Livesey, Cotton Broker, at one time of 'The Mosslands' in Breck Road, Wallasey. During their married life she presented him with a total of six daughters and three sons, two of whom entered the Church, the third following in his father's footsteps and becoming a member of the legal profession in Liverpool. It would not appear that the production of such a large family had any adverse effect on Mrs Lowndes, who finally passed away in 1915 at the ripe old age of 80, when she was living in Dudley Road, but Mr Lowndes himself died in 1900, at the age of 66.

'The Mount', thereupon became a school, still well remembered by many as Miss Whiteway's St. Hilary's School for Girls. A certain amount of demolition of the house took place but the school continued until approximately 1935, when the remainder of the house was pulled down to allow for the completion of Stoneby Drive. A gravestone in St. Hilary's Churchyard records the fact that Miss M.A Whiteway was buried there in that year, at the age of 75.

Elleray Park

Elleray Park - Formerly Seafield

This house, as was the case with several of the other mansions in Wallasey, was probably built at the beginning of the 1830s, and for many years was known as 'Seafield House'. Early maps show it to have been in the ownership of John Astley Marsden, of 'Liscard Castle', whose practice appears to have been to purchase various properties in the district with mortgage assistance, develop them if necessary, and thereafter let them. In this particular case, the earliest tenant to come to light so far was Thomas Ogilvy, a nephew of Sir John Gladstone and a partner in the prominent Liverpool firm of Ogilvy, Gillanders & Co., who was in occupation from 1836 to 1839. For some years previously, Mr Ogilvy had lived at an unidentified address in Poulton, and, as is mentioned elsewhere, was to some extent concerned in 1829 with the purchase of the land on which 'Heath Bank' in Breck Road stands, but after he left 'Seafield House' he either died or moved completely out of the area, as no further trace of him can be found. His firm for the record was still in existence well into the 20th Century.

The Thompson family, who were destined to remain at 'Seafield House' for the next fifty years or so, were first to be found in residence in 1841, when they were represented by Joseph Thompson, a Corn Broker, his wife Jane, and three children. It should be remembered that in those days, long before the construction of Elleray Park Road, the grounds of 'Seafield House' stretched with certain exceptions as far as Mount Pleasant Road.

Whilst the entrance to 'Seafield House' was situated where it's now, in Hose Side Road, (Hose Side Road was first known as Marsden Lane and later as Seaview Road) there was no direct access from the property to Mount Road. The difficulty appears to have been overcome by climbing by means of a ladder over the wall into the grounds of 'Sudworth House', which lay immediately to the east, and then out at the lodge gates.

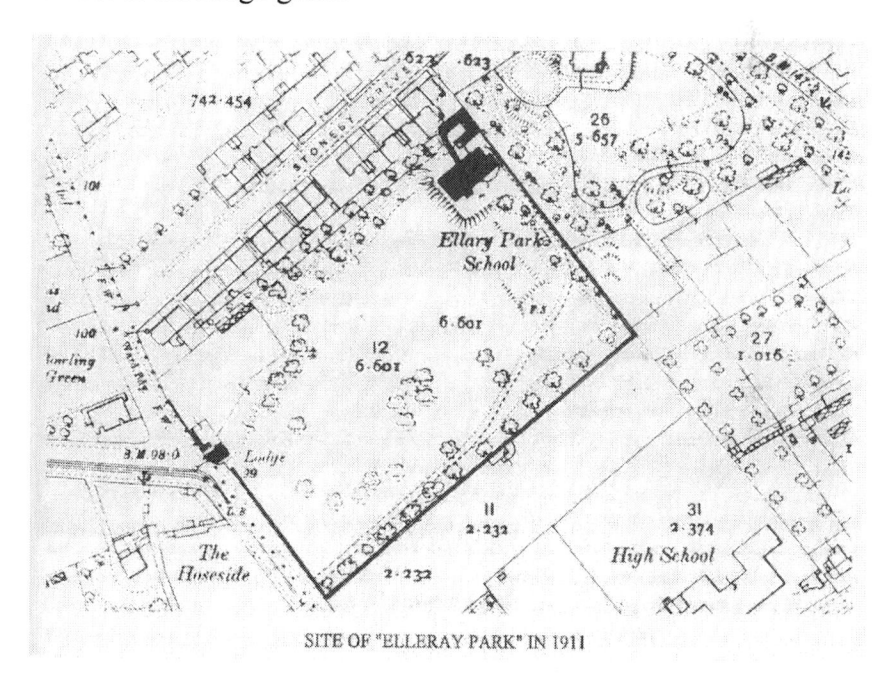

SITE OF "ELLERAY PARK" IN 1911

John Marsden, the actual owner of the property, died in 1853, and two years later his Trustees sold the house and just over eleven acres of ground to Joseph Thompson. Thompson and his wife continued to live there for the next fourteen years, but in December, 1869, when they were both in their eighties, they died within a few days of each

155

other, and were buried in St. Hilary's Churchyard. Unfortunately, a stained-glass window erected in the church to their memory was largely destroyed by enemy action in 1941.

Joseph Thompson's son, James William Thompson, a Cotton Broker, continued in residence at 'Seafield House' until his own death in 1886, at the age of 57, his widow remaining until 1889, when she appears to have let the property, first to Robert B. Steel, a Merchant, and later to Mr S. Stamford Parry, a Forwarding Agent in partnership in Liverpool with a member of the Herron family. However, in 1896, when Mrs Thompson had moved to Hemel Hempstead to live with her married daughter, the house and its eleven acres of land were sold to John Mahler, of 'Sudworth House', for £6,800.

Two years later came the big change at 'Seafield House', when the Revd. J.M Stuart-Edwards, M.A. transferred his boys' preparatory school from its former premises in New Brighton, and renamed the property 'Elleray Park'. Among the scholars prior to World War I were at least two who were worthy of mention. One was later to become Lt. Gen. Sir Miles Dempsey, Chief of the Imperial General Staff in the Second World War, and the other, the late Donald Boumphrey, had been described by Neville Cardus, the cricket critic of the 'Manchester Guardian', as it was then called, as one who, but for the Great War, would undoubtedly have been one of the finest schoolboy cricketers this country has ever turned out. Both boys were in the Shrewsbury School XI of 1912, with Boumphrey as Captain. After playing for Wallasey Cricket club for some years after the War, Boumphrey was appointed Games Master at Rydal School, Colwyn Bay, a post he retained until retirement. He died in September 1971 at Aughton, Lancashire.

John Mahler died in 1899, but 'Elleray Park' continued to form part of his estate until 1907, when his son John, as his Executor, made two sales, one, of 12,060 square yards of land fronting onto Mount Pleasant Road to Cheshire County council for £2,864.5/- (4/9d per square yard). to enable Wallasey High School for Girls to be built. The other sale, consisting of the Elleray Park mansion and 31,880 square yard of land, was to Mrs Celia Katherine Stuart-Edwards, wife of the Headmaster of the School, for £6,915.9.4d. There was Mutual Rights connected with this second sale, principally with regard to access, but in 1914 Mrs Stuart-Edwards was released from the Rights, presumably as Elleray Park Road was constructed about that time, and access problems would no longer arise. By 1923, Mrs Stuart-Edwards had died, and in that year her husband and the Trustees of her estate sold the property to Wallasey Corporation for £16,500, with a proviso that the Revd. Stuart-Edwards be left undisturbed until 1st August 1927.

When the Revd. Stuart-Edwards retired, a Mr R.C Statter assumed control of the School, but in the 1930's changing conditions necessitated a further move, and new premises were found on the corner of Warren Drive and Linksway. Some years later the school closed entirely. 'Elleray Park' was converted into a Special School, but the original house has since been demolished, and a new school built in the grounds.

The New Brighton Tower & Fairground

Back before I was born, New Brighton was a "Great" British Seaside Resort. It was more popular than Blackpool, offered many things to enjoy, and at one point in time had the highest tower in Britain. By the time I was born in 1981 it was all gone and as if it never existed. How did a booming leisure resort disappear virtually overnight?

First of all we must mention the New Brighton Tower which really was a truly remarkable landmark that featured on the New Brighton waterfront.

Here are the statistics of the Tower when it was fully complete

- **Start Date: 22nd June 1896**
- **Completion Date: 1900 (unsure of the exact date)**
- **Cost: £120,000**
- **Materials: over 1,000 tons of steel**
- **Height: 567 feet 6 inches to the top of the flagstaff**
- **Height above sea level: 621 feet.**
- **Architects: Maxwell and Turk of Manchester**
- **Builders: Handy sides and Company of Derby**

NEW BRIGHTON TOWER.

The New Brighton Tower was patterned on the world-famous Eiffel Tower in Paris. It all started when a newly formed company called The New Brighton Tower and Recreation Company Limited, with a share capital of £300,000 decided to purchase the Rock Point Estate of over 20 acres. The Tower was to be 544 feet high, with Assembly Hall, Winter Gardens, Refreshment Rooms and layout with a cycle track. The Tower was to be more elegant than Blackpool's. Shares were £1 each and the Tower would be made of mild steel.

During the construction of the Tower six workmen were killed and another seriously injured either though falls or accidents. On completion the Tower was the highest building in the country. Soon after the Tower was opened a young man threw himself off the balcony to be the first suicide from the building. Four lifts took the sightseers to the top of the structure at a cost of 6d. From there you could see for miles around including the Isle of Man, Great Orme's Head, part of the Lake District and the Welsh Mountains. The Tower is said to have attracted around half a million people in the year.

The Highest Structure and the Finest Place of Amusement in England.

General Manager & Secretary   -   R. H. DAVY.

Along with the Tower a ballroom was built and was one of the largest in the world, with a sprung floor and dance band stage. The orchestra had as many as 60 players and well over 1,000 couples could dance without overcrowding, it was decorated in white and gold, with emblems of various Lancashire towns. There was a balcony; with seats to watch the dancers below and behind this was an open space where couples could learn to dance. There was also a fine Billiard Saloon with 5 billiard tables and above the Ballroom was a Monkey House and Aviary in the Elevator Hall, there was even a Shooting Gallery!

As well as the Tower and ballroom the area was surrounded by a Tower Gardens Complex. The Tower Gardens covered something like 35 acres in all, with a large Japanese Cafe at the lakeside, where real Gondoliers had Venetian Gondolas. There was also a fountain and seal pond in the old quarry, with its rockery. Then there was a Parisian Tea Garden where one could have a cup of tea while watching the Pierrots. Towards the river end, there was an outdoor dancing platform which held a thousand dancers, where the Military

Band played, stating at 9 o'clock in the morning in the height of the season. Above the dance floor was a high wire for tightrope walking, without any safety net. The tightrope walker was a man by the name of James Hardy, who had a bet with another man that he could walk across the rope with a girl on his shoulders. He won his bet when he carried the barmaid from the Ferry Hotel across his back which was quite an interesting tale to have been told.

There were also other light orchestras which played here and at variety performances in the theatre in the afternoon. A good restaurant called "The Rock Point Castle" was situated amongst the trees, with lovely pathways to wander around. The Tower grounds had their own private Police force of up to 15 men would parade around and keep order.

However the tower did not last for long, the outbreak of the First World War the public were not allowed to go up to the top of the Tower for military reasons. In the war years the steel structure was neglected and became rusty through lack of maintenance and the cost of renovating was more than the owner could afford so sadly this became the beginning of the end of the tower. The top portion of the structure commenced to be dismantled on 7th May 1919 and was completed in June 1921. The brick portion comprising of the Ballroom and Theatre remained, together with the turrets. During the Second World War the basement was used as a communal air-raid shelter.

The Fairground remained with the Ballroom and other surrounding features until its final fate during the fire of 1969. The Old English Fairground was on a higher level which, in later years, became the motor coach park. The Himalayan Switchback Railway was a great favourite, as was the water chute, with the boats travelling down at speed into the lake. The Railway had previously been at the Brussels Exhibition. In the Lion House were 'Prince' and 'Pasha', two beautiful Cape Lions. There was also a good collection of other animals in the menagerie.

By 1961, when the photograph above was taken, the park had changed significantly, with several new rides and sideshows. The photograph was taken from the cable car ride, which whisked passengers from the beach level, to the upper areas of the park. The Beatles also around this time played the Tower Ballroom; this was proof of how popular New Brighton was at the time. The Beatles final appearance at the Tower Ballroom took place on Friday 14 June 1963 on a special NEMS Enterprises presentation of their 'Mersey Beat Showcase' series. The Beatles were supported by Gerry & the Pacemakers and five other groups.

Disaster struck in 1969. The fire, the fourth that the tower had suffered, started on Saturday 5th. April 1969. The manager and staff had left the building the night before about 8-30pm. after a routine check, the stage area was not included in their check! A police constable discovered the fire in the stage area in the west wing of the tower early next morning. In the 1970s, the area where New Brighton Tower once stood was redeveloped as River View Park

Sadly the Tower Ballroom fire in 1969 became the end of an era in New Brighton which never recovered or rebuilt after the incident. The fire was the end moment for the area with the fairground closing immediately, leaving only the New Brighton Palace as a place for small entertainment compared to the delights that were previously on offer before the fire.

New Brighton Minature Railway

On a small plot of land on the banks of the River Mersey, showman Tommy Mann ran his pleasure grounds, where in 1947 he opened an 18 inch gauge miniature railway. As you can see in the pictures it was a popular attraction. Another item lost in time.

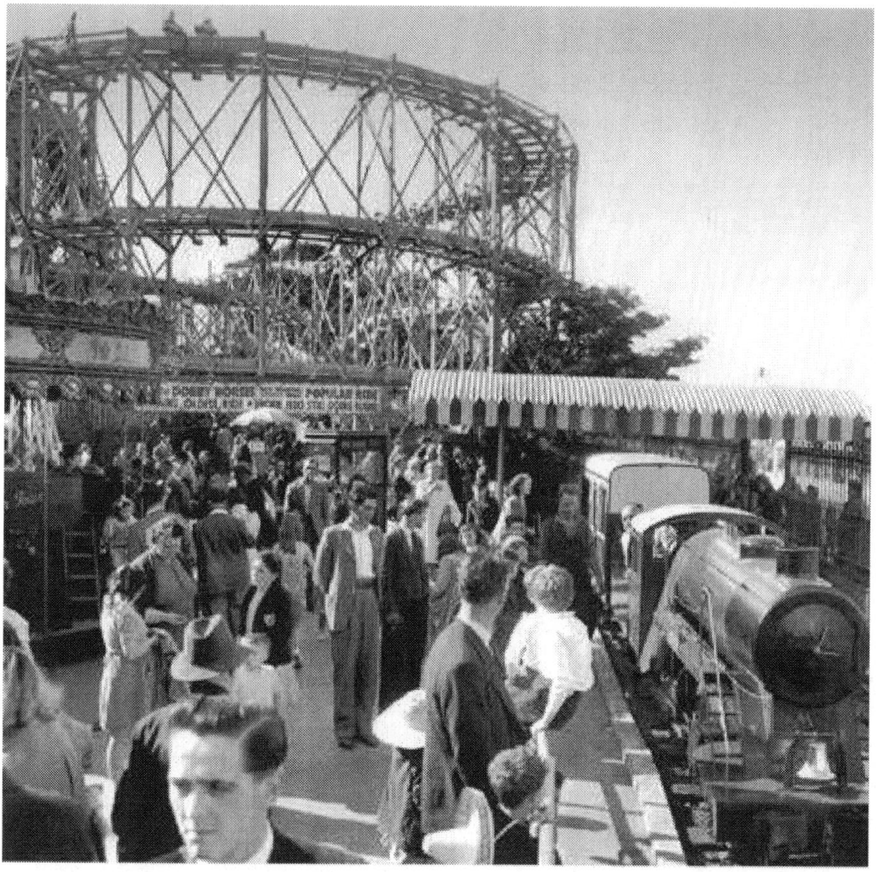

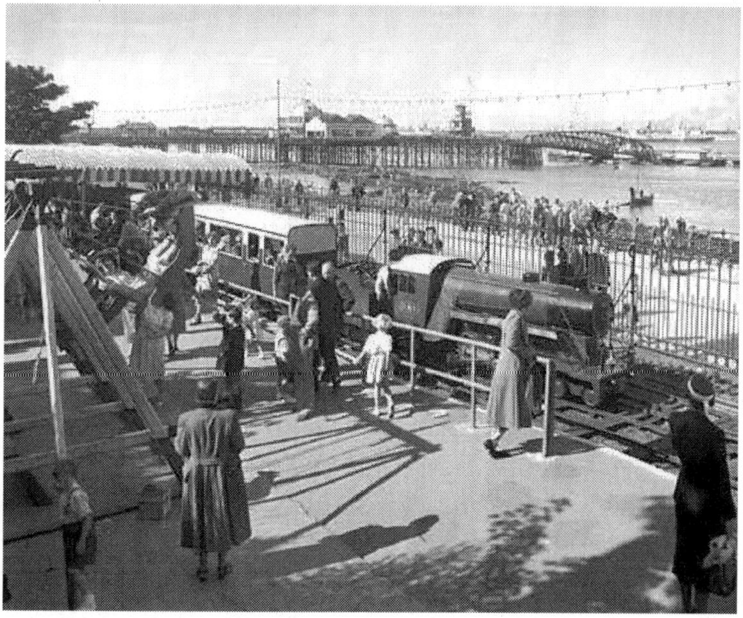

St Barnabas Home for Girls

Situated on Montpellier Crescent, Albion Street, New Brighton,(1898 - 1939) St Barnabas' Home for Girls was presented to the Society in March 1898, by Miss Whitshaw and Miss Lambert. The building had been recently decorated, and was well-equipped with all the modern conveniences of the time. The children from the small home in Stockport that was closed because of a lack of funds were transferred to St Barnabas' later in the year.

The Revd C Hylton Stewart, Vicar of New Brighton and chairman of the Home's Committee, formally opened the Home on 8 November 1898. The ceremony was attended by the Lady Superintendent, Miss Evans, the Honorary Secretary, Miss Helen Marshall, and the Matron, Miss Humble.

Each morning the 30 girls (aged 6-12) marched from Montpellier Crescent, down Albion Street and headed for the local school. Their school teachers frequently praised the girls on how clean, neat, tidy and well behaved they were.

After building alterations in 1931 St Barnabas' was thought to be the most up-to-date home in the Northern Province. The girls of St Barnabas' were evacuated to Tarporley in 1939, causing the Home to close. They later moved to Ashbourne, Derbyshire.

New Brighton Convalescent Home

The 'Convalescent Home for Women and Children' in Rowson Street, New Brighton, was founded in 1847 and was originally known as the 'Sea-side Institution for Women'. The institution was intended for the reception of women patients…'recovering from illness or requiring rest and change at the seaside' ... and was opened all year round for the benefit of patients, thus making it a "pleasant residence for delicate persons even in the most severe weather' writes Philip Sulley in 1889. He maintained that the institution was established…"to afford a comfortable home for poor women when recovering from illness at a very moderate charge"…, with the balance being met by voluntary subscription. The Home maintained a kind of two-tier system, containing 62 beds for women and children and an additional 12…'special departments for Gentlewomen…each lady having a separate bedroom'. Managed by a superintendent/matron who supervised a resident staff of nurses and domestic servants, its operation was based upon a charitable system whereby an annual subscription entitled the subscriber to nominate either one patient for four weeks or two patients for two weeks each; while, naturally, other donations were sought and 'thankfully received' by the Institution's administrators.

Morris's 1880 Cheshire Directory actually quotes the weekly terms for patients, which were: 10s.6d a week, or 6s.6d a week with subscriber's nominations, for the 62 ordinary beds, and 21s a week, or 15s a week with subscriber's nominations, for gentlewomen's departments. And when nineteenth century census returns are consulted it soon becomes apparent that both staff and patients came from rather mixed social backgrounds. It's most interesting to note for instance – in the context of listed ages, duties and occupations – these women's respective positions in the Convalescent Home's structure itself, and in Victorian society generally outside of the Home, where, once again, the hierarchy of servants is exemplified, and where it's quite possible to identify the 'gentlewomen' among the patient listings. Similarly, it's also interesting to find that the vast majority of staff and patients, regardless of position, were unmarried. The 1891 Census Report reveals that 31 of the 33 patients in the Home at the time were either widowed (five examples) or unmarried, and all eleven staff were single women; while patients occupations ranged from 'professor of music' and 'private income' to housekeepers, dressmakers and general servants, and staff ranged from nurses and cooks to ward maids, scullery-maids and waitresses.

The Sea-side Institution's foundation was in line with a substantial mid-nineteenth century increase of charitable organisation's being established throughout the rest of the country. Of course, this charitable activity could be a means of attaining social mobility and, as Margaret Simey had argued…'"through the subscription list of a charity one could display one's wealth to public view, co-operate openly with the aristocracy and thus buy a place in public life'. Whether such factors inspired the establishment of New Brighton's most noted charitable organisation is a point that is open to question, but it's true that the Institute's early patronesses did include certain members of the aristocracy, whilst the various administrative committees read like a veritable who's who of respectable middle-class society in the resort.

Electricity in Wallasey

Liverpool Mercury Saturday, 30th January 1897

Opening Of the Central Supply Station

Wallasey has of late manifested a progressive spirit which tells in tones of eloquence the enthusiasm of its public men, and at the same time testifies to the wisdom of residents in that populous district who have selected representatives animated by the one desire of jealously safeguarding and advancing local interests. But recently news came concerning the inauguration of a scheme which promises to add a hundredfold to the attractions of New Brighton - a resort which is becoming more and more frequented by the toilers of Lancashire. and which, moreover, possesses a large and growing residential population. From its pleasant shore amy be viewed daily the majestic movements of the great Atlantic liners and the passage of vessels which carry the name of Liverpool to all the ends of the earth. All the most modern accessories of a popular holiday rendezvous are shortly to be added, and a more tangible claim may be then advanced by the locality to the title of "The Brighton of the North". Yesterday, however, marked the practical development of an enterprise equally creditable to those who reside in the district which comprises New Brighton, Egremont, Liscard, Wallasey, and Seacombe. About a year ago Mr. J.H. Crowther, the engineer and manager of the Wallasey District Council, submitted to the lighting committee of that body a scheme for the illumination of the neighbourhood - including the three ferries - by electricity, at an estimated cost of £12,500. The committee recommended the council to adopt the scheme, and although some members at first ridiculed the idea, and suggested that the estimate was likely to fall below the necessary expenditure by one-half, it was eventually adopted. Yesterday, members and officials of the local authority, accompanied by numerous friends.

witnessed its successful consummation. Included in the party who assembled to see the light "switched on" were Messrs. C.G Dunn (chairman of the council), R.R. Greene (vice-chairman of the council), and W.G. Ellery (chairman of the gas, water, and electrical committee); Councillors Grace, Dr. Bristow, Bradford, W.F. Lee, J. Wright, Dr. Napier, F. Storey, J. Herron, G.J. Coombs, J. Robinson, J. Tipping, and T.V. Burrows; Messrs. W. Danger (clerk and solicitor), J.J. Burnley (accountant), J.H. Crowther (gas, water, and electrical engineer), J.A. Crowther (assistant electrical engineer), H.J. Woodfine (chief clerk), T. Moulding (assistant surveyor), W.E. Horsfall and R. Williams (committee clerks), Frederick Ash (sub-manager Wallasey Ferries), J.A. Orme (superintendent engineer Wallasey Ferries), Dr. Craigmile (medical officer), R.W. Preston, Squire Chapman, William Peskett, John Hughes, W.H. Crouch, S.G. Harrison-Dearle, J.D. Cockerton, R. Gracey, J. Ashley, Marsden, Charles Birchall, J.H. Jones, J.W. Ross-Brown. W.H. Cornish, jun., John Davies, Arthur Eillis (electrical engineer, Bolton), C.D. Taite (electrical engineer, Southport), C.J. Sutherland (electrical engineer, Hanley), C.J. Wilkinson (electrical engineer, Harrogate), R.C. Quin (electrical engineer, Blackpool), Isaac Carr (gas and water engineer, Widnes), G.H. Nisbett, J.D. Atherton, J. Atherton, J.H. Nisbett, J. Berry, Dr. Bicknell, Woodhouse. Cartwright (representing the contractors for cables), S.Z. de Ferranti, C.P. Sparkes, E.W Martin, Whiteford, (representing the contractors for engines, alternators, and switchboard), and Mr. J. Gourley (building contractor).

Vehicles were in readiness at Seacombe Ferry in the early evening to convey visitors to the Gasworks, Poulton, and thence to the supply station. The latter building, which adjoins the Liscard Pumping Station, had been gaily decorated with bunting, but the interior, dimly illuminated when the party arrived, was naturally cold and comfortless on an evening which rain and fog strove for supremacy.[19]

---

19 Liverpool Mercury Saturday, 30th January 1897

There was indeed a craving for light among the visitors, as they anxiously awaited the ceremony of the evening. Mr. C.G. Dunn (chairman of the district council) led up to it with a few appropriate observations. Many of those present, he remarked, might remember the discouraging comments which were made when gas was first introduced to Wallasey. It was then predicted that, because the district was so scattered, the gas supply would never become a paying concern. Results proved, however, that those prognostications lacked verification, as there was annually a large surplus of profit for application to reduction of the rates. (Applause). There might be some that evening who imagined that the electric light would not be a financial success because of the same reason - ("no" - but he trusted that their fears could prove equally unfounded. (Hear, hear). In conclusion, the speaker paid a high tribute to the energy, foresight, and ability of Mr. Ellery, whom he requested, amid applause, to formally switch on the electric light.

Mr. Ellery, who received a further ovation as he ascended an improved platform, said they were present to demonstrate in a practical way that Wallasey district was not behind the times. Some twelve months ago their able and esteemed engineer submitted to the lighting committee a modest, inexpensive scheme to provide a trunk line for the district, and especially to light the three ferries, at the request of their good friend, Captain Herron. The estimated cost of the scheme was £12.500, and the committee, after anxious and careful consideration, decided to recommend its adoption. He should not, however, forget the reception it met with at the hands of the council. The estimated cost was ridiculed, many members going so far as to say that the scheme would incur double the outlay stated. Nevertheless, the scheme was passed, and now, within twelve months, he hoped to show it was an accomplished fact. (Applause). He wished to add, to the credit of their engineer, that the cost amounted to £10,483 - or something like £2000 below the estimate. (Applause). This was an unique financial experience for a public body, and one of which they were proud. (Applause). On behalf of the district council, he had the honour and pleasure of switching on the electric light, which he was satisfied would eventually return a handsome dividend to the ratepayers.

Amid loud cheers and the enthusiastic waving of hats, Mr. Ellery placed his hands upon the magic switch. The effect was gradual. At first the sinuous wires in two tiny test lamps glowed red, and then, as the dynamos put forth increased power, two large arc lamps shed a steady and powerful light upon the interior, and cheering was again vociferously raised. There are two of Ferranti's dynamos in the station, and these supply the current direct to the ferries, and private consumers, the accumulator system being regarded as extravagant because of the necessary initial outlay and the evitable leakage. There are at present about 30 private consumers who will bring into requisition the full power of this plant, and in all probability tenders will shortly be invited for apparatus of double capacity. The generating station adjoins the Liscard Pumping Station, and advantage has been taken of the plant already erected on the site - the boilers, boiler house, and chimney shaft - which have proved to be of material assistance to the electric supply, without, in any way, curtailing the work plant of the pumping station. The saving effected on this head will amount to about £3000. Apart from the advantages derived from the plant already on the site, the piece of land on which this building stands may be considered as the most centrally situated in the whole district, and a more suitable place it would be very difficult to find. The system of supply is that known as the "high tension"; that is, the voltage of the station is 2000, whilst by means of transformers in the district the voltage is reduced to about 100, at which it's supplied to consumers. There is, consequently, no more danger to those using the light than there would be on the low tension system, whereas to have adopted the latter in a district such as Wallasey would have meant three districts and separate generating stations with, of course, the requisites plant, the outlay for which, apart from any first cost, may be safely be placed at £25,000 or £30,000. The plant here is capable of generating electrical energy for 5000 eight C.P. lamps, but, as it's impossible to run the whole of the plant constantly, the station is what one might call equal to a supply of 2500 eight C.P. lamps, leaving in reserve plant capable of continuing the full supply in the event of a breakdown. The building is 54 feet long by 28 feet wide, and is sufficiently large to take 2-75 kilowatt and 1-20J kilowatt steam alternators with switch board, and two sets of condensing plant. Preparation has also been made for the overheard travelling crane to lift five tons, and the building is so designed that it may be extended at a minimum cost to take in 2-200 kilowatt sets. Further preparation has been made for the erection of an additional boiler house, as well as stores and offices. The mains consist of about six miles of high tension, armoured, concentric paper insulated cables, tested to 10,000 volts, and about one and a-half miles of low tension cable of similar manufacture, tested to 2500 volts. These are laid direct into the ground, and, as a further protection, a line of bricks is placed over the cables. The engines are of a vertical type, compound condensing, capable of developing 125 I.H.P. each, and are directly coupled on to fly-wheel alternators.

The committee, as already foreshadowed, intend to put in hand without delay the extension of the present generating plant, and expect during the approaching winter to put forth a supply equal to 5000 eight C.P. lamps.

From the supply station the party drove to the Victoria Hotel, New Brighton, where they were interested to note a satisfactory display of the newly-introduced illuminist. Here dinner was daintily served, and at its conclusion an interesting toast list engaged attention. Eulogistic, but well-merited, references were made to the skill, efficiency, and energy of the engineer and manager, Mr. Crowther; the local patriotism and foresight of the chairman of the Electric Supply Committee, Mr. Ellery; the progressiveness of the district council, the promptitude and efficiency of the contractors, and the several and collective merits of neighbouring municipal electrical authorities.

New Brighton Promenade

Until 1891 the river front was open to the shore. The only built up are as being the Ferries. If a traveller on the river prior to this period looked toward Wallasey he would have seen mainly eroded clay cliffs supported by a large masonry wall (1858-1863). It was impossible to pass directly from Seacombe to Egremont via this route. At the Guinea Gap there was an actual hole in the cliff in which the tide had carved out a large hollow. From Egremont to what is now New Brighton, existed only private properties occupying the foreshore.

The Seacombe - New Brighton promenade was completed in stages, to 1901. New Brighton Ferry started in 1906. In 1931 work started on building a seawall to Harrison Drive, Wallasey Village, even by today's standards, an ambitious project. Included in the project would be an embankment 130 feet wide, 46 acres of public gardens, a marine lake (for model boats), open air bathing and subsequent roadways. With the exception of the public gardens, it was completed in 1939. The land between the railway and the promenade was left untouched due to the arrival of WW2. In fact nothing was done to this area at all until the 1990s when developers got their greedy mitts on it and built "luxury apartments". More revenue for the council and no lay out in costs! The Home Guard (Dad's Army) were located at their HQ in the School of Art. In fact some of the guard were enlisted as students too!!

Egremont Promenade

The long coastline of Egremont was for hundreds of years, open fields with commons and rocky outcrops running down to the water's edge. It had always provided a small natural harbour and has had hundreds of years of Maritime activity. The catalyst which sent Egremont from a quiet hilly harbour to a bustling borough of

Wallasey came in the form of Captain Askew. In 1823 Sir John Tobin of Liscard Hall agreed to trade some land with Captain Askew who was at that time the Harbour Master of Liverpool Docks. Naturally Sir John Tobin did not wish to give up any of his wealthier more productive lands, and it was agreed that he would trade a small portion of the rather empty and hilly Northern coastline.

And so shortly after Captain Askew built his new house in this rather empty area having previously lived in Seacombe. His new home stood out amongst the local populace which was a scattering of farms, old crook cottages and outbuildings. As was tradition in those days, it was correct to give the new house a name. Having though long and hard about it Captain Askew decided to name it after his home town of "Egremont" in Cumberland.

It wasn't long before the friendship of Sir John Tobin and Captain turned into a business proposition and would secure the future of Egremont. Sir John formed new plans for a new ferry crossing using his wealth to fund the operation and drawing on Captain Askews maritime knowledge for technical issues. Within a relatively quick time the operation was underway and the partners named their service "The Egremont Steam Ferry", drawing on the name of the Captains House at the time. In order to increase revenue the partners opened up a large hotel in the area, it was named simply "The Egremont Hotel". The hotel was a large well decorated building which stood at the end of Tobin Street near the water's edge next to the grass of Askew Close. The hotel would have given its visitors great view across the Mersey from its bedrooms or balcony's. The building itself was built at the turn of the 19th century and had to be refurbished extensively in order to bring it up to standard. The large grey hotel building was set in beautiful green gardens and drew visitors from around the country for both maritime trade and holidays. After many years the Egremont Hotel was renamed "The Egremont Institute and Assembly Rooms". Sadly, despite owing much to the popularity of Egremont; the old building does not stand today having been demolished in the 1950s.

It was from the actions of Sir John Tobin and Captain Askew that area saw a huge increase in both residents and visitors. Within years the outlook of the area had changed dramatically having been filled with superb villas and merchants housing. From this population boom the area required a name as i did not come under Seacombe nor did it fall under Liscard. It became known simply as Egremont, after the Large House and fine hotel which the settlement had been built around.

It's no wonder that with such a fine selection of architecture and influx of wealthy residents to the area that a picturesque and affluent village developed, and with it a promenade to show off its prowess. Within no time Egremont boasted one of the most beautiful promenades on the Wirral which stretched for miles skirting the river and allowing great views across the River over to the Port City of Liverpool. Today Wirral still enjoys the record of having the longest promenade in the United Kingdom, and much of this is down to the village of Egremont.

The beaches of Egremont were at one time, busy enough to rival even its neighbour; New Brighton. Families would take to the seaside for a day out and enjoy the fresh air. Families would gather for the small side shows, the donkey rides across the beach and the fresh yellow sands to build castles. It was not always families that would head down to the beach for rest and please, the Victorian believed that Sea Air was good for you, as was the sea water. Infarct during Victorian times it was not uncommon to see elderly men or sick people in their rolled up pants wading through the water. Of course these days we are much more aware and unfortunately for the, the cold water most likely caused more harm than good.

New Brighton Fort Perch Rock

During the early 1800's the various merchants and others of the area thought the Port of Liverpool should be guarded and when the old Perch Rock Light was washed away the authorities thought of the idea of having a fortified lighthouse, or having a fort which would

contain a lighthouse. It was finally agreed to have two separate constructions at a meeting held on 25th March 1825. The fort covers about 4,000 square yards and is constructed of mainly red sandstone which came largely from the Runcorn Quarries; it was floated down the River Mersey and unloaded when the tide was out. Because the stone was soft it had to be left to be weathered.

The walls were originally 24 feet and 29 feet high, but these, in some cases, were heightened to almost 32 feet, facing the river side and the towers 40 feet high. The fort had a slipway with three arches with drawbridge and a Tuscan portal bearing the Coat of Arms and the words "Fort Perch Rock". It was cut off at high tides from the mainland. The fort built on what was known as Black Rock, stood guard at the mouth of the river, shipping passing 950 yards from the battery. The fort was armed with eighteen guns, of which sixteen were 32 pounders, mounted on platforms. Six were placed on the west front, two on the east and four on the north. Single guns were placed in the towers and along the angles. There were two small guns facing the causeway. There was accommodation for 100 men, with officers' quarters and kitchen. There were also storerooms and Magazine in the centre of the courtyard at a sunken level, with a hand-hoist for lifting the ammunition.

Perch Rock Battery, New Brighton.

In the early years, the guns were smooth-bore cannon and the balls had to be heated in a furnace until they were red hot, and then shipped to the guns for firing. The idea being when they scored a direct hit they would set the enemy ship alight and set off their powder. The fort would have a practice from time to time, when the local fishermen would gather the cannon balls and return them to the fort, receiving payment for them. The fort was nicknamed the "Little Gibraltar of the Mersey".

As the Rock Channel slowly became silted, the larger ships ceased to use it and it became necessary to equip the battery with larger guns capable of reaching the range. 64 pounders were installed as a result and these were mounted in granite. The old 32 pounders were kept to guard the Rock Channel which was still being used by the smaller ships. The 4th Cheshire Company o Artillery Volunteers was established after holding an open meeting, to set up a local corp. On the 31st January, 1860 the New Brighton Company was started and it was not long before they had 60 men under the command of Captain

Henry D. Grey and his staff. Their uniform was dark blue with white facings and in full dress they wore a Busby.

At a later date, the corps became known as the 1st Cheshire and Caernarvon Artillery then, soon after the turn of the century, they joined with the 1st Lancashire Artillery Volunteers, forming the Lancashire and Cheshire Heavy Brigade. The M.O. at the Fort was Dr. J. W. Lloyd whose son, Selwin, became Foreign Secretary. In the

Second World War the unit became the "420 Coast Regiment", until they were disbanded in November, 1960.

When the Royal Artillery was stationed at the fort, there were three officers and 101 men. In 1943 there were two officers and 28 men, and finally one officer and 8 men, as a maintenance unit in April 1944. After the war, it had one officer, one master-gunner and two other ranks. Whilst the territorial's were there, they had one officer and 28 men. The Home Guard also had a spell there.

The fort controlled the Mersey Division Submarine Miners in the late 1800's. They used to lay mines both at sea and on land. Some of the men employed in the task were members of the Wallasey Ferries. In 1893 the battery was dismantled and the guns returned to Ordnance, the following year two 4.7" Quick Firing guns were delivered but due to a change of plans, as regards a second fort being built, they were installed at Seaforth Battery on the opposite side of the river. Perch Rock was to have three 6" guns installed. At the same time the Royal Engineers took over the fort and re-modelling was commenced.

The parade yard was no longer needed, as the infantry had left in 1858. It was partly filled in with sand and rocks from the beach and covered. The pits were constructed for the naval guns, which were mounted away from the walls and these were lowered so the guns could have a close range of 150 yards, Electricity was available from a new engine-room. The maximum machine guns at the fort were installed in May 1893. The 6" guns arrived in December 1897, but it was not until March 1899 that they were fully installed and ready for action. Some ten years later, between 1909 and 1910, further alterations were carried out and Mark VII guns were installed. When these were brought to the Fort, the drawbridge was strengthened to allow for the extra load. Over the next few years, search-light towers and an observation tower were built.

At the outbreak of the First World War, the war office decided to remove two of the 6" guns, one of which was later returned in 1923. Finally the armament of the fort was two 6" guns and two machine-guns, which remained until 1954. The drawbridge was removed in 1935.The modern concrete tower was used to house the Radar which was added in 1941, but this was not the only modern invention at the fort for, as early as 1895, the range-finder system operated with a lens in either tower. They could determine the distance, in a way similar to that in a non-reflex miniature camera. During the Second World War, the fort was made to appear as a sort of tea-garden from the air. The letters TEAS were painted on the roof of one of the buildings and the outer portion was painted green, to give the effect of a lawn.

In War time the fort went into action only twice in its entire history. The first was on the outbreak of the First World War, when a round was fired across the bow of an approaching Norwegian ship under sail, which failed to obey a signal from the fort. It was at the time when the Territorial's were at the fort, under the command of Major Charles Luga, who was a local dentist. He ordered a warning shot, which was way off the mark, as the gun was elevated too much. It landed in Crosby on the opposite side of the mouth of the river. They fired again, only to hit the bow of an Allen Liner at anchor! The first shell landed in the sand hills and was found by a resident, who took it to the Seaforth Battery, where the officer placed it in the Mess Room, with the words "A present from New Brighton". The Captain of the Norwegian ship thought they were just having a bit of fun. He did not know that War had been declared.

The second occasion the fort went into action was again on the outbreak of war, on September 1939, a fishing-smack came up the Rock channel which had been closed. Colonel Charles Cocks the Battery Commander ordered two shots to be fired across her bows from No. 2 gun. The owner of the fishing-smack was ordered to pay £25 for each round. The fort was dismantled in 1954, a caretaker appointed and 1958 it was put up for sale, having been offered to both Liverpool and Wallasey Corporations. It was sold by auction in 1958 for £4000. It was used for a number of years as a sort of pleasure centre, but the council objected and after the storms of 1975, it was again put on the market, the next owner with the help of the

Manpower Services Commission, restored it to something like its original 1826 design, removing tons of sand from the old parade ground, and made the Magazine into a museum of the War Plane Wreck Investigation Group.

New Brighton Lighthouse

Perch Rock, New Brighton Lighthouse, sits next to the fort, it was originally, a wooden "Perch", hence its name. A large post held a light on top and was supported by a sort of tripod. It was erected on the Black Rock in 1683 by the Liverpool Corporation. When foreign ships, passed the old perch, they were charged sixpence for its respect and to keep it in repair.

But it was often washed away and a boat had to be launched to recover it from Bootle Bay. In February 1821, the pilot boat "Liver" crashed into the perch and carried it away. It has been said that it was washed away in March 1824 and not recovered until the December. However the cost of replacing it all the time grew too expensive and it was decided to build a new one.

The foundation stone of the new lighthouse was laid on 8th June 1827 by Thomas Littledale, Mayor of Liverpool. It was designed on the lines of Eddy stone by Mr. Foster and built of marble rock from Anglesey by Tomkinson & Company. It rises 90 feet above the rocks and is considered to be a masterpiece of craftsmanship. The granite cost 1/6d a cubic foot. Each piece of stone is interlocked into the next. The whole stonework, when finished, was coated with what is known as "Puzzellani" a volcanic substance from Mount Etna which, with age, becomes rock hard. The first 45 feet is solid. A spiral staircase leads to where the keeper lived and then on to the lantern house. The revolving light was said to be the first in the country. It cost £27,500 to construct.

Work was only possible at low tide and it was not completed until 1830. Its first light shone on the 1st March of that yea and consisted of two white flashes, followed by one red, with a range of 14 miles.

The light was 77 feet above the half-tide level. It was eventually electrically connected to the mainland.

The Lighthouse last shone its light on 1st October 1973 as it was no longer needed on account of the radar system operating in the River. A local architect purchased the lighthouse for £100 on condition he maintained the construction, he tried to restore the lantern again but the river authorities thought it might cause confusion to local shipping. So he refurbished it so that anyone could stay there for a short holiday. Indeed, it was their idea to attract newly married couples to spend part of their honeymoon there at a cost of £50 a day, with champagne and flowers thrown in. With electricity being introduced, the old lighthouse has a galley with cooker and refrigerator and, on the first floor, a bathroom with shower. There is a living room and a bedroom on the next two floors. The lighthouse even has a television, just in case one gets bored with looking at the sea. A ladder has to be obtained from the fort to gain the necessary height to reach the 15 iron rungs of the lighthouse as the door is 25 feet from the base.

The Liscard Battery of New Brighton

In the 1750's the Corporation of Liverpool decided to move the Powder Magazines, used to store explosive and shot from ships in port, from their site in Clarence Street and find a more isolated site for them on the Cheshire side of the River Mersey. Accordingly, a suitable plot was purchased on the south bank of the Mersey at Wallasey and the new magazine constructed. They were renovated and enlarged in 1838-39, and were still in use until 1851, when it was decided that in future explosives would be stored in hulks further up the river at the Bight of Sloyne. The move was probably prompted by safety concerns, the land around the Magazines having become much more built up. In 1858 a battery was built on the site, and the imposing gateway with its crenulated towers, survives to this day as does the perimeter wall which now encircles several houses. Facing the south wall of the battery, on the other side of the road (Magazine Brow) are several cottages, perhaps dating from the 17th Century.

These were probably first inhabited by fishermen, but it's thought that they were later occupied by offices from the battery.

The Magazines were often referred to as Liscard Magazines and the fort as Liscard Battery, but the name Liscard later became attached to an area about a mile away where Wallasey's main shopping area is situated. A quaint circular dwelling may be seen about fifty yards from the fort's gateway, this being known as the Round House. Now forming part of a private residence, this was once occupied by the battery's watchman. Further along Magazine Brow are situated two public houses, the Pilot Boat and The Magazines, the latter having been built in 1759 and once used by sailors who were having their outward bound ships reloaded with munitions at the Liscard Magazines.

This impressive structure which is still partially standing is one of the great land marks of the area. Nestled between Magazine Lane and Magazine Brow, the old structure kept watch across the River Mersey as an additional line of defence against all manner of seaborne threats. Britain was just coming out of the Indian colonies mutiny and was strengthening it defensive positions especially for the supply lines of shipping. The River Mersey was already protected by Fort Perch rock but it was decided to build another structure which could train its guns on all vessels within the Mersey. A spot at the river's edge in New Brighton was selected. The area was just opposite the now dismantled powder magazines. Work began in 1858 on the project and the large fort was completed built from locally quarried heavy red sand stone. The fort was an impressive defensive structure capable of holding seven 10 inch guns and a small detachment of the 55th Royal Artillery.

In those days the gunners of the fort would have wore a smart navy blue frock as opposed to a full dress tunic. Each of the uniforms had a red stripe down the leg complete with brass buttons and smart black shoes. The officers of the time would have worn a white belt and sash. When the fort was first constructed the men's head wear would have consisted of fur Busby hats. This was later replaced in 1878 with a blue-cloth covered helmet complete with spike, which was again replaced in 1881 with a ball.

The forts most cunning feature was not nits, thick walls or heavy artillery, buts simply its location. The fort stood at the water's edge slightly set back, but completely hidden by a variety of foliage. From the river, the fort was not visible until it was too late and by that time it would be within firing distance. This earned the Liscard Battery the nick name of *"The Snake in the Grass"*. Fortunately for the local residents the fort was never fired against by any enemies and as time drew on the fort became obsolete without conflict. In 1912 the fort was sold to the Liverpool Yacht Club and over the years it had fallen into a sorry state of repair resulting in its demise. In addition to this many houses now occupy the site, both inside and outside of the forts walls as the photo above describes. The houses opposite the fort still stand and they also play a part in the history of the Liscard Battery. The officers from the fort lived opposite in the red sandstone house. Many of the houses along the road are extremely old, one even dating to 1747. The outline of the Battery is still visible today and is one of the many remaining features of Wallasey's past.

Discovery Of Stag's Horns Under The Bed Of Wallasey Pool

Liverpool Mercury Friday, 3rd September 1824

The labourers engaged in excavating the bed of Wallasey Pool, for the purpose of making a wet dock, have lately discovered several fine stag's horns in the most perfect state of preservation, which is surprising when we consider the length of time they must necessarily have been buried. We shall forbear to indulge in conjecture respecting the period when these remains of former days were deposited in this spot. At that time, it's probable, that what is now termed Wallasey Pool was part of a wood or forest, as, in the neighbourhood, the remains of large trees are frequently found at different depths below the surface, and also out of the ground. These vegetable remains are of very dark colour; some as black as coal, and so hard, that the farmers use them as gate posts. The horns were found nearly thirty feet below the bed of the pool. The specimen which has been committed to our care, for public inspection, consists of a single and very perfect antler, so hard as almost to defy the file. It weighs three pounds and a half, and is very elegantly branched. We had almost omitted stating a circumstance, which, if true, is fully as extraordinary as the discovery of the animal remains; and we doubt not, that some of our antiquarian readers will endeavour to ascertain whether it be in fact, as reported, that the workmen evident traces of an ancient road having once existed, twenty or thirty feet below the bed of the Wallasey Pool.

We have been favoured with the following note from a specific gentleman of this town, whose opinion we requested respecting the recently discovered horns.[20]

DEAR SIR, --

The horns found at Wallasey Pool undoubtedly belong to a stag, very similar to the stag of the present day (Cervus Elaphus). From their solidity, thickness, roughness, and the size of their antlers, they seem to have belonged to a full grown animal, that fed plentifully. Though extremely dense, and of considerable thickness, they cannot be considered as large. I have seen longer horns on the stag of these islands; and the magnificent horns in the Museum of the Royal Institution (I think between three and four feet high) are those of the American stag. The horns found at Wallasey have been regularly shed, and their points have been polished by use. They are not in a fossil state, but retain their animal matter. –

Yours, etc. T.S.T
Sept.1.1824

The horns may been seen for a few days at our office.

---

[20] Liverpool Mercury Friday, 3rd September 1824

New Brighton Pier

The New Brighton Promenade Pier was built in 1867 adjacent to the ferry pier on the north side. It was opened on the 7th September, 1867 and completed on the 9th April, 1868. It was 550 feet long and 70 feet wide. It had a pavilion where the pierrots, Aldeler and Sutton took their shows from the beach. The entrance was through the turnstiles on the ferry pier and people entered as they came off the ferry boat. In the early days, this was the only entrance the promenade pier ending some yards from the promenade. There were Smoking rooms and rest rooms on the pier and when alterations were carried out in 1913 a new pavilion was built.

The pier closed in 1923 and four years later the Wallasey Corporation became its new owners and re-opened it with its own entrance from the promenade. The whole of the pier was rebuilt in 1931 at a cost of £45,000. As in other resorts the pier had its own theatre, it was not built to high standards but some good turns could be seen on its stage. The theatre was about 130 feet in length and was used for Concerts, Flower Shows and the like. Various shows were

New Brighton Pier.

held there during the 1800's and towards the end of the century. At the end of the 1908 season the theatre was closed down for general improvements on the decor, seats and stage, there was even heating installed!! The theatre reopened on 15th March 1909. Some early films were shown between acts and a short season of plays were staged, in the winter now the theatre had heating installed pantomimes were performed with great success.

Pier, New Brighton.

As other theatres on the resort attracted larger crowds the Pavilion theatre died off and was eventually closed in 1923. The closure of the New Brighton Ferry affected the life of the promenade pier. Fortes Limited became the owners in 1968, carrying out repairs and it continued for a time, but it was not a paying proposition. After much discussion, the pier was dismantled in 1978, the ferry pier having been demolished some five years earlier.

Rutland House

Another residence that no longer greets the eye in its original forum is 'Rutland House', which stood in St .George's Mount. This house was formerly owned by Dr. William Bell, who died in 1915 at the age of 75. He had lived in Wallasey since 1866, and in that year, in conjunction with Mr Charles Crewe Chambres, of 'The Eyrie' in Breck Road, was responsible for the establishment of the Wallasey Cottage Hospital, then situated in St .George's Road. In addition, Dr Bell was a member of the Management Committee of the Wallasey High School, a Governor of Wallasey Grammar School, Hon. Physician to the New Brighton Convalescent House, and a Justice of the Peace. Whether or not 'Rutland House' was actually built for Dr Bell is not known, but it could well have owed its name to the fact he was educated at Uppingham School in the county of Rutland.

Two of Dr Bell's sons followed in their father's professions. One was Professor Blair Bell, an eminent Liverpool surgeon and cancer specialist, who lived in the closing years of the 19th Century in 'Linden Cottage', Grove Road, while the other, Edward Augustine Bell, educated at Rossall and a surgeon to the Wallasey Cottage Hospital, the New Brighton Convalescent Home and the Homes for Aged Mariners, became a Captain in the Royal Army Medical Corps in World War I, but unfortunately lost his life in France in 1916, when he was drowned shortly after returning from leave. His wife, who survived until 1967, was a daughter of Canon Cogswell, Rector of St. Hilary's, one of whose sons in turn married a daughter of Dr Bell.

'Rutland House', which had extensive grounds, is now numbers 1 and 3, St George's Mount, and it would also seem that part, at any rate, of the land was sold off to the well known Wallasey builder, Moses Hughes, in 1922, for the construction of some of the houses in St George's Park. In 1926, Moses Hughes sold over 5,000 square yards of land to Wallasey Corporation for £1,165, and this is presumably the present enclosed area in the park.

MonteBello

This house, which stood at the north corner of St. George's Mount and Atherton Street, was built about 1860 for a Liverpool merchant, Mr Charles William Harrison Pickering. Prior to moving here, Mr Pickering lived first at 'Withensfield House', Withens Lane, and later at 'Springfield House', the site of which is now occupied roughly by Vicarage Grove. In those days the new house must have commanded unsurpassed views out to sea, and it's not surprising that Mr Pickering named the property 'Monte Bello'. The grounds ran down to St. James's Road, where there was a lodge, while the stables, still standing and used residentially. They were situated opposite on the south side of St. George's Mount.

Mr Pickering, after whom Pickering Road was presumably named, died in 1881 at the age of 65 and was buried in St. Hilary's Churchyard, although he worshipped at St. James's Church, where there is, or was, a stained glass window to his memory. His widow continued to live at 'Monte Bello' until her own death in 1895, and the following year the Trustees of her late husband's Will sold the whole of the property, consisting of the house, the stables and over 6,000 square yards of land to a Liverpool Ship-owner, Mr John Karran, for £3,010. Four years later he, too, died, but his widow remained in residence for some years, finally dying at Douglas, Isle of Man, on 1907. Round about 1910, the house was leased from the Karran Trustees by Mrs Isobel Robinson, who converted it into a private hotel, still known as 'Monte Bello', and as such it continued until World War II.

In 1944 the Trustees sold off the coach-house and stables separately to a Mr Wood, who died in 1979 and the following year disposed of the remainder of the property to an Estate Company for £3,500. Ten years later it was acquired by Thomas & Caley Ltd, a local building company, the house having been demolished in the meantime, and they developed the area with the attractive smaller residences which are to be seen there today.

The Grennan

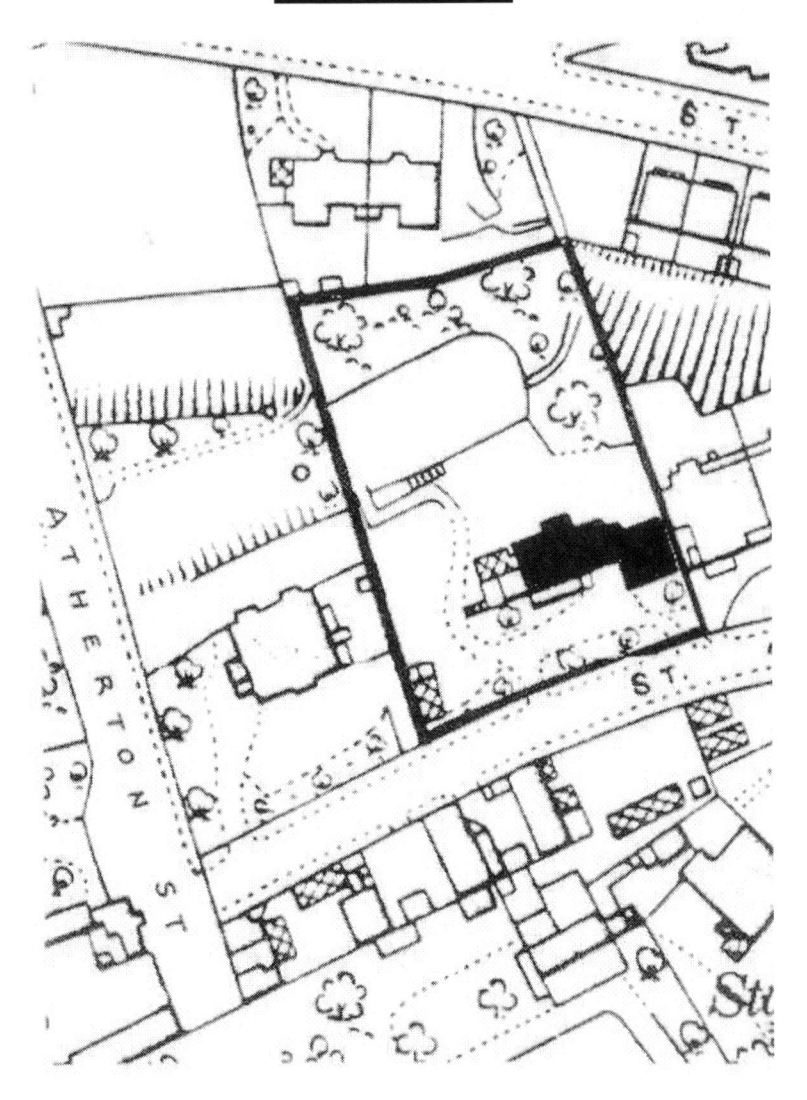

SITE PLAN OF "THE GRENNAN"

Next to the 'Monte Bello' now demolished, and probably built about the same time, stood a great house, known as 'The Grennan'. It was designed in an Italianate style, stucco rendered and painted and significant by the Belvidere, an observation tower which dominated the masard roof line. Built in the ridge of St George's Mount it commanded impressive views.

In 1860 it was in the occupation of Mr G.S Robertson, Manager and Secretary of Hamilton's Windsor Iron Works in Liverpool. According to the street directories, Mr Robertson stayed there for ten years before giving way to Mr A.T Wright, Solicitor, son of Peter Wright, at one time Clerk of the Peace in Liverpool and a partner in what became the legal firm of Wright, Beckett and Pennington. Mr Wright spent some time as Chairman of the Wallasey Local Board and a Cheshire County Council Alderman, and occupied 'The Grennan' for nearly twenty years before moving to 'The Springs' in Harrison Drive. His successor at 'The Grennan' was a Mr H.J Houghton, described as a gentleman, who in 1915 gave way to Mr Leonard Meadows, an Oil Merchant, who mingled in public life to the extent that he was Treasurer of the Victoria Central Hospital and the Wallasey Cricket Club, in addition to being a sidesman at St Hilary's Church. He was succeeded at 'The Grennan' in about 1920 by Mr G. Austin Tyrer, Wine and Spirit Merchant, who on the sporting side was capped for Cheshire at hockey in 1904, and captained Wallasey Cricket Club for seven years prior to World War I. In 1925 the house was converted into flats, but in the late 1980's was demolished for redevelopment.

Sandrock

'Sand Rock' (later 'The Cenacle') stood at the top of Atherton Street adjacent to St. George's Mount. It was built on one of the highest places in the area and before Wallasey was fully developed it could be seen and recognised from Liverpool. It was a Gothic style house with pointed windows, tall decorated chimneys and moulded parapets. The exterior walls were stucco finished etched in a stone blocked pattern and painted white or grey. The site was quite well wooded and on windy nights when the branches creaked and swayed the evening light caused shadows on the painted walls making it look quite ghostly to such an extent that when it had been vacated it acquired the reputation of being haunted. The grounds were quite extensive and originally stretched down as far as Albion Street, and over to the west almost as far as where Gorsehill Reservoir now stands. There was a lodge adjacent to the drive entrance at the top of

Atherton Street with adjoining single storey buildings which presumably served as stables and a coach house, and nearby there were greenhouses and possibly a summer pavilion. The garden to the north of the house, due to the incline of the ground, appears to have been left as a lawn surrounded by trees and bushes and with a decorative bed of flowers in the centre.

The earliest occupant so far traced was James Stringer, a partner with his father-in-law Thomas Lowry and his brother-in-law William Mann, both of 'Zig Zag House', in the form of Lowry, Stringer and Mann, (later Stringer and Mann) Merchants, Steam Sawmill and Salt Proprietors, of Seel Street, Liverpool. He was living in the house in 1850, having previously resided at 'Garden House', Garston and then 'Grassendale House', well known for many years as the home of the Lockett family, and later in Montpellier Crescent, in Wallasey. By 1853 he had retired from business, and presumably he died soon afterwards, as the name of his widow appears in 1860.

In 1868 Peter L. Henderson, Merchant, was the next occupant to be followed by Patrick Keith, partner in the well known firm of Liverpool Merchants and Ship owner's, John Gladstone & Co., who spent nearly ten years there. It has not been possible to ascertain his immediate successors, but in the 1890's there was in residence a Mr Joseph Loughran, a Colliery Proprietor, who later lived for a short time at 'Olinda', in Rowson Street, prior to that houses' conversion to its final role as Workingmen's Institute.

The first three years of the present century showed a Captain Thomson in occupation at 'Sand Rock', to be followed by Alfred Coker, the well known Liverpool ship-owner, who was there until 1907. After one further occupant, the house was purchased by a Religious Order in 1912, and for the next few years became the Convent of Our Lady of the Cenacle, a cenacle being a super-room, particularly that in which the Last Supper was held. During the First World War it was used as a military hospital, but its history subsequent to that is rather obscure. In 1932, the foundation stone of the new Catholic Church of St. Peter and St. Paul was laid in the grounds, and the building operations involved the demolition of the house.

Gorselands

This impressing house, built in a classical style with a painted stucco finish, was situated at the lower corner of Albion Street and Atherton Street, and was probably built about 1850, or even earlier. It was known as 'Gorselands', and in 1857 it became the home of Thomas Addison, a well-to-do Liverpool Stockbroker, who immediately previously had been living at 'Earlston House', now part of the Central Library, and prior to that at 'The Mount' in Mount Road. It would appear that he died some time before 1872, as in that year his wife Margaret is shown as being in residence at 'Gorselands', remaining in occupation until the early 1880's.By 1887 the house had a new owner in the person of Henry Flinn, a well known Liverpool ship-owner. Mr Flinn was born in 1820, according to one report in Sussex and to another Devonshire, but whatever was the case, he went to sea in his early teens, and by the age of 22 had obtained his first command. He later founded the firm of James Flinn & Co., sailing ship-owners, and in 1870 became a partner in the firm of Flinn, Main & Montgomery, founders and managers of the Liverpool & Mississippi Steamship Company, later to become the Mississippi and Dominion line, better known as the Dominion Line. This Line, which had been incurring losses, changed hands in 1894, and was ultimately incorporated into the International Mercantile Marine in 1902, the better ships being transferred to the White Star Line, which company by that time had become a member of the group.

Henry Flinn, then a widower, retired in 1895 and died in 'Gorselands' the following year, leaving two daughters and two sons, one of whom, F.W Flinn, was a Justice of the Peace, living at 'Grassheys' in Grove Road until the 1930's, when that house was demolished to make way for a new road called 'The Aubynes'. For the record, Henry Flinn was of the Catholic faith, and was buried at St. Swithin's, Gill Moss, which in those days was a small village well out in the country beyond West Derby. After his death, 'Gorselands' was presumably sold.

Some years later, Mr. F.Glynn Baker, late Housemaster of St .Cyprians Eastbourne, started a Preparatory School, in January 1914 to be exact, known as 'Somerville School for Boys'. Pupils were taken as boarders from the ages of 7-14½ years. Classes were presumably on the ground floor and dormitories on the first floor. In the grounds were two large playgrounds, cricket nets, lawn tennis courts and gardens. The pupils were taught French, Algebra, Geometry, Latin, Carpentry, Rifle Shooting, and Swimming. There was also a Cadet Corps, and a Band Board and tuition for three terms per year came up to 30 guineas per term.

There was also a Lower School for juniors and Girls on the opposite side of the road in a smaller detached house run by the headmaster's sister Miss Ruth Glynn Baker. The house still exists today's as a private residence and is known as 'Rockland', now number 173 Victoria Road.

It's use as 'Somerville Junior School' did not last very long and it eventually reverted back to its former role of a dwelling. The main school was demolished before World War II when in charge of a Mr Baddeley and was replaced by modern houses. However some parts still remain and these are the stone boundary walls and the beautiful gate posts marking the original entrance to 'Somerville' alias 'Gorselands' and these are situated in Albion Street. When the house was first built the views from the site must have been quite splendid with the area around it undeveloped, and with the level of ground floor taken from Albion Street the building was set up high above Victoria Road.

The Penny Illustrated Paper and Illustrated Times Saturday 28th May, 1887

A Burglar and His Yacht

The Cheshire Police were on Monday engaged investigating the antecedents of a man who gives the name of William Moody, and who was arrested on Saturday, charged with burglariously entering the premises of Mr. Peter Davies, known as the "Pioneer" Stores, [Brighton Street] Seacombe. Mrs. Davies saw the man enter her bedroom, and screamed out, awakening her husband, who leaped out of bed and seized the burglar. An investigation revealed that the prisoner had poisoned the watch-dog and secured some valuable property, including £30 actually taken from Mr. Davies pockets. He was furnished with a complete set of housebreaking implements.21

Now comes the remarkable part of the story. The police, continuing their investigation, discovered the prisoner was occupying a luxuriantly-fitted yacht now at anchor at Tranmere. There valued

---

21 The Penny Illustrated Paper and Illustrated Times, Saturday 28th May, 1887

property, including dressing-cases, jewellery, and articles of vertu, which it's believed are proceeds of previous burglarious raids. One curious find was a South Eastern Railway Company's dividend for £41, payable to Joseph Beaumont Stockwell. The prisoner, it appears, bought the yacht from a Cheshire gentleman a short time back for a considerable sum of money.

The purchase of the yacht was an adroit move by which he calculated confidently on eluding the police, for when the chase became inconveniently close it was easy to avoid it by retiring to the snug berth which he had thoughtfully provided for himself in the vessel, and then, lifting the anchor, proceeding to sea.

The fellow, who is of slender build and dressed in the garb of a sailor, has been remanded formally by the Cheshire magistrates until Friday.

Berrow's Worcester Journal Saturday, July 30 1887

A Burglar with a Yacht

At the Chester Assizes, on Tuesday, William Moody (20) was indicted on three separate charges of burglary. Prisoner pleaded guilty to one – namely, to burglariously entering the dwelling house of Mr. Davies, of Seacombe, and stealing £28. He pleaded guilty to charges of burglary at Knutsford and Blackley.[22] *Prisoner had bought yacht at Birkenhead, which was floating in the Mersey, and when he was captured on a charge of entering Mr. Davies's premises, the police found a number of valuable articles on board. One of the articles recovered was a railway's dividend warrant, payable to Mr. Stockwell, of Blackley, and the prosecution alleged that when he entered that gentleman's residence he also stole a lady's gold watch*

---

20 Berrow's Worcester Journal Saturday, July 30 1887

and chain, two gold brooches, and several other articles of value. It was decided, however, to convict upon the count to which prisoner had pleaded guilty, and not go into the other charges. The Judge, in passing sentences, referred to the prisoner's extraordinary career of crime, remarking that that he had been found guilty of the same sort of thing many times before. In 1884 he received a long sentence for burglary, and after serving it committed another burglary. In 1886 he had another sentence, again for burglary, and, after serving another sentence, commenced the same thing again. Society must be protected against this sort of thing, and he must have a long period in which to reflect upon what a wicked fellow and what a fool he had been. It was no longer a question for a few months; it had now come to years. The sentence must now be five years' penal servitude.

Borough Road

Victoria Road was one of the four original roads of Poulton-cum-Seacombe, and became the main shopping area for the small village of Seacombe until Liscard was built up between the two World Wars. The fire brigade requested a change in name to avoid confusion with

Victoria Road, New Brighton. The road was re-named Borough Road in 1918.

Looking at Borough Road in the 1920s we begin right down at the bottom of the road which was the railway station. T.F Williams and Son's, coal merchants were once on the site. Mrs. Louise Jackson had the Queen's Arms public house at No. 2. Coming up the road on the left-hand side there were a number of businesses. The 'Wallasey and Wirral Chronicle' was established in 1888 and was published on Wednesdays (a halfpenny) and Saturdays (one penny). They later moved to the Primitive Methodist Chapel in Brighton Street.

Next door was the old tea rooms which were run by Mr. Atkinson which were later taken over by Tony Ecceo. The 'Leasowe Castle' Hotel was in the hands of Bill Bryan and a few years later Bob Crawford became the landlord, followed by Charlie Canner. Bill Ferney was the pawnbroker and coming up the road were the 'Echo', 'Daily Post' and 'Mercury' offices and Mrs. Owen was a 'tallow chandler' at No. 53. The 'Wallasey News' (Wallasey Printers) were next door. The first issue appeared in the newsagent at 3rd November 1899. They, too, published twice-weekly. On Saturday there were twelve pages for a penny and on Wednesday it was halfpenny with four pages. This firm eventually moved to Church Road.

'The Wallasey News' was established by Messrs Willmer Brothers of Birkenhead to replace the Wallasey edition of the 'Birkenhead News'. In 1918 it was bought by the Wallasey Printers. Ernest Keel was the managing director and Edwin Peace was his associate. Mr. Peace was a solicitor in Liverpool and served the town as Mayor of Wallasey in 1916/1917.

William Clarke, printer and plumber was at No. 57. The business was established in 1846 by John James Clarke. He came to Wallasey from Bentham in Yorkshire and was the father of nine children. Garrick Studios were at Nos. 77 and 79, where Bert Cooper was the photographer. he carried out a wide variety of work was a specialist in marine, legal and survey photography. He also produced the 'Anchor' picture postcard series. Next door was the Imperial Penny

Bazaar, which was run by J.H Burrows and Sons. There were a collection of shops including boot shops. Pegrams. the grocers, Johnsons, the dyers, the Misses Ellen and Rose Smith had their confectioners shop at No. 95 and Jack Holdsworth was the butcher. Woodson's Stores (grocers) and Lockley's baker shop on the corner of Stanley Street, which later became Boot's the Chemists.

At the bottom of Stanley Street was the blacksmith's, Harding and Son, later Tom Dunnicliffe had the smithy. On the other corner of Stanley Street in Borough Road was the Maypole at No. 103 and next door was Waterworth's (later John Skirrow) the greengrocers, followed by Oliver's the fishmongers. This business was originally owned by George Turtle. One advertisement ran "If you want to buy a rabbit go to Teddy Turtle's". A rabbit cost no more than sixpence in those days.

Next to Shepherd's Dairy/Grocery was Bertie Moore, the butcher, who had taken over from Eastman's. Lunt's the bakers were next; Brown's became the Shoe Warehouse and Ted Evans' became Dick's Family Boot Stores, which was owned by G. & W. Morton. In later years this business moved towards the bottom of the road to Nos. 73 and 79. Tom Parker was a baker at No. 121, with the butchers next door. Arthur Stretch had the drapers and Mrs. John's the tobacconist/stationer's next to the chandler was Jim Marl, the grocer, who had taken over the shop from Jack O'Brien on the corner of Hatherley Street. When W. Singleton and Son's the bakers gave up the premises they were taken over by the Co-operative Society on the opposite corner.

Among the other shopkeepers in the road was Chris Curry, the butcher which were later bought out by Guest's, Israel Soloman, the draper, McCarthy and Elliot the grocers which became John Newall's grocery. Maxwell's dairy, Bennett's chemist and Mrs. Hart's laundry and when this shop closed Mrs. Graham opened up an ironmonger's shop. Then Foster's took over John Simpson's greengrocery at No. 139.

Alf Derbyshire had the butchers and Scott's the bakers. Mr. Albert Tatler had the druggist.

On the right-hand side, coming up from the bottom were several businesses; Mr. George Longworth had his cycle shop at No. 30. Mr Byrom took over the premises in the 1930s. John Abraham had the butchers next door. E.H. Wright, the bakers was at No. 38. This firm went on to be one of the town's leading confectioners who had their bakery at 12 Demesne Street. They specialised in supplying the shops and functions, etc., with small cakes of every description. Bill McQuire was a wheelwright and blacksmith in Smithy Lane. The 'Griffin' Hotel was on the corner of Smithy Lane where Bill Donnelly was landlord. Arthur Dodwell took over from him a few years later. Mary S. Davies had the public house at one time. Labouchere had a book shop and next door was the chemist (Budden's) when Mrs. Charles Richards was the manager. Mrs. E. Durden had the 'Hat Box' at 48a. Franklin Jones had the dairy and after a couple of more shops there was George Burrows, the leather goods shop. He also sold clogs and boots. Boots sold from 3s. 10d. to 18s. 0d. a pair. The shop was on the corner of Brighton Street. Mr. Maurice Thomas was the manager of the Joint City and Midland Bank. Mr. John Greenwell became manager in the 1930s. Among the other businesses in this part of the road were the fish and chip shop run by Archie Chippendale, Arthur White the stationer and Joe Scott, the butcher. Bob Leenam was landlord of the 'Stanley Arms' hotel and in the 1920s Reg Prichard took over, followed by Jim Horsley. The hotel once had a balcony and next door was 'Belle Vue', with steps leading up to the front door. The hotel once boasted a bowling green, on the opposite side of the road there were strawberry fields in the days long before the shops were there. Morris Davis was the proprietor of the Strand Tailoring Company. They had a little ditty on the back of the tramway and bus tickets which went like this:

"When I was a lad
I went with my Dad
and always got clad
at Davies 78 Borough Road
Now I'm a Dad
and have many a lad
we all get clad
at Davies 78 Borough Road"

And at No, 82, George Williams had a top shop called the "Wallasey Grotto", which became the Doll's Hospital where one could take a broken doll and have it repaired. Next door, Miss Ogden always had a nice selection of ladies' blouses in her window and the housewives would stop and see the latest fashions. Mrs. Williams had the Water Lilly hand Laundry, with William Lawrence's outfitters at No. 90. Next came Grosvenor Place and Grosvenor Square. Prince's Dairies were by the theatre.

www.historyofwallasey.co.uk | Borough Road, 1925

Still standing today was the former Irving Theatre. Opened in 1899, today it is the Embassy Bingo & Social Club. Continuing up Borough Road, Mrs. Dickinson had the florists and Jack Dobbing was the barber at No. 144. The business was later taken over by Mr. Daniels who was demobbed from the army after World War II and opened the shop on the 18th December 1945.

Jim Hyett ran a cabinet-making and upholstery business next to Dobbings' (Mrs. Dobbings was a milliner) and Leyland's, the pawnbrokers, had two shops one being on the corner of Florence Road. On the opposite corner was Devine's grocery business. There were drapers and bakers, butchers and confectioners - all doing well in the 1920's. Near the top of the road was a cooked meat and pork butchers, which was run by the two Tushingham brothers. This was the same family as Rita Tushingham - the well-known film actress and star of '*A Taste of Honey*'.

The Irving Theatre

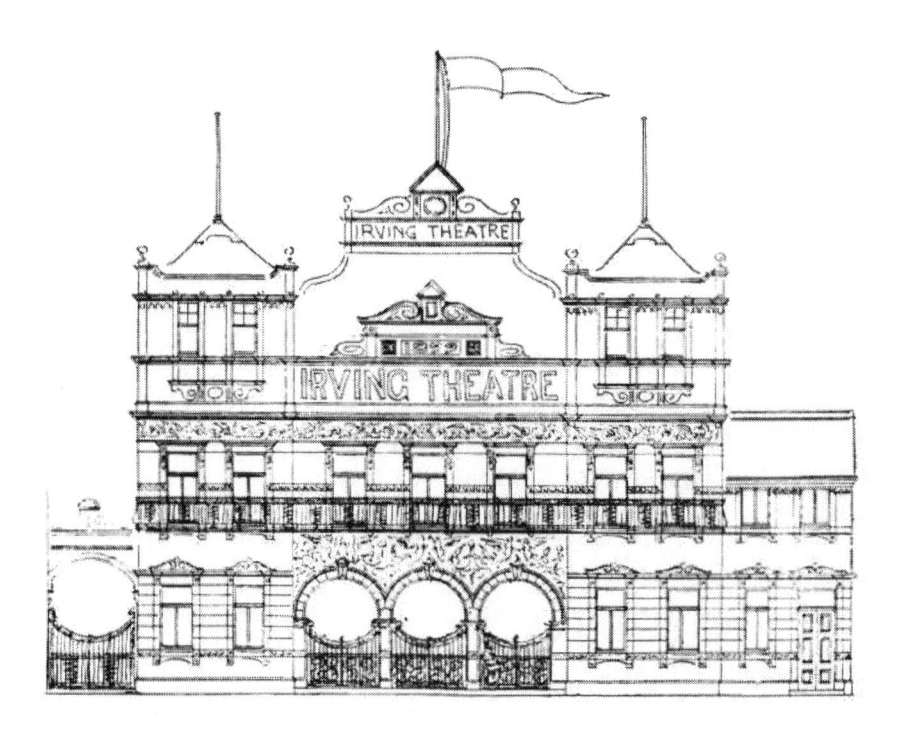

The Theatre in Borough Road, Seacombe, stands on a site once occupied by Hope House and its gardens. It was opened on 18th December 1899 by Sir Henry Irving, who allowed his name to be associated with the building on the strict understanding that the best of legitimate drama would be produced there. Mr J. Kierman, in applying for a licence, declared that accommodation had been provided for 2,500 persons and that fourteen dressing rooms were available.

The theatre opened with The Sign of the Cross and other plays were *A Royal Divorce, The Little Minister, The Only Way,* and *Charley's Aunt.* In 1901 *Uncle Tom's Cabin*, in which Harry Bedford portrayed 'Uncle Tom', was described as one of the best presentations local people had had the opportunity of seeing for a long time.

In October, 1902, Mr J.H French became manager, and under his administration musical comedy and pantomime were introduced; *Floradora* was performed twice in one year, and a company of juvenile artistes presented *The Sleeping Beauty* in February 1907. Among the cast was Wee Georgie Wood, then a talented boy of eleven and a fine mimic of well-known music hall celebrities. In the show was another young man, thought by his contemporaries to be rather too old for the show (as he was then in his teens) and decidedly 'untalented'. After a conference it decided to give this boy the part of a golliwog; in fact it was considered by some that he was given a part at all only because his father owned three of the four theatres and the producer did not want to offend him. So instead young Stanley Jefferson was 'suited'. The name, which meant nothing to anyone then and means nothing to people now, was later changed to Stan Laurel of the Laurel and Hardy partnership.

During the summer months the theatre showed silent pictures, reverting to theatre again in September 1908; in the ensuing months the following plays and musicals were presented: *School For Scandal*, *The Walls Of Jericho*, *The Merry Widow*, and *The Still Alarm*. The last play, which incorporated a special engine-house scene, had live horses harnessed to a real fire-engine on the stage. Ironically, a week later, on the 19th December 1908 for caused £1,000 worth of damage which necessitated closing the building for nine months for repairs and renovations.

On the 13th September 1909, the Irving theatre opened as 'The King's', with Mr Robert MacDonald's play of the year *The Dairymaids*. During 1910 variety became part of the repertoire and was very popular. Nevertheless, plays. Musical comedy and pantomime still held their place with a large section of the audience, and programmes were of a very varied nature.

On Easter Monday, 1912, Mr Ludwig Blattner took over the management and the theatre was renamed 'La Scala'. A new feature was the introduction of the Cosmopolitan Orchestra, under the direction of Blattner himself. Pictures were then so much to the fore that the building was advertised as 'The Philharmonic Cinema', and the only artiste of note who appeared at the theatre in person was Charles Coburn, 'The Man who broke the Bank of Monte Carlo'. 'La Scala' seemed to be losing some of its attraction, and a new general manager, Mr John Gaffney, was appointed. Under his guidance the theatre appeared to gain a new lease of life. Variety, revue, and occasionally a straight play provided the main forum of entertainment. In 1917, the play *Casta* was presented, with Albert Chevalier playing the chief character 'Eccles'. The company was declared to be one of the best to ever visit Wallasey and caused a box office boom. In May, 1918, the 'one and only' Dr Walford Bodie came to the theatre, and the same year the Wallasey Police Minstrels, for one night only, gave the last show to be presented at 'La Scala'.

On Monday, 12th August 1918, the grand opening of the Wallasey Hippodrome was announced, after the building had been 'substantially improved and handsomely equipped.' Mr A.J Morgan of the Salon Company Orchestra, and the name was changed once again - this time to the 'Casino'. Variety continued to be the only form of entertainment offered to patrons, but the new regime did not last very long. On Monday, 3rd September, the theatre opened its doors again as the Hippodrome. Among the items included on the programme this time we find Mr F. Rowland-Tims, F.R.C.O, playing the largest movable stage organ in existence, in a scena *A Musical Romance*. Miss Hettie King, described as the world's greatest male impersonator, visited the Hippodrome in 1924, followed by a return visit of Dr Walford Bodie, 'the Radio King'.

During the first half of 1926 the theatre returned completely to legitimate drama; the change of policy was very popular, at least for a short time, as in August the Hippodrome became known as the 'Irving Repertory Theatre', under the management of Mr A.L Bayley. The new repertory era lasted only until December; some of the plays presented were *The Temptress of Paris*, *A Bill of Divorcement* and *The Price of Coal*.

When the repertory season finished the theatre became known as the 'Irving' again, even though it was used for variety shows. In 1928 the Gordon Circuit acquired the theatre, spent £1,500 on improvements, and opened it under the managership of Mr Claud King on Easter

Monday, 1928, as the Hippodrome. In 1929 Wilkie Bard appeared in two of his famous sketches *The Cleaner* and *The Night Watchmen*. The Hippodrome was again closed for a time, until opened by Mr F.V Ross, in March 1930. Shortly afterwards it closed down again, this time until 1934, when it reopened with Mr Pat Collins, as proprietor, and 'Dick Batch' as manager. Sid Dooley's revue *I'll Be Seeing You* was the opening attraction, Wal Langtry, himself in the cast, presented his own road show *Fun Mixture* later in the month. During the week commencing 24th December 1934 the revue *West End Scandles* commenced its provincial tour at the Hippodrome having come straight from the Garrick Theatre, London. The chief comedian was none other than Tommy Trinder. Billy Merson, who song 'The Spaniard That Blighted My Life' made him world famous, was top of the bill in a week's variety show in April 1935.

However, notwithstanding the high standard of entertainment, the days of the Seacombe theatre were numbered. Live entertainment was being supplanted by moving pictures everywhere: on 2oth April 1936, the building was taken over by the Buxton Theatre Unit, to be operated as a cinema, and was renamed the 'Embassy'; subsequently it became one of the North-Western Group of Cinemas. Twenty-three years, owing to a lack of public support, it was closed on 21st March 1959.

New Brighton Floral Pavilion

In its heyday New Brighton was the accepted rendezvous for theatre goers and with seven theatres, was rich in live entertainment. From the 1890's to the outbreak of World War Two and shortly afterwards, hundreds of top stars trod the boards and enthusiastic audiences filled the seats of The Tivoli, Winter Gardens, Tower Theatre, Pier Pavilion, Palace Theatre and the Victoria Gardens Pavilion. Over the years these wonderful theatres, one by one, shut their doors. In 2006 the Floral was facing a similar fate.

Determined to keep the dream alive, the theatre management embarked on an ambitious development campaign that has revived this majestic venue to her former glory. Though she may look different to when she opened her doors in 1913, the magic and charm that has prevailed over nearly a century is evident as you walk through the new doors. Rebuilt as part of an exciting regeneration programme for 'Brand New Brighton', the Floral is living proof of the power of live entertainment in uniting communities through culture.

A pianist is playing to the audience in this photograph of the Bandstand in Victoria Gardens, **New Brighton** whch opened 3 May 1913 as an open-air summer theatre. In 1925 a glass structure enclosed the theatre and it then became the Floral Pavilion

The Picture below is how the Floral Pavilion now looks today following a new and modern building being erected on the site. The theatre closed in 2007 and was demolished as part of the town's £60 million Neptune Project redevelopment plans. The building was rebuilt to a new design and reopened in December 2008. The first act to perform at the venue after reopening was Ken Dodd, who has had a long association with the Floral Pavilion, making his first appearance in 1940. As well as an enlarged theatre auditorium, seating over 800, the complex also provides for conference facilities and a large multi-purpose lounge area.

The Tivoli Theatre

This legendary theatre stood at New Brighton for only 40 years but in that short space of time was host to many famous acts from around the world. When the theatre was opened in 1914 New Brighton was already renowned for entertainment and as such the Tivoli Theatre had to fend off rivals such as the Tower Theatre and the Winter Gardens Theatre. To do this the company who ran the Tivoli hired Fred Ross who had previously been responsible for the success of the Tower Theatre, and hoping to follow suit; they in turn hired him. Ross helped bring many famous names to the theatre over the following decade and the theatre was an outstanding success. The theatre closed in 1955 and remained derelict for some time before vandal managed to break in and cause a fire. The extent of the damaged was so great that the structure was deemed unsafe and it was demolished several days later.

The Pier Pavilion

In Abel Heywood's description of New Brighton Promenade and Pier in his *Guide to New Brighton and Birkenhead*, 1892, we read, 'Running at the back of the centre of the Pier is a covered saloon 130ft. in length and varying in width from 28ft. to 34ft. - it's available for bazaars, flower-shows, concerts, balls etc.'

In 1899 Adeler and Sutton's Pierrots, following the success of their shows on the shore, transferred to the Pier and created a 'sensation' there.

GEO. CHRISTIAN'S ROYAL SCARLET PIERROTS,
NEW BRIGHTON, 1915.

In 1900 the summer season lasted until 22nd December. Just prior to this date a special attraction was advertised: 'The Pier Pierrots Amalgamated Company of Star Artistes', who were to appear after a successful season at the Agricultural Hall, London. Also a special engagement was announced for twelve nights only of Malcolm Scott, who was to appear with Charles Harvey 'in the screamingly funny duets', *A Weak Woman* and *The Lady and the Ship*. Prices of admission were - Reserved seats 1s, unreserved 6d. Which was inclusive of the Pier admission.

In 1902 the lessees were 'The Summer Entertainments Syndicate Ltd.', and the presentation for the summer season was once again Adeler and the Sutton's Pierrots. The programme consisted of comedy, songs and pianoforte playing. In 1903, 'that eccentric, excruciatingly funny artiste' Mr Malcolm Scott made his second appearance. Scott was a dame comedian of a female impersonator, and had been described by Lupino Lane, the silent movie comedian, as "one of the most brilliant performer of his time."

During the next few years Adeler and Sutton's Pierrots went from strength to strength, building up their reputation and creating a good impression wherever they went. In a guide issued in 1909 we read 'the Pavilion is under the management of Messrs Adeler and Sutton, who hold a unique position in the world of entertainment, in as much as they branches in nearly every seaside town and watering place in the country. The concerts given in the Pavilion are of a special type and are recognised as the nursery of the stars of the lighter side of the stage.'

In the 1908 season Berr Erroll appeared, giving what was described as, 'a remarkable female impersonation.' Another entertainer was Miss Mona Vivian, known as 'Wee Mona.'

In 1909 the interior of the Pavilion was completely reconstructed, redecorated and heated throughout. 'Pierograph' pictures were shown to supplement the stage shows, but this novelty was short-lived. The Russell Rosse Repertory Company paid a visit, including in their repertoire *A Pair of Spectacles* and *A Fool's Paradise*. In 1910 Pelissier's The Follies gave performances at the theatre.

The first pantomime to be introduced at the Pier Pavilion was *Dick Whittington,* which ran for a week commencing 8th January 1912, and was immediately followed by *Aladdin.* In April of the same year The Scamps gave a performance, and among their cast was the famous actor and comedian Leslie Henson. In April 1913 it was announced that a new pavilion was to be built on the Pier at the promenade end, and that there would be a clear walk from the new pavilion to the sea front. The Pier Company was to provide the entertainment in future instead of leasing the building as in former days.

During the 1914 season many concert parties visited the Pier Pavilion including 'Ideals'. 'The Europeans'. 'Sequins', and the 'Poppies'. They were followed in 1915 by the 'Zeniths', 'Curios', 'Nobodies', and the

'Gaieties'. The opening show in 1916 was presented by Douglas Farber's London Company 'Glad Eyes', and 'The Mountebanks' opened the season in 1917. The Pavilion remained open during the whole of the war years . presenting the usual concert party or Pierrots troupe, with visits from well-known companies.

The Chrysanthemums Pantomime Society, then in its infancy, presented *Cinderella* in 1921, followed in 1922 by *The Babes in the Wood* and *Robin Hood*

The pier was closed in 1923 and four years later the Wallasey Corporation became its new owners and re-opened it with its own entrance from the promenade. The whole of the pier was rebuilt in 1931 at a cost of £45,000.

The closure of the New Brighton Ferry affected the life of the promenade pier. Fortes Limited became the owners in 1968, carrying out repairs and it continued for a time, but it was not a paying proposition. After much discussion, the pier was dismantled in 1978, the ferry pier having been demolished some five years earlier.

The Winter Gardens Theatre

Albert Douglas, a member of the well-known theatrical family, came to Merseyside on business in 1907, and realising how little entertainment there was in Wallasey, decided to stop. With Mr H.E Jones as a partner, he leased the Conservative Hall in Atherton Street and renamed it Alexandra Hall. Shows were presented every Saturday evening beginning with the Horbury Hand Bell Ringers as the chief attraction on 19th October 1907, the takings were 51s.9d. After a few weeks it was decided to open nightly, but the financial return was even worse.

In February 1908 the name was changed to the Winter Gardens, and palms were placed round the auditorium to justify the appellation. An orchestra was introduced, and programmes included variety, silent films and plays; but loses were still considerable until the John Riddling Opera Company came for a week. The theatre was packed for all performances, and from then onwards business increased. Among the stars to visit the Winter Gardens were Laurence Irving, who appeared in a one-act play, and Edward Terry who played in *Sweet Lavender*, *Liberty Hall* and other presentations.

In 1909 a limited company was formed to purchase the building, and alterations on a major scale were commenced in March of that year. A 'Circle' was provided, and an entirely new stage measuring sixty feet by thirty-three feet was installed, with adequate new 'flies' and a modern electric lighting system. After closing only four weeks and three days, the theatre was reopened; the work had proceeded day and night, and the last sections of the stage floor, and slating of the stage roof, were completed just 10 minutes before the doors opened. The attraction was a variety show. The following Monday, Moody Manners' Opera Company began a two-week's season with Zelie de Lussan starring in *Carmen* and *Samson and Delilah*. Plays and musicals predominated afterwards, and two artistes who frequently appeared were Ethelbert Edwards (afterward Henry Edwards of film fame) and J. Hamilton Stewart. In 1911 Owen Nares made his first appearance, being paid five pounds per week to take the lead in *Old Heidelberg*, which later formed the basis of *The Student Prince*.

During the Great War the theatre remained open and in spite of many difficulties made a modest profit. In 1919 Albert Douglas became sole manager director, with his eldest son A.C Douglas as general manager. It was not unusual for London success to visit New Brighton before going on to Liverpool, and from 1919 onwards many famous stars appeared including the following: Sybil Thorndyke, Edmund Given, Leon M. Lion, Bobby Howes, Fred Terry, Julia Neilson, Martin Harvey and Matheson Lang. Musical productions included: D'Oyly Carte Opera Company, Carl Rosa Opera Company, *No, No, Nanette, White Horse Inn, Street Singer and Maid of the Mountains.*

In 1924 the younger side of the management wanted to rebuild the theatre on modern lines, but this was vetoed by the older side. However, in 1929 all the directors agreed on rebuilding and work was commenced in February 1931. The Winter Gardens was reopened the following June and for three months was exceedingly successful; then came the world financial crisis and the theatre, in common with all other places of amusement, suffered badly. During a week in March takings fell to forty-seven pounds. Shortly afterwards there was one week of closure, but Albert Douglas decided to reopen and reimburse the Limited Company, if necessary, for any losses. His efforts were successful, and once again business reached a steady and profitable level. One of the most popular features was the annual summer visit of the Liverpool Playhouse Company. Audiences had the pleasure of seeing such well-known and popular artistes as James Harcourt, Wyndham Goldie, Ena Burrill, Marjorie Fielding, Ronald Squire, and Arthur Chesney.

Emilyn Williams paid two visits to the Winter Gardens, the first time appearing in *Night Must Fall*. Every night audiences included coach loads of people from North Wales where the play had been widely advertised. His second appearance in Wallasey in *The Corn is Green* produced the largest takings in the history of the theatre, over £2,000 gross.

Vincent Douglas, youngest son of Albert Douglas, wrote his first play *The Jeffersons* when he was eighteen years of age. The original production was in New Brighton and afterwards it toured for many years with great success. His other plays included, The Partners, The Optimist, Perfect Wife, and Christmas Dream. The death of this promising young playwright on his twenty-sixth birthday was a tragedy.

In 1936 the theatre was sold to the Cheshire Picture Halls Ltd, but Douglas remained managing director for twelve months and advisory director for a further twelve months.

With the outbreak of war in 1939 the Winter Gardens had to close down, and the performance on the night before the declaration of war was the last with which Douglas was associated with the theatre. Douglas died soon afterwards on the 19th February 1940. He had bought to the town entertainment seldom seen outside London, He knew many great actors of the day and was sadly missed. He was aged 78 and had been a life-long teetotaler and was also a non-smoker. In 1942 the Winter Gardens reopened with the BBC broadcast Florence de Jong playing the organ. 'Guest Nights' for amateur talent became a popular feature of the cinema.

After the war the Winter Gardens passed over to the S.M Associated Cinema and in 1954 to the Essolco Circuit. Although at this time it was used mostly as a cinema, programmes were still varied and repertory drama was produced by the Nita Valarie Winter Garden Repertory Players in 1954 and again for short season in 1956. In the latter year the 'Essoldo Follies' also appeared in revue and the theatre for a little while was peopled by 'live' performers.

The theatre was put up for sale and had a reserve of £15,000. Television had arrived and, like everywhere else, it had an effect on the town's dozen cinemas. The building remained closed, then reopened as a bingo hall for a period.

The building was later demolished and sheltered housing now occupies the spot.

The Palace Theatre

The Palace Theatre, on the Marine Parade, formed part of an ambitious scheme to give New Brighton a grand amusement centre. In 1881 it was announced that on Whit Monday the 'New Brighton Aquarium, Baths and Hotel Companies' splendid new Salt Water Baths would open, the manager was Mr J. Nolan. By 1882 entertainment were provided daily during the season, many of them being in the form of sacred concerts. On Good Friday, 1883, the following artistes appeared: Madame Rose Hersea, Miss Frances Armstrong, Mr Vernen Rigby and Mr Bantock Pierpoint. The Palace band and choir of seventy were conducted by Mr W.I Argent.

By 1885 the site consisted of the Grand Concert Hall, the Small Concert Hall, the "finest ballroom in England", Skating Rink, Aviary and Grotto. Entertainment of all types was given, from classical music to variety.

In October 1887 Mr C.B Roylance Kent made, on behalf of Mr W.T Malood, an application for a theatrical licence for the Jubilee Concert Hall (a licence was necessary in those days before anything approaching a 'play' could be performed). He stressed that only the best of drama would be presented there; that Mr Malood, being the son of a Congregational minister, was a most was a most suitable person to run it; and that all precautions in case of fire, etc., had been taken, In spite of his eloquence the licence was refused.

The year 1982 saw the visit of the original 'Baldwin Cat' which, it was stated, climbed up a rope to the ceiling fifty feet high, attached itself, and made a parachute descent. About this time the title 'Palace and Pavilion Theatre' was first used.

Mr Charles Coburn, the celebrated comedian, made his first appearance at the Palace in 1894. The theatre was crowded for every performance and Mr Coburn made many return visits in subsequent years.

In 1895 the Palace was under the control of the 'New Brighton Palace Company'; the theatre was then extremely successful and only first-class artistes were engaged. The following year the building was purchased by a Manchester syndicate who planned to float a company with a capital of £140,000 in order to erect on the roof what was described as, 'the largest wheel in the world' alter the style of that at Earl's Court. The company was to be called 'The New Brighton Graydon Castle, Great Wheel and Towers Company', and the wheel was to contain forty-two carriages, each to accommodate forty passengers. A new theatre and salt water baths were also to be erected. Unfortunately this ambitious project never materialised.

By 1899 operettas, musicals and plays were all being performed at the theatre, some by London companies, and all by well-known performers.

There is little doubt that the opening of the Tower Theatre had disastrous effects upon the Palace, although it managed to keep going. In 1903 it was the first hall in Wallasey to show animated pictures. The company responsible for this enterprise, 'New Century Pictures', controlled the Mount Pleasant Picture House, Liverpool.

Under the Wallasey Tramways and Improvement Act of 1907 the land and property were acquired by the Corporation for the sum of £41,500.

By 1908 animated pictures were firmly established at the Palace, although variety turns were still a feature, and this type of 'mixed' programme seemed to be quite popular.

The mixed entertainment continued throughout 1909-10, although the programme showed a slight preponderance of 'live' entertainment. Will Hay, described as an eccentric comedian, appeared in 1910, and included in the same bill was Sid Santo in his novel musical scene *The Breakdown of the Nine-thirty Express*. In October a full orchestra was introduced to aid the artistes, with Mr Arthur Lynn as musical director. Sandy Powell played at the theatre in 1911, achieving great popularity.

In 1913 (before the building of the Tivoli Theatre) the Tivoli Company Ltd. acquired control of the theatre and ran it in conjunction with the Victoria Gardens. The original idea was to rebuild the Palace, construct an arcade and erect a large hotel. However, owing to difficulties which had arisen over the building of the Tivoli, the plan had to be abandoned. The Corporation then asked for tenders for the tenancy of the theatre, and the highest (£520), that of Mr. Ludwig Blattner, was accepted. Mr Blattner renamed the building 'The Gaiety', and carried out many improvements and renovations. Under his administration the programme's contained more pictures than 'live' entertainment, and the Royal Bohemian Orchestra was engaged to play at every performance. A series of Sunday orchestral concerts was introduced, and Mr. A.Delmonte, the orchestra leader, became manager in 1914.

In April 1916, the greater part of the Palace site was destroyed by fire, but luckily, after desperate efforts by the firemen, the skating rink and the Gaiety Theatre were saved. The name of the theatre reverted to The Palace again in 1920. Later in the year it became known as 'The Palace Picture Playhouse', finally finishing as 'Collins' Palace Cinema'.

It was decided to close The Palace Theatre after its final performance on 11th December 1926. Soon afterwards the Palace was demolished and a car park occupied the site until August 1939 when Wilkes'

Palace Amusements opened. The War office took over the building during World War II and used part for storage space with secret munitions factory operating under the building.

After the war the 'New Palace' was a success with holidaymaker's with new exciting rides such as the "Moonrocket". During the summer months, Wilmer Wilkie's' Circus opened next to the New Palace. This was replaced by a permanent family funfair.

In the late 1980's Go-Karting was introduced to the Palace but closed in 2001 and in 2003, after redevelopment, 'Adventureland' opened which is an indoor children's play area that includes a 25 foot climbing wall, ball pool and giant inflatable's.

New Brighton Palace

In June 1876 a new company was formed, it was called *The New Brighton Palace Co* and it had a share capital of £100,000. The aims of the company were to build a new entertainment centre in the up and coming resort of New Brighton. Land alongside the beach was acquired and work started on laying the foundations for the buildings; however work soon came to a stop and it seemed unlikely that the project would be completed. A local resident, Mr Laurence Connolly saw the possibilities and bought the site, he completed the buildings and the Palace opened in 1880. In the winter of 1880 a new salt water bathing pool was added. During the 1882 season, the Palace averaged 10,000 visitors per week. Major changes were made for the 1883 season.

The Liverpool Mercury, 22nd March 1883 described it as follows:

The Palace, Winter Gardens and Grotto, which have been built by Councillor Connolly, promise to prove a highly popular place of recreation amongst the many holiday makers who visit New Brighton in the summer months. Extensive alterations and improvements have been carried out during the past winter, and every effort has been made to render the Palace and its accessories a thoroughly attractive pleasure resort.

The whole covers an area of about three acres, a portion of this space being occupied by splendid sea water baths. In the Palace proper, the "great hall" which has an area of 22,000 square feet, has been completely re-decorated since last season, and has been converted into a charming salon for music and dancing. The walls have been painted by Mr T.W.Grieve, of London, who has depicted a succession of picturesque views of English and Irish scenery from Kildare to Richmond.

The ceiling has also been elegantly decorated, and the columns and pilasters have been adorned with mirrors. In the Winter Gardens the greenhouses have been plentifully stocked with tropical and other plants, and they already look bright and beautiful with a variety of blossoms. A spacious open air skating rink has also been constructed on the roof of the concert hall, there has also been provided a recreation ground for children, a well stocked aviary and monkey house, and a smaller concert hall.

The most attractive addition, however, is an agreeable grotto, which will afford a cool and refreshing retreat in warm weather. It has been constructed by Mr James Cross of Southport and Manchester, and measures 140 feet by 120 feet. The grotto contains a large waterfall, extending from end to end, a distance of 131 feet, and several cascades intertwined with enarchments. Between the archways play fairy fountains of Swiss design. In the centre is a recess constructed of coral and other grotesque formations, and in the middle of the recess a fairy fountain showers crystallised sprays of water. 23

Rugged rock work, relieved with rich ferns, gives the grotto a charming aspect, and the effect is enhanced by the water-jets from many fountains of varied designs erected at different elevations. The crypt is supported by over forty iron columns, all richly embellished in rustic fashion to represent trees, and these have been surrounded with hardy ferns and mosses of various kinds, whilst the fountains and artificial rivulets have been abundantly supplied with mosses, lichens and aquatic plants, numbering altogether over 12,000. Two advertisements were placed in The Era, a London based weekly paper covering theatrical matters, in January 1883, the first offering for rent 1,600 square yards at the Palace for a Circus or similar; the second advert was looking for "New and Sensational Entertainments and Side Shows" for 1883 the season.

The opening on Good Friday 1883 was marked by a grand concert and a variety show. This was the pattern followed for many years with entertainment of all types being provided, from classical music to variety. As the reputation of the Palace rose, due in no small part to the quality of the sacred music concerts on Sunday afternoons, many famous classical musicians and singers; and many popular variety acts appeared. In order to perform a play in those days, a licence was required. The Palace applied for a licence in 1887, but the request was turned down. In 1896 the building was bought by a Manchester syndicate who planned to build a giant Ferris wheel on the roof. The wheel would have had 42 carriages, each of which would have held 40 passengers. This was never built. When the tower

---

23 Liverpool Mercury, 22nd March 1883

theatre opened in 1898, business at the Palace was drastically affected but the theatre managed to keep going, in 1903 to increase the number of patrons, it became the first hall in Wallasey to show animated pictures.

In 1907, Wallasey Corporation used its powers under the Tramways and Improvement Act to buy the notorious 'Ham and Egg Parade' and most of the other properties, including the Palace, which fronted onto the river. A new, wider, parade and sea wall were built. The newly formed Tivoli Company took control in 1913, their plan was to rebuild the Palace and build a new arcade and hotel, and however these plans were abandoned when problems arose over the building of the Tivoli theatre. The next tenant was Mr Ludwig Blattner who renamed the building the Gaiety and carried out many improvements. Towards the end of the nineteenth century, a Birkenhead rope maker named George Wilkie joined a travelling fairground. After 12 years with the fair, he leased at least part of the Palace site and set up a fairground.

A Joy Wheel was located next to the theatre; Joy Wheels were a popular, though short-lived, novelty rides in the early part of the twentieth century. Riders sat on a low, conical disk in the centre of the enclosure, the disk rotated at increasing speed, gradually throwing the riders off. The wheel was surrounded by tiered seating to enable spectators to watch.

In 1916 much of the site was destroyed in a disastrous fire, only the theatre and the skating rink were saved. There is little information on the Palace complex at this time, but it seems likely that the site was split up into a least two parts, the theatre being run by Mr Blattner and rest of the site by Mr Wilkie. There are also very few records as to what was in the fairground, although it's known that Mr Wilkie bought a second hand Burrell Traction Engine after the First World War The cinema, which by now had a separate entrance in Virginia Road, closed at the end of 1926.

In 1936 Mr Wilkie demolished what remained of the old Palace complex and put up a new building to house an indoor fairground. The building was called the New Palace and was completed in 1939. While a new roundabout was being built on the promenade, workmen discovered some unmapped caves, Mr W Wilkie had the caves dug out and constructed blast proof rooms in the caves. A munitions factory was set up and production started in March 1942. The weekly output of the small factory under the promenade was 250,000 machine gun bullets, 25,000 shells and 1,400 press button switches for aircraft radios. After the Second World War, the indoor fairground prospered, and in 1949 the Wilkie's opened a circus on a piece of land next to the New Palace (the area which would later be occupied by the Bright Spot amusement arcade).

Some of the rides remained in the New Palace for many years; one of the best known of these was 'The Jets'. The Jets were an early example of a 'rider-controlled' machine, the rider used a lever to control a pressure valve which raised and lowered the arm. The machine in the New Palace was the third one built, and was bought new in 1955. The Jets remained in the New Palace until 1995 when it was sold. Over the years the ride was 'modernised', the original 'jet planes' were replaced with 'space ships', and the lattice arms were panelled. Another long standing ride was the Waltzer; this was originally built in 1938 and was bought second-hand by Mr Wilkie, in 1950. This was the last Waltzer built before the Second World War the Waltzer was sold in 1997. Both these rides are now in preservation, and it's a testament to the care given to these machines that they, and many other rides owned by Wilkie, are still in existence. Other rides didn't stay as long in the fairground, Wilkie bought his 1959 Autodrome second-hand in 1985 and it only remained until 1990.

In the 1960s, as with everywhere else in New Brighton, trade at the New Palace fell off. The fair struggled on for many years but by the 1980s things were getting desperate. In the late 1980s David Wilkie took over running the New Palace and much of the fairground was cleared out to make space for a go-cart track to be built. This brought in new customers and improved the situation. The go-cart track was closed in 2001, and David Wilkie had the Bright Spot arcade and much of the New Palace demolished. The facade and the shops at the front remained. The New Palace, now an outdoor fairground, continues still under the control of the Wilkie family. Below is the Picture of how the New Palace looks today, with the Bright Spot demolished and replaced by a small outside fairground. The building now also houses a night club as well as the traditional cafe with a donut stall catering the indoor arcade housed inside the remaining part of the building.

St Peter & St Pauls Church

A well-known landmark, the "Dome of Home", a cathedral-like domed building dating from the early 1930s and standing high above the River Mersey opposite the Liverpool shoreline, and which got its name from sailors returning to their Scouse homes. St Peter and St Paul was threatened with closure in 2008, but a self-help group SOUL (Save Our Unique Landmark) was set up to pinpoint the importance of this fine local iconic landmark. Even so, in August 2008 it did close despite pleas from the congregation. But at length the prayerful persistence of the SOUL group paid off and the church was partially reopened in March 2011.

St Peter and Paul's Catholic Church is a Grade II listed Church in Atherton Street, New Brighton, Wirral, England. It has a green dome. The church was founded by a priest called Father Tom Mullins. Born in Ireland, he studied for Priesthood in Lisbon, Portugal. When Father Tom got back to the Wirral, he was serving at a church (now demolished) in Hope Street. He went on to pursue his dream of constructing the church. When construction was finished New Brighton was becoming a very popular resort. The church opened in 1935.

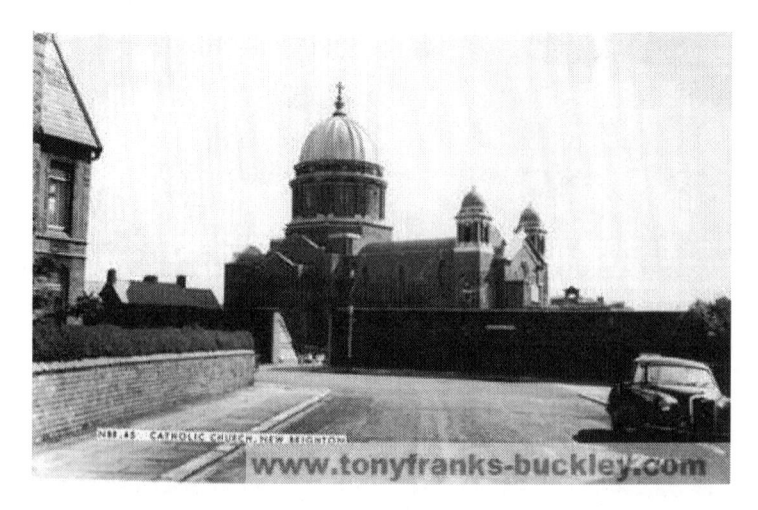

Serving Priests:

1. Father Tom Mullins 1935-1945
2. Mgr Canon Maurice Curran V.G 1945-1960
3. Father John Quinn (1960–1983)
4. Father Joseph Prendiville 1983
5. Father (later canon) Robert Fallon 1983-1990
6. Father Anthony Myers 1990-1996
7. Father Michael Wentworth 1996- 2006
8. Father John Feeney 2006–2008 (church closed)
9. Canon Oliver Meney 2011-

Wallasey & Major Sea Disaster Connections including Rake Lane Cemetery

With thanks to the hard work of John Robinson and the friends of Rake Lane cemetery, this is their work and I claim non as my own.

Many of the graves in Rake Lane are memorials to the victims of disasters at sea. These include Titanic, Empress of Ireland and

Lusitania. But in Liverpool Bay there were three other tragic incidents: the submarine Thetis, in 1939; the pilot boat Alfred H Read, in 1917 and another pilot boat, the Charles Livingston, in 1939.

History of the Cemetery

In December, 1876 a committee was formed to select a site for a municipal cemetery in Wallasey. The decision depended upon the suitability of the soil and fifteen sites were surveyed, including Mill Lane, Grove Road and Seabank Road. At least eight different sites were seriously considered. Nearly two years later three sites, at Manor House, Earlston and the land at the Grammar School, were still in the running. They ranged in value from ten to eleven thousand pounds. Eventually, the Earlston site was chosen and the cemetery officially opened in 1883, after completion in 1882.

Cornelius Smith was an engine fitter at Cammell Laird's shipyard. He was one of the men lost on the submarine Thetis when she sank, in Liverpool Bay, in 1939. Many of the victims of this disaster were buried on Anglesey, but two men were brought back to Wallasey and interred in Rake Lane Cemetery. Close to Smith's grave is the headstone recording the loss of John Griffiths, also a Cammell Lairds engine fitter. There were 103 men on board. Only four men managed to escape. In the tower of St Mary's church, behind the Priory in Birkenhead, there is a memorial to the men of the Thetis. All the way up the staircase, inside the tower, are the names of each individual who was lost on the Thetis. .

The Liverpool pilot boat Alfred H. Read was built in 1913. At the beginning of the First World War two of the pilot boats were taken over by the War Office for use as Examination Ships. In the early hours of 28th December, 1917, the S.S. Alfred H. Read struck a mine on the Bar station. She sank almost immediately. Of the forty-one men on board, only two were saved; nineteen pilots, eight apprentices and six crew members were lost, as well as six men employed by the Admiralty. At least seven victims of this disaster are buried at Rake Lane Cemetery.

The Liverpool pilot boat Charles Livingston, built in 1921, was lost on Saturday, 15th November, 1939. When the vessel ran aground Second Master/Pilot Ernest Bibby was in charge. The weather was bad and deteriorating. The situation was made worse due to the imposition of war conditions: the considerable dimming of the Bar Light and the channel buoys. Just after midnight, Second Master/Pilot Bibby lost sight of the Bar Light, the only means available for positioning the ship. Thus began the appalling events that ended in tragedy. With Pilot Bibby in charge, the ship ran aground near Ainsdale at 3.30 am. Unfortunately, signals were transmitted stating: 'Ashore between Bar Light Vessel and Ormes Head,' causing great confusion for the rescuers, as she was actually off Ainsdale beach. Four men managed to reach the shore, but it was more than ten hours before the last six survivors were taken off the grounded ship. Of the thirty three men on board, ten were saved, including Pilot Bibby. Twenty three drowned. Seven of them are buried here, in Rake Lane cemetery.

Captain William Turner went to sea at the age of thirteen. He joined the Cunard Line in 1883 and became a Cunard captain in 1907. On May 1st 1915 the Lusitania left New York for Liverpool with Captain Turner as her master. At 2.10 p.m. on the 7th May a German U-Boat torpedoed the Lusitania. The captain of the U-Boat was staggered by the effect of his single torpedo: the superstructure at the point of impact and the bridge were torn asunder, fire broke out and smoke enveloped the high bridge. In the chaos only six of the forty eight lifeboats were successfully launched. The ship went down in eighteen minutes. One thousand two hundred and one people were lost. Seven hundred and sixty four were saved, including Captain Turner.

The Admiralty had informed Lord Mersey that, "It's considered politically expedient that Captain Turner . . . be most prominently blamed for the disaster". However, in his summing up, Lord Mersey said Captain Turner "exercised his judgement for the best. It was the judgement of a skilled and experienced man, and although others might have acted differently and perhaps more successfully, he ought not . . . to be blamed." Turner continued with Cunard until 1921, when Winston Churchill (ex-1st Lord of the Admiralty) published The World Crisis in which he inaccurately and unjustly blamed Turner for the Lusitania disaster. Unable to face the renewed publicity and criticism, Turner retired to Crosby, but was buried in the family grave in Wallasey in 1933.

Captain Stanley Lord was born in Bolton in 1877. When he was thirteen he went to sea in sailing ships. On the 5th April, 1912 Lord, now captain of the Californian, sailed from London, his destination Boston, U.S.A. Nine days into the voyage, his ship encountered an ice field. Lord, mindful of his training that a captain must never endanger his ship, wisely gave the order; "stop engines" at 10.21 p.m. on Sunday, 14th April. There was no other vessel in sight at that time. Lord stayed on the bridge until midnight and then turned in. Sometime after 2 a.m., distant white rockets were sighted. These were the distress rockets sent up from the Titanic, which had struck an iceberg at 11.40 p.m.

At the Inquiry Captain Lord stated that his ship was nineteen miles distant from the Titanic but, with no evidence to back him up, this was refuted and the Californian was blamed for not going to the rescue immediately. Before the Titanic hit the iceberg the men on watch had seen no sign of another ship. It wasn't until half-an-hour later that they saw a ship steaming towards them, which then veered away. This could not have been the Californian because she never moved.

Following the Inquiry, Captain Lord felt that he had suffered an attack on his seamanship, integrity and humanity. He resigned from the Leyland Line, but within a few months took a job with the Nitrate

Producers' S.S. Company, for which he was a captain until 1927, when he retired.

Unfortunately, in 1958 the film A Night To Remember told the story of the Titanic and again blamed the Californian for not going to the rescue. Captain Lord, now aged eighty, tried to get his case reopened to clear his name and the Mercantile Marine Service Association Council agreed to defend his reputation. However, the Board of Trade decided that it would not be in the public interest to reopen the case. Sadly, Captain Lord died long before the exact position of Titanic's final resting place was found. This discovery bore out his assertion, at the Inquiry, that his ship had been nineteen miles from the Titanic when she was sinking.

Captain Henry Wolsey Johnson was born 9th August, 1821 at Oswego, New York. He was married twice, his first wife having died at sea. After he left the sea he became a New York harbour master. When he was about sixty years old he came to England and was employed as an agent for the Midland Railway Co., based in Central Station, Liverpool. Captain Johnson's grave is one of the earliest in Rake Lane Cemetery. Find out more about the history of the cemetery at www.wallaseycemetery.co.uk/

Wallasey Hero of the Battle of Britain

Flight Sergeant Ray Holmes ran out of ammunition when he was in the thick of a 'dog-fight' over London on Sunday, 15 September, 1940. So he decided to ram his Hurricane fighter into a Dornier bomber. This caused both planes to crash, but Holmes and some of the crew members of the bomber managed to bail out. Holmes landed near the Oval Cricket Ground and it's said that he then called in at a nearby pub for a quick pint. All this caught the imagination of the public and he was feted as having saved Buckingham Palace from being attacked.

Flight Lieutenant Ray Holmes, who died in 2005, delivered the coup de grace to a German Dornier 17 bomber near Buckingham Palace in one of the most celebrated episodes during the Battle of Britain. The German bomber had taken off from France at 10am on Sunday September 15 1940, which is now regarded as the climax of the battle. After joining up with a formation at 15,000 ft it headed for central London, its crew avoiding RAF fighters when crossing the coastline near Dungeness; then an engine started to malfunction, and the bomber dropped behind the main force.

As it neared its target it came under concentrated attack from fighters near Battersea. It was set on fire by Hurricanes of 310 (Czech) Squadron; and two of the crew bailed out.

Holmes, a sergeant at the time, then appeared on the scene to deliver a further attack, causing the Dornier to break up, and forcing the German pilot to bail out. A large piece of the bomber fell in the forecourt of Victoria Station, a scene depicted - with considerable artistic licence - in the film Battle of Britain. The stone façade of the station bore the scars for more than 40 years.

Afterwards, Holmes stated that his aircraft had hit something during the attack, and he was forced to bail out over Chelsea. On landing in Hugh Street, he was told by onlookers that his enemy had crashed at Victoria. He was led to the Orange Brewery 100 yards down Pimlico Road for a swift brandy before being dispatched to Chelsea Barracks. Following a visit to an Army doctor and then the mess for a few more drinks and a bit of warranted line-shooting, a taxi took him back No 504 Squadron at RAF Hendon.

The attack, during in which Buckingham Palace was also bombed, captured the imagination of the public as well historians. Last year archaeologists unearthed parts of Holmes's Hurricane for a Channel 5 television documentary, in which Holmes visited the site near Buckingham Palace Road and was shown the fighter's control column or "joy-stick" which he had last held 64 years earlier. Appropriately, the firing button was still set to "FIRE". The aircraft's engine was recovered, and it's now displayed at the Imperial War Museum. The son of a journalist, Raymond Towers Holmes was born on August 20 1914 at Wallasey, Cheshire. He attended Caldy Grange Grammar School, West Kirby, where he excelled at cricket and rugby, then became a crime reporter. He joined the RAFVR as an airman pilot in 1937 and trained at Prestwick and Barton in Lancashire.

Holmes went to No 504 Squadron at Wick in June 1940. The squadron flew south to Hendon in early September, and it was soon involved in some of the heaviest fighting of the Battle of Britain. After he was commissioned in June 1941, 'A' Flight of No 504 became No 81 Squadron at Leconfield, East Riding, and the pilots were kitted out for an unknown destination. They flew to Glasgow, and embarked in the aircraft carrier Argus, which carried crated Hurricanes. On September 1, the squadron flew off in groups and landed at Vaenga airfield near Murmansk, northern Russia. Operations were flown until November, when Holmes and his fellow pilots taught Russians to fly the fighters. In December the RAF contingent sailed for England, leaving the Hurricanes and their equipment for the Russian Air Force. After returning home, Holmes spent the next two years training student pilots before he went back to operations, flying high-altitude Spitfires with No 541 photographic reconnaissance squadron at Benson. During this period he acted as a courier, carrying papers for Winston Churchill when he was preparing for the Potsdam Conference. Holmes left the RAF in

November 1945, having been mentioned in dispatches and given the Air Efficiency Award.

After the war, Holmes turned down a suggestion that he become an airline pilot, and returned to journalism in Liverpool, where he established his own agency which specialised in court reporting. He also took agricultural photographs in colour when the technology was in its infancy, retaining his own laboratories for processing and working closely with Kodak, which was impressed with his innovative ideas. But eventually he could not keep up both journalism and photography, and opted for the former. Taking notes with a fountain pen in perfect shorthand, Holmes became a father figure at Liverpool crown court, teaching young reporters the proper way to bow before a judge. After retiring at 80, he maintained a keen interest in journalism while devoting time to golf, woodwork and gardening. He wrote an autobiography, Sky Spy (1989).

In 2004 the Wirral Borough Council bestowed the Freedom of the Borough on Holmes, the chief executive stating that he could "think of no one upon whom this honour could have been more fittingly bestowed". On the day Holmes died, flags flew at half-mast in his honour in the Wirral, and his widow received a message from Buckingham Palace expressing the Queen's sadness on hearing of his death. Raymond Holmes married Elizabeth Killip in April 1941. After her death he married, in 1966, Anne Holmes, who survives him with two daughters from his first marriage, and a son and daughter from his second.

Wallasey & The World War Two Blitz

NEW BRIGHTON from the Air

The first bombs in Wallasey fell on Adelaide Street, Poulton, on the 10th August, 1940, about half an hour after midnight. Seven high explosive bombs wrecked property, killed four people and seriously injured four others; in all there were thirty-two casualties. Around midnight on August 17th, Liverpool had its first bombs. Wallasey suffered again on August 30th, and the last day of the month brought a comparatively heavy attack on Liverpool, Birkenhead and Wallasey. Among the first places to be hit were Adelaide Street, Cliff Road, East Street, Field Road, Florence Cottages, Gorsey Lane, Ingleby and Ladyewood Roads, Lily Grove, Mill Lane, Stroud's Corner, Rake Lane, Palatine Road and St George's Mount; the Town Hall was damaged on 31st August. In September, Wallasey was bombed nine times, in October three times and many times in November. To illustrate the danger to the ARP workers, on September 17th a bomb struck an AFS post killing eight members of the AFS inside it. After a heavy raid on November 28th/29th there was a lull until December 20th, the beginning of the Christmas raids. The raids started about 6.30 p.m. on the 20th, became heavier on the night of the 2lSt and eased somewhat on the 23rd. At this period 119 people were killed and 91 seriously injured.

With the New Year, attacks lessened for a time, but in January there were three raids. Then followed a period of more than a month of peace and quiet and thankfully, no bombings. February brought two raids on the 15th and 24th; and a fortnight later came another very heavy attack. About 9 p.m. on the evening of March 12th flares were dropped, and on the nights of the 12th, 13th and 14th the Cheshire side of the river took the brunt of the attack. In Wallasey within two hours of the first onslaught water for fire fighting failed completely, the trunk main having been fractured by a bomb.

The electricity works at Poulton were damaged and the two gas-holders at the adjoining gas works rendered useless. This was Wallasey's worst raid of all: the bombing was widespread, with great damage to property. The areas of heaviest destruction included Church Street, Lancaster Avenue and Fox hey Road.

A very large number of houses were made uninhabitable and eleven churches were hit. The death roll totalled 174, with 158 seriously injured; in addition 10,000 people were made homeless. The ARP services worked devotedly and unceasingly during the raids 'an example to the whole country', were the words used by Mr Herbert Morrison, Minister of Home Security when on a visit to Merseyside.

The above image is of the Wallasey Town Hall which took a direct hit. One of the strangest episodes of all blitzed Britain occurred when Lancaster Avenue and Wimbledon Street were bombed in the early hours of March 13th and thirty people were killed, most of them in a communal shelter. On Sunday morning, March 16th three and a half days later, a rescue party 'heard what they thought was a kitten's faint mew below them in the debris. Listening in silence they heard it again, it was a baby's cry.

Getting feverishly to work, the three men made their way towards where a child of a few months was lying buried and half choked with dust. Moving like cats themselves, lest one ill judged gesture should loosen a pile of debris on to the child, they finally reached it, gave it first aid, wiped the dust from its mouth and released it. The child had lain there three and a half days, from the time the bomb exploded in the early morning of the fateful March 13th to the moment of its rescue—almost incredible, but true.' The baby's parents had both been killed, their bodies protecting the child from harm. The baby was taken to the Victoria Central Hospital (pictured below) where she responded to treatment and is alive and well today.

Intermittent raiding took place until the beginning of May when a series of attacks continued for eight successive nights. Some heavy damage to buildings occurred, and the Royal Daffodil II was sunk at her moorings at Seacombe Stage. But although there were 7,500 people homeless after the raids, Wallasey suffered comparatively less than other Merseyside towns, only three citizens being killed as against 1,500 in Liverpool. Germany soon afterwards was involved with Russia on the Eastern Front and Merseyside was never again raided in force; the last raid, recorded as number 43 took place on 1st November 1941 and caused damage and casualties in the Vyner Road, Prospect Vale and Beverley Road area.

The picture above shows an Anderson Shelter situated over the road from the Wallasey Town hall which took a direct impact during the Blitz.

The above picture is a monument commemorating those who lost their lives was erected in Rake Lane Cemetery. The inscription read:

'*This memorial is erected to honour the 324. Non-combatant residents of Wallasey of whom 51 rest here who lost their lives by air attack from the enemy during the Second Great War, 1938-1945. In Wallasey, as a largely residential town, houses and people bore the main weight of the attacks. In addition to the killed, 275 were seriously injured and more than 600 less seriously. Houses totally destroyed numbered 1,150, and 17,000 were damaged; in fact, it would have been difficult to find a house in the older part of the town that had escaped damage entirely. There were 500 'alerts', and 658 high explosive bombs, including 17 parachute mines, are known to have fallen on the town, together with thousands of incendiaries.*

Another War Memorial situated on the promenade next to Vale Park. There are many places situated around Wallasey that remembers the heroes and the fallen of the two great wars.

Wallasey Naval Base by John Saville

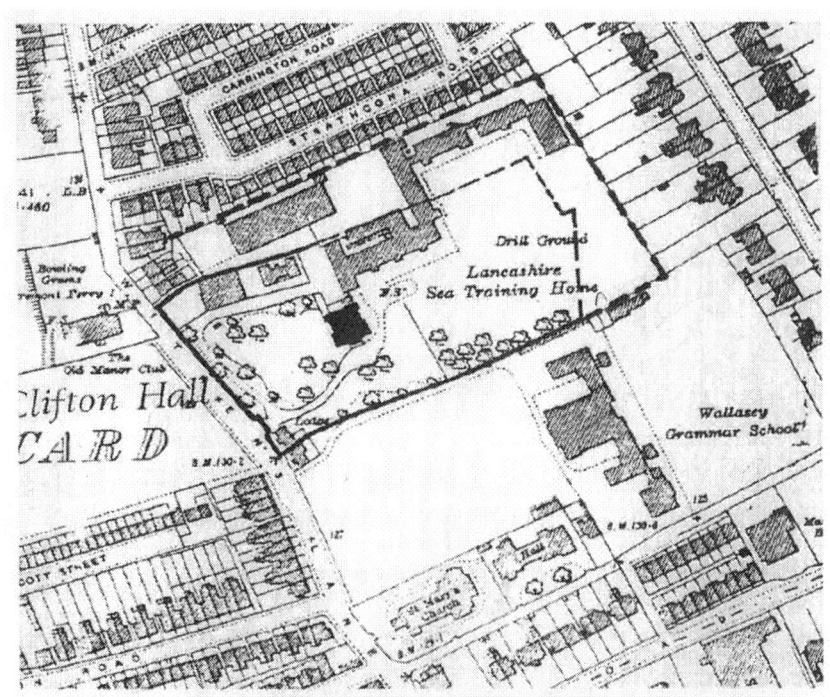

The site of the Training Home is now occupied by new homes in Brookthorpe Close

The former Royal Navy training vessels which were moored in the River Mersey are well recorded in both word and pictures on the internet. These were once 'wooden walls', sailing ships which had served in the fleets of Victorian Britain and looked very much like the ships in which Nelson had achieved his famous victories. 24

Perhaps best remembered was HMS Conway on which many future Royal Navy officers received their first introduction to nautical life. A similar establishment was HMS Indefatigable, a charitable institution founded in 1864, which provided to train boys in poor circumstances to become merchant seaman, while the Akbar was a reformatory ship for protestant boys and the Clarence served a similar purpose for Roman Catholic 'Young Offenders'. The Clarence

---

24 'The Making of Seamen' by Norman W Howell, 1997

suffered the fate of being burned down to the waterline by its inmates in January 1884!

Perhaps less well remembered was the sea training establishment based on land in Liscard. Wallasey, and which was known by all, locally, as 'The Navy League'. Firstly, it has to be to be discovered what exactly was meant by 'The Navy League', this term was recalled in as applying in the 1940's to 'The Navy League Sea Cadets', and while Sea Cadets were, and still are, well known, quite what the 'Navy League' part of the 'Homes' title meant, was still a mystery.

The Navy League grew out of a perceived need for promoting and advocating a strong British Fleet. In the Victorian reign imperialist tendencies were more pronounced in several countries, including Germany and other European 'Great Powers'. In Britain there was a firm belief in this country's status as world peace keeper and upholder of a superior Empire. In 1894, a series of newspaper articles set about raising the awareness of the importance of the sea to Britain and a reaction to these was the formation of the British Navy League with the purpose of lobbying the Government to maintain Britain's lead over other countries so far as naval power was concerned, and in particular to increase the number of 'Dreadnought' type battleships being built in order to keep ahead of naval construction in Germany.

At the same time, Britain's mercantile marine was easily the largest in the World, and with particular importance locally, fully one seventh of all the world's shipping was registered in Liverpool. Commentators lamented the fact that Britain's demand for seamen was so great that suitable crewman were not available in sufficient numbers from 'home grown' sources and as a result foreign seaman were having to be employed, while, at the same time, large numbers of potentially useful British youths were unemployed due to their lack of suitability for a sea going life.

It was against this background that The Navy League, with its dedication to keeping Britain's superiority in both the Royal Navy and the Merchant Marine, decided to set up a shore establishment to train these boys for a sea going life, with an emphasis on the discipline necessary for both services, and where better than on Merseyside, the home port to so many British ships.

The Navy League decided to set up its Merseyside training establishment in Liscard, Wallasey, and chose one of the 'mansions of old Wallasey' for the location of the sea training school. 'Clifton Hall', in Withens Lane, had been built in 1844 and had, for many years been the home of a succession of wealthy local people. Many had these has close connections with the sea going life of Merseyside, being ship-owners or otherwise being involved in the maritime commerce of the port. One of the last of these was a Captain John Herron who was at one time Chairman of the Wallasey Local Board and after whom one of the Wallasey's Council's Mersey ferryboats was named. After the death of Captain Herron, his son sold Clifton Hall and approximately five acres of surrounding land to The Navy League for £28,000. A foundation stone was laid on the 18th October 1902 by Lord Strathcona and the 'Lancashire and National Sea Training Home For Poor Boys' was opened on the 2nd October 1903, although the 'poor' was dropped in 1916. 25

The homes were originally intended for poor homeless boys between the ages of thirteen and sixteen who had to be of good character and conform to the physical standards laid down. Friends of the Navy League could donate £25 to endow a hammock at the home, but some donated £500 for a hammock forever. There was an impressive list of sponsors of the establishment and donations and gifts were frequently welcomed. In addition to Clifton Hall, which became the home of the Captain Superintendent, a number of buildings were erected in what had previously been the grounds of the house. Some of these additions were built over a period of time but as it fullest extent the campus consisted of, besides Clifton Hall, The Liverpool Navy League Home, The Cheshire Home, The Hertfordshire Navy

---

25 'The Old Mansions of Wallasey' by J.S. Rebecca

League Home, The Sir Alfred Jones Memorial Home, The Heath Harrison Technical Instruction Wing, and The Sir Alfred Read Gymnasium. Instruction was given to the boys in Mathematics, Science, Geography, English, History, Seamanship, Boat work, Signalling, Rule of the road at sea, Wood and Metal work, Physical Training, Boxing, Swimming and outdoor sports. As can be imagined, with a large complement of boys, much of the space was devoted to dormitories, and in its later years, after the 'Navy League' had left Wallasey, and when the buildings had been adapted for use as a Further Education College, 'Old Boys' would visit and locate their former 'bed spaces' in the classrooms.

The intention was that once they had reached the requisite age, the trainees would be placed in either the Royal Navy or with a shipping company of Britain's Merchant Marine. For example, Hertfordshire had sent 67 boys to the School for training up to the end of 1914. Out of this number 13 had entered the Royal Navy, 2 joined the Royal Navy School of Music, 24 went into the Merchant Navy, 7 were taken away from the School as unsuitable and 21 were still undergoing training. 26

The list of subjects quoted above gives an idea of the regime which prevailed at the School and given that the instructors were ex Navy personnel, there would be no doubt that discipline would be strict. The need for discipline would be very necessary for those who would go to sea, in both, the Royal Navy and the Merchant Service. A series of photographs, taken at the time for a national magazine shows not only indoor instruction in the classrooms and workshops, but also such activities as gun crew drill and bayonet practice. Religion, still very much a mainstay of society was not neglected and Church Parades, to the nearby St. Mary's Church was a regular feature.

The boys of 'The Navy League' were a well known presence in Wallasey. The establishment maintained a fine 'silver band'

---

26 Personal recollections - Noel. E. Smith, Harry Nickson and Dr. Peter S. Richards

composed of some of the boys themselves. This often took pride of place at various local events and prominent amongst these were the Gala Day and Tattoo which was a great event in the summer. As many of the boys did not have families the Home invited neighbouring families to come along. Deck chairs would be placed for people to sit and watch the events. A local resident recalls pillow fights over water, a 'slippery board', rather like 'walking the plank' and a greasy pole. At the end of the afternoon prizes would be given to the winners by the Commander, who dressed in full uniform complete with sheathed sword. Of course, the band, attired in naval uniform, played throughout.

Nautical activities played a large role in the life of the boys and none more so than the traditional naval discipline of rowing. There was scope for practice on the waters of the nearby docks, or on the River Mersey itself. The school had an eight oar gig, which beat everything in sight, including the Indefatigable. In the Report of the Indefatigable for 1939, it was stated that 'A cutters race against the Lancashire & National Sea Training Homes was won by them'. (The Liscard boys). In tune with the nautical theme, on the Drill Ground there had been built a scaled down sailing ship with a mast to enable the boys to practice climbing and sailwork.

The Homes continued to provide training throughout the years, a report in 1917 showed that out of a total of 497 boys, 195 went into the Royal Navy and 302 into the Merchant Service. During the 1920s and 1930s, the trainees were a very visible presence in Wallasey but by the end of the 1930s, war clouds were beginning to gather. The boys had to dig up land at the back of the Homes so that air raid shelters could be built. Air raid precautions were practised and early in the war a large bomb fell near to the gymnasium and one of the dormitories and of course the risk of loss of life to the boys was too great to contemplate by allowing them to remain in Wallasey. Following the air raid the Officer in Charge sent all of the boys to their respective homes and they were recalled in October 1941, not to Wallasey, but to Ravencrag, Howtown, near Penrith. The officers reported back to Ravencrag, with the exception of the Cheif Officer who stayed at the School in Wallasey to receive boys en route to the Royal Navy or the Merchant Navy Shipping Pool.

By 1943 it had been decided that a merger of the Lancashire and National with their old rivals, the Indefatigable would be beneficial. As with the other training ships in the Mersey, the Indefatigable School had been evacuated, in their case, to Ruthin.

The joint school, after the war, re-convened at Plas Llanfair in Angelsey, the Wallasey premises passed into the hands of Wallasey Corporation who intended to re-open it as a Further Education College. During surveying operations it was found that Clifton Hall, the former nucleus of the School, was riddled with damp and it was subsequently demolished. Some of the School buildings shown in the old photographs also disappeared, but enough was left of the establishment for 'old boys' to identify familiar locations. Following a recent reorganisation of Further Education, the Wallasey site was declared surplus to present day requirements and all of the buildings were demolished. Today there is no evidence of the Hall, or of the School but memories remain of a now long vanished part of Wallasey's history.

By John Saville with thanks and credit to him.

Margaret Boode

Margaret Boode was the daughter of Reverend Thomas Danneth the rector of Liverpool. She was the widow of a West Indian plantation owner, and took up residence in Mockbeggar Hall now known as Leasowe Castle in the year of 1802. Margaret Boode had a good reputation as a helper of shipwrecked sailors, many of whom were lured onto the dangerous rocks in the area by wreckers. In addition she was well known for other charity works and promoting Christianity within the community. Their large house provided an ideal place to aid such unfortunates, both in size and situation.

On the 21st April 1826, Margaret Boode was carrying out her daily duties and travelling along Breck Road in a horse & carriage. For reasons unknown, the horse shied and Margaret Boode was thrown from her carriage and killed instantly aged 52 years. As a mark of respect a large Gothic style obelisk made from lime stone was erected some 25 years after in 1827. At the bottom of the monument an inscription read:

Near this spot Mrs. Boode of Leasowe Castle was killed By a fall from her pony carriage April 21st 1826 May ye who pass by Respect this memorial of an awful dispensation And the affectionate tribute of an only child To Perpetuate the clever mother's memory Beyond the existence of that breast Which will never cease to cherish it Ah, may the sad remembrance which attachés to this spot Impress on everyone this salutary warning In the Midst of Life we are in Death Erected in 1827, mother-in-law of Colonel Cust of Leasowe Castle.

The obelisk was moved in 1914 further down the road to make way for road widening of Breck Road. It stayed there for many years and was damaged by German bombers in WW2 during which it sustained shrapnel damage and the top of the needle broke off and fell onto the floor. Sometime after, and for reasons unknown; the obelisk was removed and a single plaque was placed on wall nearby which was placed on a wall and bears the following inscription:

"This memorial was erected in commemoration and to mark the place in Breck Road where Mrs BOODE of LEASOWE CASTLE was killed by a fall from her pony carriage on 21st April 1826. Due to road widening it was moved to this site in 1914".

The legacy of the Boode family went on for many generations and her daughter married Queen Victoria's Master of ceremonies, Colonel Edward Cust in 1821.

The Mosslands

SITE OF "THE MOSSLANDS" IN 1926

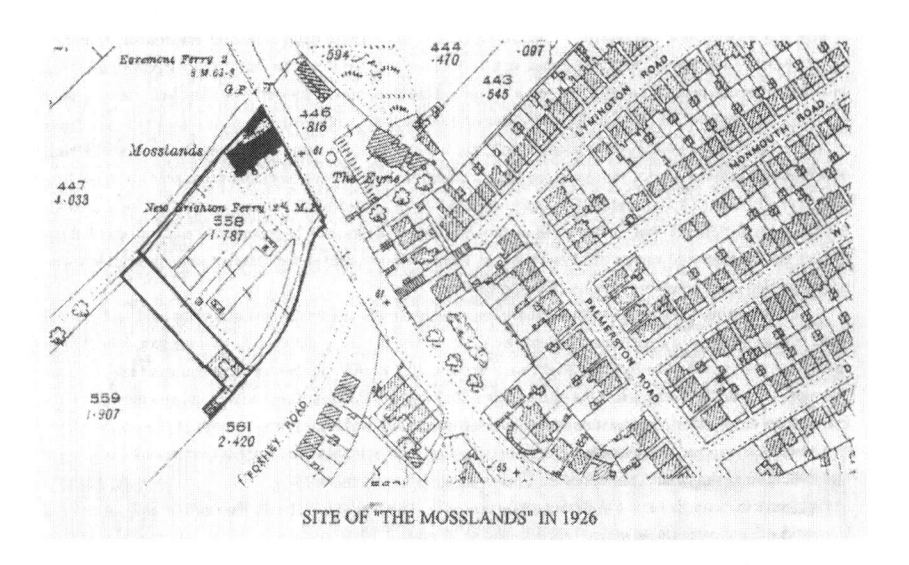

The old Bidston footpath used to start from Breck Road. It remained unchanged for many years and was a pleasant stroll before the construction of the Bidston Dock was undertaken and the surrounding land requisitioned for tipping purposes. the house in the photograph, later known as 'The Mosslands', appears to have begun life in the 1830's as 'Pool House', when it was in the ownership of Mr James Livesey, Cotton Broker, who later lived at what is now the University Hostel in Holly Road, Fairfield, Liverpool. The name 'Pool House' was a logical one, inasmuch as the Wallasey Pool in those days extended as far as Warrington's Bridge, when in later years the Club House of the West Cheshire Golf Club stood, on the Breck Road side of the railway.

Round about 1853 Mr Livesey, who was evidently a man of means as some years previously he had paid £100 for the use of pew in the old St Hilary's Church, gave way to Major William Chambres, Stock and Share Broker, hitherto of 'Hillside', a house standing in Breck Road further to the north, and it was at this stage that 'Pool House' was renamed as 'The Mosslands'. Major Chambres acquired his rank when Queen Victoria gave permission for the formation of Volunteer Regiments, he being the first captain to be appointed in the area. That he was a popular man was evidenced in 1880, when on his removal to 'The Grange' in Grove Road he was the recipient of an illuminated address from 317 members of the working class of Wallasey Village, which ran like this :-

"Sir - on hearing that you were about to leave this neighbourhood. We, the members of the working class of Wallasey Village, felt that an opportunity had occurred of expressing our sincere regard for you and your family whose many acts of kindness and neighbourly love towards us have endeared you us to all, connected as you have been from your earliest years with our village. We, hearing in mind the innumerable tokens of the neighbourly feeling you have ever entertained towards us, cannot but feel the warmest interest in your welfare, and we now rejoice to learn that you are still going to remain with us. We heartily pray that the Divine Protection may rest upon you, your esteemed lady and your family, and hoping that you may be abundantly blessed with health, long life and prosperity.

We remain, on behalf of 317 members,
Yours most sincerely,
Richard Clough, John Williams
Edward Williams, John Davies"

October A.D. 1878
The next occupant of 'The Mosslands' was Thomas Livesey, son of James Livesey, the original owner, and himself a Cotton Broker. It's

on record that when he moved over from Huyton, his gardner, with his wife and seven children, followed him and took up residence in the old School House on the Breck. One of the children was Tom Ibbetson who was caretaker at the Peers Institute and Verger at St. Hilary's Church for many years. Thomas Livesey's stay at the house came to an end in 1886, when business difficulties necessitated his sudden departure for New Zealand on a non-return basis. His successor was a Mr Joseph Brewin, a coal merchant in a large way of business which at one time held the lucrative contract for coaling the Wallasey Ferries.

On Mr Brewin's death his daughters remained in occupation until the early years of the last century, when they were replaced by a Mr Harries, a metal merchant, who owing to the defalcations of his partner was declared bankrupt shortly afterwards. In an effort to recover his money he pursued the fugitive partner to Canada, but in 1906 news came that he had succumbed to heat at Hamilton, Ontario. In the meantime 'The Mosslands' had been purchased in 1904 by Mr R.L Sandie, a Soap Manufacture. Mr & Mrs Sandie were very well-known in the district, Mrs Sandie continuing in residence after her husband's death in 1923 until the property was sold for development in 1935, and she moved out to Raby Grange, where she died in 1963 at the age of 91. 'The Mosslands' is now commemorated by the Drive of that name.

<u>Eric Idle</u>

Little has been said about Eric's time in Wallasey but as one of the famous faces of British comedy he must get a mention. When Eric Idle turned three, his mother moved the family from his new home in Wallasey. There he attended school at St. George's Wallasey until he was nine years of age. Even though it was only a brief time he spent in Wallasey I am sure that he seen it at its best.

Pirates and Smugglers of Wallasey

Although mostly associated with Cornwall, smuggling was a common occupation in poor seaside communities along all the coasts of Britain. Like many forms of crimes, it came about as the result of legislature, when Edward 1 placed a customs duty of wool exports to Europe, a duty that increased throughout the Hundred Years War, in order to fund the king's attempts to become King of France. He customs service was primarily concerned with collecting duties, but as time went on, illegal trade increased, particularly in the 17th and 18th centuries when smuggling reached industrial proportions. Wool exports were criminalised in 1614, and made punishable by death in 1661. Smugglers began to arm themselves against the dreaded Revenue men, who were soon provided with 'cutters' to patrol the coasts. (*Wirral Smugglers, Wreckers & Pirates - Gavin Chappell*)

Wallasey forms the northerly corner of the Wirral and has always been somewhat remote from the remainder of the Wirral. A town without a centre, visitors had difficulty finding their way about; locals prided themselves in being a breed apart. In the 18th and 19th Centuries all of North Wirral was remote and cut off from more densely populated areas.

Wallasey was more isolated than most and it gained a notorious reputation as a haunt of smugglers and pirates. The headquarters of local smuggling was a house that once stood on the river front between Lincoln Drive and Caithness Drive on what is now Egremont Promenade. Built in 1595 by one of the Mainwaring family beside what was at that time Liscard Moor, on the high water mark of the River Mersey, it went through a number of different names including the Half Way House, The Whitehouse and Seabank Nook. Next to it were 3 houses, some of which remain, called Seabank Cottages. The house became a tavern during the American War of Independence, when American and English privateers roamed the ocean and John Paul Jones raided Whitehaven in Cumbria.

The tavern gained the nick name Mother Redcap's after Poll Jones, who always wore a red cap or bonnet. Its normal title was The Half Way House. It was officially this until late into the 19th century.

One of the ports of call of the Smugglers transferring contraband across Bidston Moss was the Ring 'o Bells, now Stone Farm, in Bidston. Owned by a local family, some say the Radley's, others the Pendleton's. In the mid 19th Century Mary Radley or Pendleton married a Simon Croft under which the Ring 'o Bells became as notorious as Mother Redcap's. It also had a well established reputation for Hm 'n Eggs! It's described in The Adventures of Christopher Tadpole! Simon Croft kept his own pigs but became something of a drunkard. A lively and mixed crowd used the establishment including prize fighters Tom Sayers, Jem Mace and 'Tipton Slasher'. Four years after his death, in 1864, Lady Cust (Leasowe Castle) prevailed upon Squire Vyner, the lord of the manor, to revoke the licence. Bidston has been 'dry' ever since. Sept 2010. Note: I have had an email from Victoria Hart who tells me that the pub was indeed a Radley pub. She goes on: I can confirm that it was Mary Radley who married Simon Croft. Radley is my mother's maiden name and I have been researching my ancestors. Mary and Simon are buried together in St Oswald's cemetery. Also I know that

The Ring 'o Bells Inn was owned by the Radleys - the first I can trace back to is James Radley (B: 1756) and Peggy Fog (B:1766-D:1837). I am not sure of the dates they were at the inn but Mary Radley was one of their 12 children. I also know that the Inn was originally nicknamed the Ham and Bacon house as the Radley's would cure their own ham and they were carefully preserved from damp.

On occasion revenue men may be found to be waiting near the moss for contraband. In such cases, the contraband was taken along the edge of the Moss and around to Saughall Massie, to a Mill, which stood in what is now Action Lane, Moreton. One such tale relates that a revenue man lay in wait as he had been tipped off that two barrels of rum were to be carried that night across the Moss to the Ring 'o Bells. As the carter approached the Revenue man leapt out of hiding and challenged the carter. You have rum in those kegs!! Nay, its ale - the Ring o' Bells has run out and I'm taking them some. On checking contents, it was indeed ale. The smugglers had got wind of the revenue man and switched the rum barrels for ale!!

Another instance was when Revenue men saw two men removing bales from the area of a wreck. After a pursuit, the bales were found to contain cabbages and ferns. The real stolen bales had vanished by the time the Revenue men returned to the shore. Mother Redcaps finally closed its doors in 1960 after an unsuccessful short lived nightclub venture, and was demolished in October 1974. During demolition the famous 'smuggler's well' was discovered by the workmen, they found lots of bottles, jars and flagons and they wanted to inform the museum authorities! The foreman insisted that the 'hole' be filled in and treasures of lost artefacts were found were lost again. He threatened to sack anybody who told the museum! Sadly there are too many of these short sighted idiots around and much has been destroyed here and elsewhere that could have been saved. Maybe the foreman had found something he would rather not be made public? Who knows? (*Information taken from Wirral*

Smugglers, Wreckers & Pirates, a 2009 publication by Gavin Chappell which is on sale at local bookshops and Amazon.)[27]

The prayer of the Wirral Wreckers was tragically answered on many occasions. At the foot of the old Wallasey Parish Church tower lie two weather worn and almost forgotten gravestones, concealing a tale of one such shipwreck on the Wirral shore. An apt resting place, looking out, as it does, over Leasowe Castle and the Wirral shore, the waters of Liverpool Bay and the very sandbank where disaster struck. On Christmas Day, 1838, the packet ship "Pennsylvania" set sail from Liverpool bound for New York. She proceeded to the mouth of the Mersey to await the first favourable wind. She was a superior and fast sailing freight carrying vessel, with cabins commodious and elegantly fitted.

On this voyage there were 40 people on board, of which 5 were passengers. On the 12th day of Christmas, a Sunday, she finally put to sea on her fatal voyage. It was 10.30am and there was already a strong wind blowing from the southeast. The ship had a good run as far as Point Lynas, off Anglesey, which she reached by 9pm. Then she was totally becalmed for some 10 minutes, the proverbial lull before the storm.

The wind freshened from the southeast, and soon after midnight the Pennsylvania was in the midst of a hurricane. It was the 13th day of Christmas. The storm continued unabated throughout the Monday. About the Pennsylvania efforts were made to clear the damage, and turn the ship about. When daylight came on Tuesday, Captain Smith, her Commander, tried to put back to Liverpool. On reaching Ormes Head, a course was plotted for the Mersey Lightship. Unknown to the Pennsylvania, however, the floating light had parted from its mooring the previous day. Normally it was anchored off the East Hoyle Bank to help guide mariners safely into the Horse and Rock Channels.

---

27 Gavin Chappell - Wirral Smugglers, Wreckers & Pirates, a 2009

The newspapers of the time were suspicious:

"To say the violence of the gale drove her from her moorings is absurd. The floating light .... makes its appearance .... so regularly in the Mersey with every onslaught of the elements ...... (That one might suspect) those who tended it felt so deeply for their own personal safety in times of danger that they quit their post. Again, during the past gale when most needed to guide vessels in distress, has this vessel parted her moorings. It's scarcely two months since she parted her moorings before a gale and came into port. To us this is very extraordinary and inexplicable"

The Pennsylvania still bewildered by the absence of the Lightship, dropped anchor off Hoylake, about three miles from the shore. It was now 1.30pm on Tuesday. Before another anchor could be dropped however, the vessel swung around, drifted, and struck the Hoyle Bank. The force of the gale rammed her into the bank 8 or 9 times, and she started to take on water rapidly. Strangely, two other packet ships, the St Andrew and the Lockwoods also struck the Bank, not more than half a mile apart.

James Stonehouse, writing in 1863 says:

"Many a fierce fire has been lighted on the Wirral shore on stormy nights to lure the good ship onto the Burbo or Hoyle Banks, there to beat and strain and throb, until her timbers parted ...."

In an attempt to reach the shore, the Pennsylvania's jolly boat was launched into the gale. Aboard it were 5 passengers, including one William Douglas, as well as the Chief Mate, Lucas B Blydenburgh, and several of the crew. Those worn gravestones in a Wallasey churchyard tell only too well the fate of that little boat. Only one of its occupants survived. Meanwhile back on the wreck of the Pennsylvania, the long boat, the only other prospect of escape, was lost in heavy waves, which also swept the Captain overboard. It was 3pm Tuesday.

Much of the hull was now underwater. The remaining crew climbed desperately into the rigging where they were to cling for dear life for 19 hours. It was not until 10 am the next day that the steam tug Victoria took them off, except that is, three of the crew who had literally been starved to death of cold and hunger in the rigging during the night. 21 were saved from the wreck, 19 drowned. From the wreckers of the Wirral shore, the storm had come as a belated Christmas present. Liverpool newspapers commented:

"We lament to find that these infamous wretches, the wreckers, have been at their fiendlike occupation, plundering what the elements have spared, instead of seeking to alleviate the calamities of their fellow creatures. The wreckers who infest the Cheshire coast were not long in rendering the catastrophe a source of emolument to themselves. The property of the passengers and crew where plundered by them to an alarming extent. The Steward, who had in his trunk, sixty watches and other articles of jewellery, found on regaining the vessel that the whole of it had disappeared". Some reports placed the value of the cargoes carried by the Pennsylvania and St Andrew as high as £400,000, so it's hardly surprising that the wreckers chose the Pennsylvania as their "especial prey". The Pennsylvania had suffered most, her state cabin has almost entirely been stripped.

A number of plunderers were, however, taken into custody. One in particular, a John Bibby, boatman, is worthy of our interest. When apprehended he was found to have forty yards of new cloth, valued at £12, folded round his body. In his fishing boat were found books, a large and handsome cruet stand, and a black coat, a pair of trousers, a pair of drawers and much else.

It transpired that the coat had belonged to the late Captain Smith and the cruet stand to the same ship. The trousers belonged to Mr Thompson, its sole surviving passenger. The owner of the drawers was never ascertained. Bibby claimed in court that the cloth had been given him by a man on the Pier Head. Nor had he any idea how the other articles had found their way into his boat. He was fined £27. In default of payment he was to be jailed for 6 months. He might have considered himself lucky, for it was an age when a not unknown penalty for wrecking was public whipping or even transportation. William Douglas, one of the 5 passengers, who along with the First and Second Mates, tried to escape from the wreck. However, the ill fated boat did not live long in the tempest. About midway between the vessel and shore, she swamped, and all on board was thrown into the sea. He succeeded in reaching the shore, he was immediately taken to Leasowe Castle but he only survived a short time. The Captain and First and Second Mates were also drowned. It was thus reported,

"His mortal remains (Lucas Blydenburgh) were attended to the grave by all American Captains in port, as well as by hundreds of seamen. The sight was most mournful "The Inscription reads:"Sacred to the memory of Lucas B Blydenburgh of New York, Mate of the Packet Ship Pennsylvania, who was drowned near Leasowe Castle after leaving the wreck during the Memorable Gale on January the 8th 1839. Aged 40 years"

Max Moeller Director of Research Services The Historical Society of Pennsylvania 1300 Locust St. Philadelphia, PA 19107 has replied to a question from me asking about ships images, he states that: I have found two images reproduced in published sources (both of which should still be available in bookstores) of the U.S. Ship Pennsylvania . Neither of the originals are owned by HSP.28 They are: "Launch of the U.S. Ship Pennsylvania", a wood engraving by R.S. Gilbert, July 1837 – private collection (reproduction found on page 271 of Russell Weigley's Philadelphia: A 300 Year History, 1982); and "View of the Launch of the U.S. Ship of War Pennsylvania", lithograph by Lehman & Duval after G. Lehman, 1837 – Library of Congress (reproduction in Edwin Wolfe's Philadelphia: Portrait of an American City, 1990).

28Kenneth Burley, Philadelphia: A 300 Year History, 1982

The following extract is taken from the book "Portrait of Wirral" by "Kenneth Burnley".

One hundred and fifty years ago this stretch of coast was renowned for its wreckers; robbers and smugglers who would lure the Liverpool-bound vessels on to the sandbanks using decoy lights and flares. Once ashore, the wreckers showed no mercy towards the unfortunate crew and passengers; if their lives were spared, their cargoes and belongings were not. But not all wrecking was deliberate; winter storms claimed many ships, and local people were quick to arrive on the scene to salvage what they could. Henry Aspinall, of Birkenhead, wrote this vivid description of a severe storm in 1839: On 6th January 1839, the day was fine; a fair wind blew for outward-bound ships. Many left the Mersey under sail, among them the St Andrew, the Lockwoods, and the Pennsylvania, first class packet ships, loaded with valuable cargoes and emigrants together with a few saloon passengers for New York. On the morning of the 7th, the barometer fell to a very low point. The vessels had almost reached Holyhead, when suddenly the wind changed to the north-west and blew a hurricane. The three vessels at once put back for the Mersey, the only shelter in such a gale. Unfortunately the wind veered dead north-west, and took the three vessels on to the Burbo and West Hoyle Banks. The sea rose to a fearful height, and the vessels settled in the sand until they were literally smashed to pieces. No boats could live. The moment they reached the water they were swamped and all on board were washed away. Many were drowned and washed ashore at Leasowe, Hoylake, and the neighbouring coast. Such a sight I never saw before or since, nor should I like to. The scene deeply impressed. The beach was covered with wreckage and dead bodies. I vividly recall the latter. . It was, indeed, a most pitiful sight. To this day, in old Hoylake cottages, may be seen cupboards, doors, satinwood fittings, and glass and ebony door handles, washed up and appropriated by the finders, sad relics of a catastrophe which caused a great sensation in the district.

Mother Redcaps

Mother Redcaps is undoubtedly one of Wallasey's most famous land marks. The old white-washed, short; stumpy looking building was built by the Mainwaring family in 1595 on the river bank. It was a bold stone building with walls nearly three feet thick. The house was known by many names over the century's, names such as the Halfway House, the White House, Seabank Nook and several others.

The name Mother Redcaps came about in the 1700's when an elderly lady in her autumn years was the owner and proprietor of the tavern, and was well known for always wearing a red hood or cap. The tavern was frequented by sea farer's and smugglers as it was well known that Mother Redcap was trustworthy and allowed contraband to be hidden within the tavern, albeit im sure for a fee or cut of the profit. The activities of mother red cap over the years are well documented and in essence, she provided the first bank service to appear in Wallasey. She would store goods and currency within the building and sometimes even pay out prize money to the locals of which was be trusted to her as a neutral party.

The actual building looked like no more than a small white cottage, although this was the image that she wanted to portray; however inside it was a far different matter. Accounts shows that the front door was made of solid oak, five inches thick, studded with square headed nails. The remains of the door, although much decayed, were found in the cellar by Mr Kitchingman when making alterations in 1888. There were indications of it having had several sliding bars across the inside, and slots were also found at the sides of the lower windows as though at one time strong shutters had been fitted to them.

Immediately on the inside of the door was a trap door into the cellar under the north room. It would seem that by forcing the front door, it would withdraw the bolt to the trap door, thus letting the intruder fall eight or nine feet to the cellar floor, rendering them immobile at the very least. The way into this cellar was concealed by a rough wooden lid with the remains of hinges and shackles at the sides and entry could be gained from the back of the staircase in the passage from the south to the north room. Under the house stairs seven or eight steps led down into this cellar. If the front door lid or trap were down, the visitor, unless he turned to the right or left into the south or north front room, would proceed (there being no lobby) straight upstairs, and if anyone were in the cellar at the time he could run up the steps under the staircase and get out at the back of the house, there being a narrow doorway at the top of the steps into the yard. When the front door was open the entrance to the south room was a closed by it.

Behind the stairs was a door leading to the old kitchen at the back of the house and so into the open backyard. In this yard was a well about twelve feet deep, dry and partly filled with earth. There seemed to have been a hole made at the west side of the well, appearing to lead into the garden, but probably leading into a passage, to be referred to later. There was a small stream of good water at the back of the house, which supplied the house and also the small vessels that anchored off here. There was a primitive brew-house at the back, and even down to about 1840 the house was noted for its strong, home-brewed dark ale. There was another large cave or cellar at the south end of the house; indeed under the greenhouse (1930) it sounded hollow, and the coarse mosaic was laid on the top of large, flat, sandstone flags placed over this hollow. This cavity was entered by a square hole with steps as though it were an old dry pit well. Part of the yard was in reality the roof of a large cavern, composed of flagstones carried on beams.

On it stood a large manure heap, and a stock of coal and coal scales completed the disguise. This coal was supplied by flats and was retailed to the inhabitants of Liscard and Wallasey. When the cave was used for the reception of any goods that were better kept from the public gaze, the coals and a few odd barrels were manoeuvred so as to conceal the cavity, and the appearance of any disturbance of the ground was obliterated. At the end of this cave was a narrow underground passage (mentioned in some books as leading to the Red Noses) which led to a concealed opening in a ditch that ran down from the direction of Liscard. It's probable that this tunnel joined the one from the old well in the yard. The ditch was a deep cutting as far as a pit that was about halfway up what is now Lincoln Drive. At the edge of this pit grew a large willow tree, with long overhanging branches which formed an excellent concealed look-out commanding the entrance of the river. The trunk of this tree was sawn in sections in 1889, and when Lincoln Drive was cut through the pit, the root was rolled down the hill to the garden where for twenty-three years it formed a rude table in the summer-house. A cutting from this tree was planted by Mr Kitchingman in 1890 at the back of the house and grew higher than the house itself.

The beams inside the house on each side of the fireplace were of old oak, but as some were too decayed to keep they were removed; two, however, were retained. The one in the north room is quite sound, almost blue-black and as hard as steel. The chimney breasts are of great area inside, and in the two ground floor rooms were cavities (near the ceiling over the oak beams) with removable entrances from the top of the chimney breasts inside the flues.

In the south room there was a cavity hardly sufficient to conceal a person of more than small stature, the wall of which had to be pierced when Mr Kitchingman made the small staircase to the studio. There were a few other small cavities in the walls papered over where the sailors, it was said, hid their wages and share of prize-money. An artificial harbour stood next to the old cottage (1865) and remains still across, under the promenade. It formed a shelter for boats stored on its south side, and could be made higher by sliding boards between thick posts. Sometimes with a north-west gale and high tide the water flowed into the cellar.

There was a wooden seat across the strand in front of the house composed of thick timbers from wrecks. It had a short wooden flagstaff at one end with a large plain wooden vane at the top. This vane was supposed to work round with the wind but it was in reality a dummy; the staff fitting down into a round wooden socket in the shingle could be turned in any direction and was used by the smugglers for signalling. When the vane pointed to the house it meant 'Come on,' and when pointing away, 'Keep off.' At the other end of the seat was another post, with a sign hanging from it adorned with a portrait of Old Mother Redcap holding a frying pan on a painted fire, and underneath these words:

All ye that are weary come in an take rest,
Our eggs and our ham they are of the best,
Our ale and our porter are likewise the same,
Step in if you please and give 'em a name.
- Mother Redcap

This post acted as a kind of counterpoise to the vane. The old seat and sign were seen by Mr Kitchingman's father when, in his twentieth year (1820), he stayed there for a short time. When this house was built about 1596, rumour has it that it was the only building on the river front between the old Seacombe Ferry boathouse and the old herring curing house at Rock Point, now New Brighton. The house became a tavern in the Privateering days of 1778-90, and was much frequented by the officers and crews of the

Privateers,2 the Redcap, 16 guns; Nemesis, 18 guns; Alligator, 16 guns; Racehorse, 14 guns; Ariet, 12 guns; and other small vessels made use of the good anchorage known as 'Red Bet's', opposite the house.

A small cannon, punched with the broad arrow, was unearthed during Mr Kitchingman's alterations. It had a spike welded on the end to replace a wooden handle, long since decayed away, to turn the gun in the desired direction. It was evidently a bow-chaser from some Privateer. It was placed by Mr Kitchingman in his garden, together with the remains of two flint muskets found near, and of about the same date.

Another interesting find was a 'Nine-hole stone', supported by a pedestal of brick. Nine Holes is a French game, halfpence being thrown at the holes, and was the forerunner of bagatelle. It was supposed that this stone was fashioned by some French sailors (possibly prisoners of war confined in Liverpool and on parole). This was the suggestion of old Captain Griffiths, aged eighty-five years, and an inmate of the Home for Aged Mariners. He recognised the stone and told Mr Kitchingman that he had played on it when quite a boy and called the game 'Bumble puppy. Stonehouse, writing in 1863, and describing the activities of the Pressgang about 1797, says:

"The men used to get across the water to Cheshire to hide until their ships were ready to sail. Near Egremont, on the shore, there used to be a little, low public-house known as Mother Redcap's, from the fact of the owner always wearing a red hood or cap. The public-house is still standing and I have often been in it. "And had their entire confidence. She had hiding places for any number. There is a tradition that the caves at the Red Noses communicated in some way and somewhere with Mother Redcap's. The men used, on returning from their voyages, to deposit communicated in some way and somewhere with Mother Redcap's. The men used, on returning from their voyages, to deposit with her their pay and prize money until they wanted it. It was known or at least very commonly believed that Mother Redcap good deal of prize money on their account, yet none

of it was ever discovered. Some few years ago, I think about ten or twelve had in her possession enormous (for her) sums of money hidden or put away somewhere, but where that somewhere was, it was never known, for at her death very little property was found in her possession although only a few days before she died a rich prize was brought into Liverpool which yielded every sailor on board at least £1,000. Mother Redcap's was swarming with and many a strange story has been told and scene enacted under the old roof.
"sailors belonging to the Privateer directly after the vessel had come into port, and it was known that the old lady had received a good deal of prize money on their account, yet none of it was ever discovered. Some few years ago, I think about ten or twelve (1850), a quantity of Spade Ace guineas was found in a cavity by the shore. It has always been a firm belief with me that someday a rich harvest will be in store for somebody. Mother Redcap's was the resort of many a rough hard-hunted fellow, and many a strange story has been told and scene enacted under the old roof."

Smugglers and pirates were a real threat in the 1700's particularly to the Wallasey area, adored by both. They would often take wealthy residents and ransom them for money. There reputation also shows that they were also keen on kidnapping the poor and keeping them on board against their will to help out with labour on their vessel. This could also be said of the smugglers nemesis, the Royal Navy.

The Royal Navy notoriously picked up young and able men and recruited them into the ranks many times against their wishes, but the great terror of the sailors was the press other side of the Black Rock that they might conceal themselves in Cheshire, and many a vessel had to be brought into gang. Such was the dread in which this force was held by the sailors that they would often take to their boats on the port by a lot of riggers and carpenters sent round by the owners for that purpose."

Two entries in the Wallasey parish registers, both in 1762, refer to the risks the sailor ran. Under the date of 29th March, appears, ' William Evans drowned in endeavouring to escape from a cutter lying at ye Black Rock'; and again on 6th November, 'John Goss sailor drowned from ye Prince George tender in his Majesty's Service', the tender being the ship to which the men were sent immediately on being 'pressed.'

In his notes Mr Kitchingman says:

"Except in Mr Stonehouses Streets of Liverpool there does not seem to be any information to be obtained from writers about this spot. I can readily understand this as it was so out of the way and used for such secret purposes. I came on the scene and rooted it out for myself". In another place, he says: *"My father lodged at Mother Redcap's in 1820, and many of the notes of the old house here set out were made by him in that year"*.

Encamped on the Leasowes awaiting embarkation for Ireland. There is a tradition that at the time of King William's and a place from which pilots boarded vessels, besides being put to other uses. In 1690 the troops of William III were encamped on the Leasowes awaiting embarkation for Ireland. There is a tradition that at the time of King William's embarkation, dispatches were conveyed in a roundabout way to Chester, from Great Meols to Mother Redcap's, and then by fishing boats up the Mersey to Stoke and Stanney, instead of from Meols via Parkgate.

At an earlier period a small privateer called the Redcap cruised between here and Ireland. She took several dispatches for King James's partisans up to Stoke and Poole on the secluded upper reaches of the Mersey where some of the old Roman Catholic families resided.

Mr Coventry, a pilot well versed in Wallasey and Liscard folklore, stated that he had been told by his ancestors that several of King James's adherents, landed at Mother Redcap's. On one occasion three persons of some distinction were hurriedly landed from a ship. Horses were in readiness, and without a word the travellers rode off rapidly towards 'The Hooks'. Very soon afterwards a boat with an armed crew came from up river and made a hurried search. Mr

Coventry said that the explanation his father heard at the time was that these refugees had made their escape from Ireland and were intending to proceed for refuge up the river towards Stoke or Stanney, but the tide being out, horses had been obtained here. The armed boat had been lying in wait higher up the river above Seacombe Point, and discovering the probability of a landing being made at Mother Redcap's, hurried down the river to intercept it.

The smuggling went on in this area for century's and storeys denote that on one occasion when the smugglers were desirous of getting a cask of rum or some other merchandise away from one of the hiding places, but were prevented by the unwelcome presence of a duty officer. So it was arranged that one of the smugglers was to creep down to the shore from the Moor, and lie down in his clothes in the water, at the edge of the receding tide. The attention of the solitary officer at Mother Redcap's was called to the supposed body which had been washed ashore, and he made his way to it as quickly as possible. He had removed the watch, and was going through the pockets when the corpse came to life, sprang up, and laid out the surprised officer with a swift blow from a melee weapon. By the time he had come to, the rum had been removed from Redcap's, and started its journey to the moss at Bidston.

No blame could be attached to the 'drowned man' who stated:

"He was walking along the shore, when he must have had a fit, for the next thing that he became aware of was that he was lying in the sand with his pockets being rifled. Thinking he was being robbed by a stranger he attacked".

On another occasion a ship with tobacco on board was wrecked, and the watching officers saw two men run from the part of the wreck on the shore, along the beach northward, with two small bales as though they were about to depart for the Wallasey side. It took some time on the soft sand to overtake them, and when they were caught the packages were found to contain cabbage leaves and ferns. In the meantime their friends had made free with the real tobacco in the wreck.

Old Mr W. Whittle told Mr Kitchingman about 1896 that there was a great dispute concerning the right of way on the premises about 1750. It seems that when a dead body was found on the beach it was brought here and taken in by the back door. On removal for interment, on account of some superstition it was taken out by the front door. Certain people claimed that if twelve bodies passed through in one year it gave a right of way for living people to pass through the house at any hour, day or night. An attempt was made once and once only, for a fierce fight ensued.

Whittle at one time had an idea of purchasing this cottage, but hearing this story which came from his wife's grandfather, he consulted Mr W. H. North, senior, about the legality of the supposed right of way; but Mr North only laughed at him. Doubtless the attempt referred to was a dodge on the part of the coastguard to obtain right of entry into the house. Mr W. Coventry once told Mr Kitchingman he believed Mother Redcap was a comely, fresh-coloured, Cheshire-spoken woman, and that she had at one time a niece to help her, who was very active but very offhand in her manners, and who afterwards married a Customs officer.

The first steam voyage across the Atlantic from Liverpool was made in the year 1838 by the City of Dublin Company's steamer Royal William, 617 tons, and 276 horse-powers. She left the Mersey on 5th July. A party of the Liverpool Dock trustees and ship owners assembled at Mother Redcap's to witness the departure, and a cannon was fired from the front of the house as a farewell salute when the steamer passed on this side of the river to enter the Rock Channel. Mr J. Askew, the harbour-master, and Captain Dobie, of Messrs Brocklebank's ship Rimac, made speeches, and the belief was expressed that the vessel would not get beyond the Cove of Cork.

THE PROMENADE, EGREMONT.

Mr J. Kitchingman was, it's said, born in the house in Withens Lane, lately the Horse and Saddle Inn. When he retired from Warrington, where he practised as a solicitor, he purchased and restored, in 1888, Mother Redcap's which had previously been a fisherman's cottage. He gave the land in front of it, when this portion of the promenade was made, on condition that it should not be used as a thoroughfare for carriages. When Royalty came to open a new addition to the Navy League Buildings, the royal and other carriages did drive along this part of the promenade, which so annoyed Mr Kitchingman that instead of leaving his house to the district, he left it instead to be used as a Convalescent Home for Warrington people, as his family belonged to that town. As it was not suitable for this purpose, the powers were obtained to set aside the will, and the property was sold. Mr Robert Myles became the purchaser, and he opened it as a café, bearing once more the name of Mother Redcap.

The small white cottage style tavern was demolished in 1885 and was rebuilt in 1888 in a mock Tudor style although it did continue being a public house. This is the taller building with spires which can be seen several old pictures that eventually became the café. Unfortunately this building also demolished, this time in 1974 to make way for flats. Nothing now remains of Mother Red Caps except the solitary archway that marked the entrance, a bygone to a time of smuggling and maritime history.

The pathway in the picture below led from Wallasey Village to the Ring 'o Bells in Station Road Bidston, a smugglers route. There is a story about a customs man who, having been tipped off that there was to be a 'brandy run' across Bidston Moss, lay in wait for the smugglers. But they had found out about the tip off and substituted the brandy barrels for ordinary ale. They were stopped and obviously nothing was found! In the midst of the Moss was a bridge formed from whale bones, but eventually they sank into the marsh and vanished. All this area is now built on and Industry and Motorway now dominate. The railway line in the above image is the stem line from Seacombe Ferry to Bidston. The signal box is at the junction leading to Wallasey Village station.

Fortunatus Wright The Wallasey Privateer

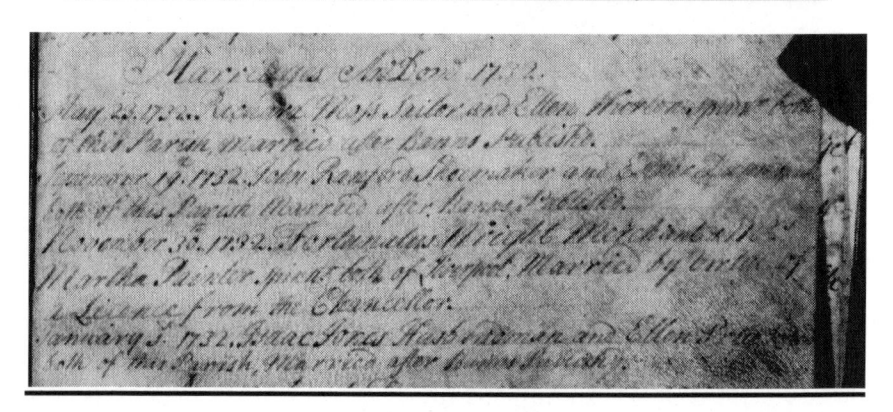

Fortunatus Wright was the most famous British privateer commander and Liverpool's favourite hero during the first half of the eighteenth century. His exploits against the French during the War of Austrian Succession and later at the start of the Seven Years War would rival any adventure of Drake or Raleigh, and yet he is largely forgotten nowadays. He was a colourful mixture of rogue and swashbuckling hero, by all accounts a likeable villain.

We know that his father was a mariner – Captain John Wright – and that he died in 1717, because of a gravestone is in St. Peter's churchyard in Liverpool. The gravestone also records that the Captain "gallantly defended his ship for several hours against two vessels of superior force". We don't know very much about the early life of Fortunatus, except that he born in 1712 and became a brewer in Liverpool. We assume he learnt his sea-craft from his father.

In November 1732, at the age of 20, he married Martha Painter and had three daughters by her, including Phillipa who later married the grandson of the diarist, John Evelyn. Martha died a just a few years later. In November 1736, at the age of 24, he married Mary Bulkeley, who was already pregnant with his child.

War of Austrian Succession (1740 – 1748)

This ranged from 1740 until 1748, and throughout this time Letters of Marque were issued to merchants wishing to engage enemy shipping. We know that after marrying Mary Bulkely in 1736, FW went off to Italy and based himself there for the next twenty years or so, engaging in trade and later Privateering - financed by the merchants in the English 'colony' there.

Fortunatus Wright soon became a figure of controversy. In 1742 he was challenged at the gates of the city of Lucca (near Pisa in Northern Italy) and was ordered to give up his weapons. He refused and held a pistol to the head of one of the guards. Another 30 soldiers arrived and restrained him, and was arrested and held prisoner in his Inn for 3 days. Although he was eventually let off, he was forbidden to return. He moved to Leghorn.

Leghorn (or Livorno) is in Tuscany, a province of northern Italy. In the mid eighteenth century Austria was the dominant foreign power in Italy and Leghorn was supposedly a neutral port where merchants from all countries could trade and refit their vessels etc. There was a large English 'colony' based in Leghorn, and it was these merchants that paid for the fitting out of a privateer vessel for Fortunatus Wright.

We should go back to 1746 and relate one last anecdote that is so typical of the character Fortunatus Wright was. A French vessel, double the size of FAME had been sent into Malta to hunt him down. Huge crowds of French sympathisers lined the coast as the two ships reappeared after a noisy and furious engagement. The French vessel was seen to be towing the badly damaged FAME, and as they rounded the headland the French flag was raised on the leading ship. A great cheer went up from the French - at last the scourge of the Mediterranean had been defeated. Suddenly, as the ships entered the harbour, the French flag was lowered and the British flag raised high above it – the French ship was in fact a prize to the British privateer, with its crew imprisoned in the hold and FW at the helm! On his father's tombstone in St Peters' Church, Liverpool is included the following inscription: 'Fortunatus Wright, his son, was always victorious and humane to the vanquished. He was a constant terror to the enemies of his King and country.'

The Red & Yellow Noses

An outcrop of red sandstone known locally as the Red Noses, there are also yellow noses nearby. Here there are wide grassy area for camping and playing games and nearby a miniature golf course and tennis courts and at the other side of the railway Warren Park Golf Course and Harrison Park.

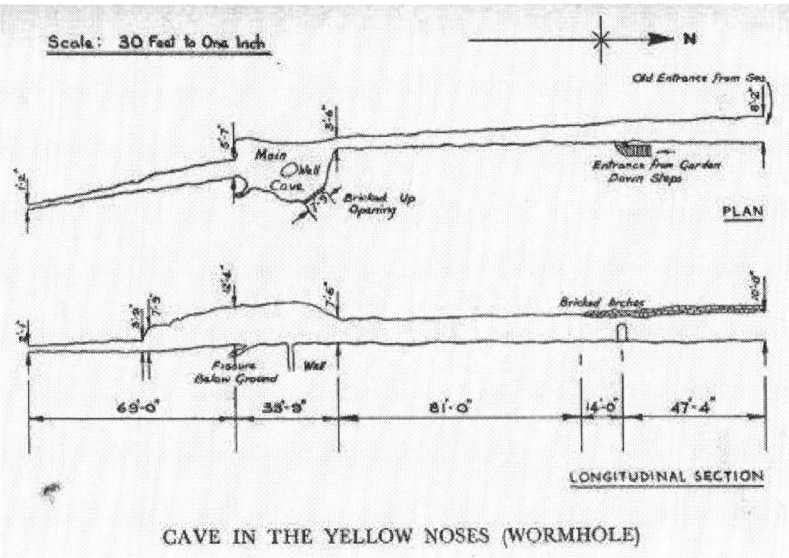

CAVE IN THE YELLOW NOSES (WORMHOLE)

The Red Noses are also famous for the involvement in pirating and smuggling in the 16th and 17th century, where people would hide in the Rocks and they lured ships onto the rocks and sandbanks at the mouth of the Mersey using lanterns on donkeys and beacons. The ships wrecked off Wallasey and New Brighton were then plundered and their cargoes stolen. Often sailors were drowned or murdered but that did not deter the wreckers.

Cheshire Cheese Inn Wallasey Village

The old Cheshire Cheese

On the right-hand side of Wallasey Village when travelling from Poulton, we have the 'Cheshire Cheese' public house which, although rebuilt, dates back to the 1600's. The present building was erected in 1885 and, not long after this date, Ted Bryant was the landlord. During the First World War, Robert Davies was the licensee and Bill Bryan was there in the 1920's. Years ago they served home-brewed ale and one could get bread, dairy and milk cheese there.

The Cheshire Cheese is a proper, old-fashioned local pub in the oldest part of Wallasey, The Cheshire Cheese is well known locally for the strong characters that stand on either side of its bar In the 17th century, it was the regular stopover place of William of Orange (later King William III) as he sought reparation from the House of Stuart and launched attacks on Ireland from the Wirral.

The Cheshire Cheese is said to be Wallasey's oldest recorded inn. The present day building does not date back more than 80 years but there are records of the name existing as far back as the 1500, at which time Wallasey would have looked much different. The previous building stood near old Folly lane in a row of cottages but was demolished in 1885 for the purpose of road widening. Nowadays, it's a lovely – and deceptively large – neighbourhood pub with a pleasant beer garden and a dedication to hand- pulled real ales. It even hosts an annual beer festival.

The Clarence Hotel

The Clarence Hotel has been established for over 150 years. The pub was originally a coach house but through the generations, it has served many other functions such as a post office and slaughter house, before becoming the pub it's today.

The Magazines Pub

The Magazine Hotel' was built in 1759, but over the years several alterations have been carried out. The pub was originally called 'The Black Horse' and the old house plate had the initials of R.T and the date. The hotel has a concealed cellar which was used by the old Press Gang. There was once a cock-fighting pit behind the hotel which had circular wooden seating for sailors and locals who would arrange and bet on bird fights. The Mags was often frequented by top-hatted gentlemen, city clerks and shipping people, many of whom arrived in horse-drawn cabs and were known as 'bay window customers'

The Pub had to have an urgent refurbishment in 2010 following an electrical fire. Fortunately, very little History was lost to the flames. Two witch's broomsticks used to hang from the ceiling near the main fireplace. According to local legend, if something were to happen to either of them, something bad would happen to the Pub. One of the broomsticks was stolen just before the fire. The remaining one is now re-instated, further out of reach, and has a toy witch perched on it. Here is the full story regarding the fire.

The landlords of a Merseyside Pub which was almost destroyed by a fire believe a mysterious curse is to blame. The blaze at the 250-year-old Magazine Hotel in Wallasey caused £200,000 worth of damage and left managers Linda and Les Baxendale living in a caravan for three months. A small fabric witch figure which hung from the ceiling of the main bar was stolen two nights before the fire. And with a History of accidents befalling those who dared to touch it, the couple are convinced the two are connected.

The official cause was a power surge which blew up the Pub's fuse box, starting a fire. Linda, 59, said: "Part of the History of the Pub is the two witches and a little devil, all made from brown felt, which were hanging by the bar. "No-one knows exactly how long they were there and we don't know who gave them to the Pub but we think they were there for at least 100 years." They were covered in cobwebs and dust because we were told that if anyone touched those bad things would happen to them." The Baxendales have managed the Magazine Hotel, known locally as the Mags, since 2000 and Linda also ran the Pub between 1980 and 1993 with late partner Phil. When they first moved in they received an anonymous phone call warning them not to touch the witches. She said: "We found out that a decorator took them down while he was working here in the 1970s and then was involved in a serious car accident at the top of the road. "Phil once happened to touch the witch by accident and the following day he fell through a trapdoor leading to the cellar and broke his collarbone.

"Someone else fell over the following week and broke both his knees. It's spooky." Linda says she was convinced something terrible would happen after she learned about the theft. She said: "One of my bar staff, Charlie, saw a man take the witch from the ceiling on the Friday night and run out. He wasn't a regular because they all know the story.

"I suppose I am superstitious because I used to say to the witches 'I tell people not to touch you so look after me' but when I found out

one had gone I said 'oh God something bad's going to happen now. "We live above the Pub and on Sunday we woke up about 7.45am to the sound of smashing downstairs. "I thought someone had broken in and was using a baseball bat until Les went downstairs and found it was a fire. "It was terrifying. If it wasn't for the prompt response of the fire service the Mags might have burned to the ground."

The remaining witch and devil were found in the scorched remains of the bar after the fire on April 18 but Linda says they have since vanished. A friend bought the couple a replacement witch from Pendle which now hangs in their place. They are celebrating the Pub's re-opening with a beer and cider festival next week which will include a special brew, Witches Revenge. Linda said: "What happened was so strange that I thought I'd better put the new witch up – just in case."

The Pilot Boat Inn

The areas of New Brighton and Wallasey have always been home to a wide range of pubs and taverns. Some of these pubs go back to the days of smuggling and ship wrecking and have a murky past!
Recently found, following a change in ownership. The Pilot Boat Inn, uncovered something more spectacular and mysterious.

Wirral Globe, 22nd November 2012

Mystery of Jake Bolt's coffin

THE owners of a Wirral pub are calling on local history buffs to help them find out more about a mystery coffin lid discovered there.

The Pilot Boat in Magazine Brow, Wallasey, dates back hundreds of years and is thought by many to be haunted.[29]

New licensee Kate Darroch is now keen to find out the story behind the coffin lid of a sailor and his painting hanging on a wall in the cellar.

The pub is known to have once housed a mortuary and the body of teenager Jake Bolt, whose name is on the coffin, is believed to have been examined there in 1749.

Now Kate and her colleagues are hoping to find out more information about him, and even track down any distant relatives.

She said: "The lid and Jake's painting is hanging on our wall and we were told upon moving in that it's never to be removed.

"It's quite spooky, but also very interesting and we've found many ancient documents in the cellar, which used to be used as a mortuary for fishermen and sailors.

"We don't know anything about Jake really, so it would be great if there are any historians out there who could offer their expertise and help us to learn more.

"If he is a local lad, there's also a chance we may be able to find his distant family, which would be incredible."

---

[29] Wirral Globe, 22nd November 2012

The Jolly Sailor

Poulton's Jolly Sailor

On the right of this picture is the Jolly Sailor Inn, in Limekiln Lane, Poulton. A tall mast stands in its tiny garden.

Dacie and *John,* Agents, No September 4, 1813

Notice is hereby given, that application is intended to be made to Parliament in the ensuing session, for leave to bring in a Bill for dividing, allotting, inclosing, and draining the commons and waste lands in the several townships of Wallasey and Poulton cum Seacome, in the county of Chester, and for allotting, dividing, and draining a certain common pasture called Wallasey Pasture, in Wallasey aforesaid, and for making a road over Bidston Marsh, in the said County, from the said townships of Wallasey and Poulton, to communicate with the townships of Bidston and Moreton and also for allotting, dividing, inclosing, and draining a piece of land called the Carr, otherwise Newton Carr, in the parish of West Khby, in the said county.—30

---

30 *Dacie* and *John,* Agents, No September 4, 1813

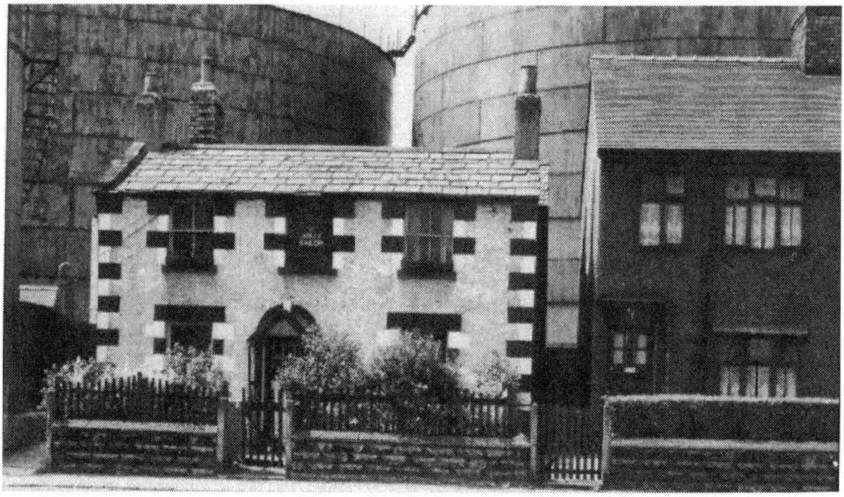

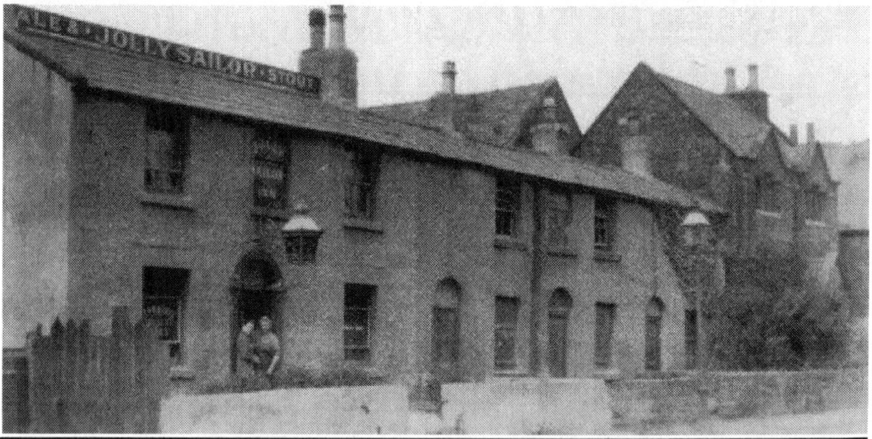
JOLLY SAILOR
STOUT

The Black Horse Inn

It's believed that the Black Horse Inn took its name from a horse entered in a race at Leasowe Racecourse in the 1700s by Lord Molyneux. The Inn had cobbled paving along the frontage, with a mounting block at one corner. A small building, used as a mortuary, stood at one side, so sometimes the landlord was woken up at night to admit a body - sometimes they weren't even dead - just drunk and from Birkenhead. The sixpenny beers sold at the Inn came from Richard Spragg's Wallasey Vale Brewery, which stood at the top of Leasowe Road. It dated back to the 1850s

In front stood the whitewashed house belonging to it; today the shops numbered 37 and 39 Leasowe Road occupies the site. The old Black Horse Inn was demolished in 1931 when the present ornate building was erected. The picture above is taken looking down Leasowe Road with the old bridge in the distance; Spraggs Brewery is to the left where West Wallasey now stands.

In 1920 a football team from the Black Horse made it all the way to Wembley in the last 'Drinkers Cup' final.

Here they are above pictured at a reunion in 1966 - they played The Jolly Sailor from Botherington and won 4-3 in extra time. The trophy - a copy of the Kaiser's helmet can still be seen behind the bar to this day. The Pub is now known as Sheridans

The Ship Inn

How it looks now, and the following photo is how it looked then.

Cheshire Observer Saturday, 2nd January 1892

The Publican and the Bona Fide Travellers

Samuel Spicer, landlord of the Ship Inn, Breck Road, Wallasey, was charged with committing perjury at Liscard Petty Sessions on the 17th February. Mr.Colt Williams, with Mr.Yates, prosecuted. and Mr.Marshall defended.

Mr. Williams, in opening the case, said that on the date named prisoner was summoned for supplying liquor to two men, Clare and Burgess, during prohibited hours. On Sunday morning, 31st January, the men came to the house and were supplied with two pints of beer each, and when they were having the second pint five policemen in plain clothes entered the house, and disclosing their identity asked prisoner who the men were, and he led them to believe they were bona fide travellers. The prosecution alleged that the prisoner took no precautions to ascertain whether the men were bona fide travellers until after the constables came and said who they were, and he then put questions to the men, and ascertained from them that they came from the Alexandra Dock, Liverpool, and had slept on a flat there the previous night. Before the magistrates prisoner gave evidence on his own behalf, and swore that when Clare and Burgess came to the inn, and before the constables arrived, he questioned them as the distance they had come, and where they had slept the previous night. The men Clare and Burgess gave evidence against Spicer, and as a result he was fined £3 and costs. Clare and Burgess were also convicted of being on licensed premises during prohibited hours.

John Burgess, flatman, Birkenhead, deposed to having gone to the Ship Inn with Clare on the morning in question. He asked for two pints of beer. Before witness had tasted his second pint the police officers came in. When witness went to the house Spicer said nothing to him about having stopped serving travellers from that side of the water. He did not ask them anything. Neither of them told him that they had slept on a flat at the Alexandra Dock the night before. Witness had come from his own house. When the police officers came in they asked who witness and Clare were, and Spicer said. "oh, they are right enough; they are from Birkenhead". After the officers came in nothing was said to Spicer about the Alexandra Dock. It was to the officers it was said by Clare, and in the hearing of witness. Witness remembered Spicer and a young man named Bell coming to his house on a subsequent Sunday. Spicer said to him "Jack, I want you to go to Mr.Thompson - (a lawyer) - and tell him you slept at the Alexandra Dock". Witness replied, "I shall do nothing of the sort".

Cross-examined : Clare and he were flatmen at the same flat. On the Sunday they went to the Ship Inn. They did not say a word to Spicer before they asked for two pints of beer. Witness did not ask Spicer of they were within the limits for a drink. That happened on the previous Thursday. On that day they walked to the Ship Inn for the purpose of asking Spicer if they would be within the limits for a drink if they came there on the Sunday morning. Spicer said to witness. "Jack, when you come in my house you must go out when I tell you, and mind no one else. He told them if they came there on the Sunday they would walked the necessary distance. Witness heard Clare say to the officers that he had slept at the Alexandra Dock the previous night, but witness knew that he had been fined for being drunk on licensed premises in Birkenhead, and also for being drunk and disorderly.

Mary Burgess, wife of the previous witness. recollected prisoner calling at her house on the Sunday morning, and asking her husband to say he had come from the Alexandra Dock.

Thomas Clare, Craven Street, Birkenhead, captain and owner of the flat "Margaret", corroborated Burgess's evidence.

Cross-examined : If he had said he came by Seacombe Ferry that morning it was untrue; and he did not remember saying anything of the sort when before the magistrates. He did not say to Mr.Thompson that he had not slept at home on the night of the 30th January. He told him plainly that he had slept at 45, Craven Street. He could not remember rightly what he said, because Spicer took them away, and they had something to drink, and were confused. It was after they had had the drink that they saw Mr.Thompson, and then witness was drunk.[32]

His Lordship said he had been considering the nature of the evidence during the luncheon adjournment, and the whole case must depend upon the statement of these men as to what Spicer said to them. It would be rather dangerous to act upon their statements unless the prosecution had some other evidence.

Mr .Williams said when he opened the case to the jury, he told them they would have to rely upon the evidence of Clare and Burgess.

---

32 Cheshire Observer Saturday, 2nd January 1892

The jury having conferred together, the Foreman said they were agreed that the evidence was conflicting.

His Lordship : I think so too.
A Juror : There is no sufficient evidence to convict.
His Lordship : I am of the same opinion.
The jury then acquitted the prisoner, and he was discharged.
Mr.Colt Williams said he proposed to offer no evidence in the charge of perjury against Charles Alfred Bell, nephew of the prisoner.

The jury then returned a formal verdict of not guilty against Bell, and he was discharged.

This concluded the criminal trials.

The Plough Inn

The Plough Inn was at the bottom of Mill Lane and was built in about 1870 and became a beer house at No. 27, selling Yate's Ale. It used to have cast iron railings mounted on a small wall in front. On one side of the building as you entered the parlour there was sawdust sprinkled on the floor. In 1889, W. Thomas Grey was the landlord who was followed by George John in 1897. Margaret Heald took charge in about 1912. The name of the pub was under the eaves and was still place long after it was used as a beer-house. Eventually the inn was converted back into a house again.

The Nelson

The old Nelson Hotel in Grove Road was a small two storey building. It was demolished and a new large pseudo-Tudor-looking hotel was built in its place and opened in February 1935, costing £25,000. The present hotel has an inn sign of Lord Nelson while, inside there is the Trafalgar Room. In actual fact, the licensed premises are named after a family bearing the name of Nelson.

This Extract is from the book "Almost an Island" by Noel E Smith
"Thomas Peers son named Alfred, held the license, whilst also being licensee of the Old Black Horse, who put Joseph Belce in Charge of the Nelson. It was not unusual to see the barman or another brushing the blown sand away from the doorway".

The old inn was built as a house by Thomas Peers, Nelson being his wife's maiden name. His son, Alfred held the licence, whilst being licensee of the Old Black Horse, who put Joseph Belce in charge of the Nelson. 33

The Boot Inn

The Boot Inn actually existed in Elizabethan times. It was reputed that it got its name after a boot containing gold which had been rescued from a robber by the landlord and returned to the rightful owner. Originally *The Boot* was a small white washed cottage, which stood on the rough road leading to Wallasey Village. This was knocked down and a two-storey building was erected in its place. The increase of traffic caused congestion so the local authority suggested road widening and so a new "Boot Inn" was built to the rear and in 1925 the old one was demolished. After renovation work the Boot Inn was renamed as 'Turnberry's" in 2004 but in 2008 after decreased sales and awareness it was renamed back to its former name.

---

33 Almost An Island - Noel E Smith

The Lighthouse Inn

The old Lighthouse Inn in the village was built between 1827/1830. Originally the inn was two cottages dating back to the 18th Century and was first licensed in c1860. The inn, which was later knocked into one building, together with three adjoining cottages and one acre of land to the rear was purchased by Birkenhead Brewery in 1900, for £3,340. The old building was replaced with a modern public house, being built in 1966.

The Travellers Rest

The Traveller's Rest was made of sandstone and had two small rooms; the bar parlour and the news room. This was one of the properties that had been earmarked in the widening and straightening scheme, prepared by the Corporation as far back as 1906. The Traveller's Rest had closed down by the outbreak of war in 1939, by which time half the property had been acquired by the Corporation. The go-ahead for demolition of the war-damaged or derelict property was given in 1946. The site is now occupied by St. Mary's College, which opened in 1973.

The Pool Inn

The Pool inn was previously situated on the crossroads of Poulton not far from old Mr Birds House. The building is 2nd or 3rd generation of the inn built c1880, with the original dating back to the beginning of the 18th century. The original building is said to small 2 storey edifice which was possible used as a dwelling previously. The last building that we seen up until a year ago, was a Victorian structure built around the turn of the 20th century. It was built from fine sandstone blocks washed with lime and strong sash windows. On the opposite side was the villages pinfold, which is where the lost animals in the village would be placed until there owner could find them. It's described as a circular pen, built from large stones with an entrance gate on one side. But, unfortunately like many more local pubs in Wallasey. The Pool in has shut its doors for the last time and was quickly knocked down, probably to be replaced by social housing.

Grosvenor Ballrooms

The history of the Grosvenor Assembly Rooms in Grosvenor Street, Liscard is closely associated with the adjacent building on the corner of Manor Road and Grosvenor Street, now the 27 Social Club but which was previously the Wallasey Concert Hall.

The Concert Hall was built in 1875 by a local entrepreneur and businessman James Joseph Brewin and the building quickly became the centre of the social life of the expanding District. There was a large Ballroom/Concert Hall on the first floor reached via a grand staircase. The building originally had a large glass veranda at the front under which carriages could drive and the ladies in their fine dresses could alight and not get wet when it was raining.

Apart from Grand Balls, Dances, Orchestral and Choral Concerts in the spacious main Hall on the first floor, the various rooms in this large two storey building were used for all manner of and Social Events. Meetings of local businessmen and Societies, Public Meetings, lectures and debates, Weddings and Receptions, Bizarre, Whist Drives and numerous private functions were all held in here. It was advertised as "An up-to-date Hall for up-to-date People" and rooms could be hired for between 1 and 4 guineas per night (1905).

In his booklet, "Sandstone and Mortar - More of Old Wallasey" Noel Smith explains that it was in this building that the Wallasey High School (now Weatherhead School named after Canon Weatherhead one of the founders) was started in September 1883. The school hired two large rooms on the ground floor. The school had 14 girls in the first term, which increased to 60 in the second year of operation and soon moved to new larger premises on the corner of Manor Road and Stringhey Road. At the back of the building there were extensive Tennis courts which could be hired. It was here that Harrowby Tennis Club was based before they moved lower down Manor Road next to the Masonic Hall

By 1905 the Concert Hall was proving inadequate to for all the numerous demands made upon its resources and the proprietor planned a new hall and Ballroom, which could accommodate 200 dancers, with a frontage on to Grosvenor Street. This new hall, which was to be constructed on part of the tennis courts, was to be called the Grosvenor Assembly Rooms. A firm of Liverpool architects, Messrs T T Wainwright were commissioned to design the new building which was constructed by a local contractor, Mr J Bellis of Liscard.

The new building was ready for use on 1st March 1906 and could be hired for 4 guineas per night. With the completion and opening of the Grosvenor Assembly Rooms and its large airy Ballroom, the ground floor hall at the Concert Hall was refurbished and redecorated (in pink) and was reserved for less smaller Balls, Dances and Receptions. This Ballroom could accommodate 70 dancers.

The Grosvenor Ballroom saw some very special Beatles nights. Run by promoter Les Dodd, Their first appearance was as the Silver Beatles in June 1960, booked by Allan Williams - and Allan will be here as a special guest on 28th August 2004. It was also here that the Beatles turned up without drummer Tommy Moore and John Lennon asked for a drummer from the audience. Up stepped a big teddy-boy called "Ronnie" who sat behind the kit and no one dared tell him to go! The Grosvenor is looking for Ronnie - no luck so far. The Beatles appeared here on his 18th birthday in 1960.

> **GROSVENOR BALLROOM**
> The Grosvenor Ballroom to-night introduces a new series of summer Saturday evening dances for youthful patrons, when the all-star outfit The Silver Beetles will be playing.

It was also here that Chas Newby made one of only a handful of appearances with the Beatles after returning home from Hamburg without Stuart Sutcliffe. This was the prelude to the Litherland Town Hall gig.

Poulton Hall

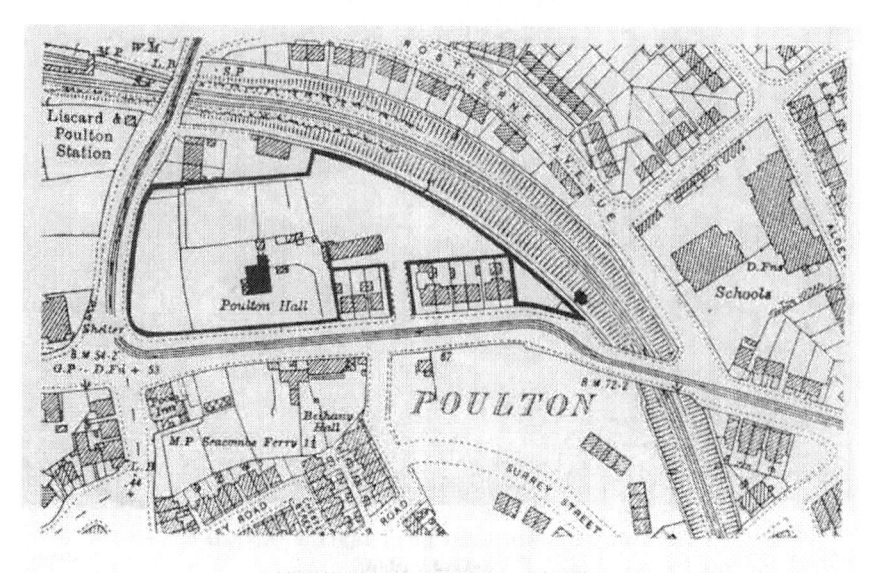

THE SITE OF "POULTON HALL" 1925

The Poulton of the old days contained several houses worthy of attention, the principal being Poulton Hall, constructed between 1790 and 1800 on the site of a seventeenth-century farmhouse. It was situated at the corner of Mill Lane and Poulton Road, and at one time formed part of the Mainwaring Estates, being mentioned in a Deed of Settlement executed by James Mainwaring of 'Bromborow' in 1816. In 1839, when the property was owned by the Executors of Thomas Parry, late proprietor of the old Seacombe Hotel, William Smith, a Merchant, was living at the Hall, but a better-known resident was Daniel Buchanan, a Cotton Broker, who moved there from Toxteth Park in the 1840's. He had something of a reputation as a lampoonist, and was author of a somewhat scurrilous poem on the occasion when the local Volunteers, under Major Chambres, visited Leasowe Castle to be presented by Lady Cust with what was understood would be a silver bugle, and were so disgusted by their reception and the poor quality of the gift that they were promptly marched away again by their Commanding officer. On another occasion, when the Rector of

St. Hilary's, Revd. Frederick Haggit, returned to Church after a short absence sporting a moustache, the congregation thought he was developing High Church tendencies, so Mr Buchanan wrote offering him £150 for the Church Schools if, before the following Sunday, he would fulfil three conditions, namely:-

1. *Shave off the moustache*
2. *Restore Tate & Brady's Hymns*
3. *No eastward position when celebrating the Communion*

Although Mr Haggit was greatly incensed, after some thought he replied to Mr Buchanan saying that if he would come to Church on the following Sunday, he would see that the first condition had been observed, but the other two matters of principle and could not be altered. Mr Buchanan thereupon sent him a cheque for £50, and regretted that it could not be for the full amount of £150. Mr Buchanan remained in residence at 'Poulton Hall' until his death in 1884, at the age of 74, when he was succeeded by Mr A.C Hopps, an Oil Merchant and member of a well-known Wallasey family. As it turned out, he was the last occupant of the property, because the Hall was demolished in 1933, and dwelling-houses were built on the site. The name is commemorated by Poulton Hall Road.

Sommerville House

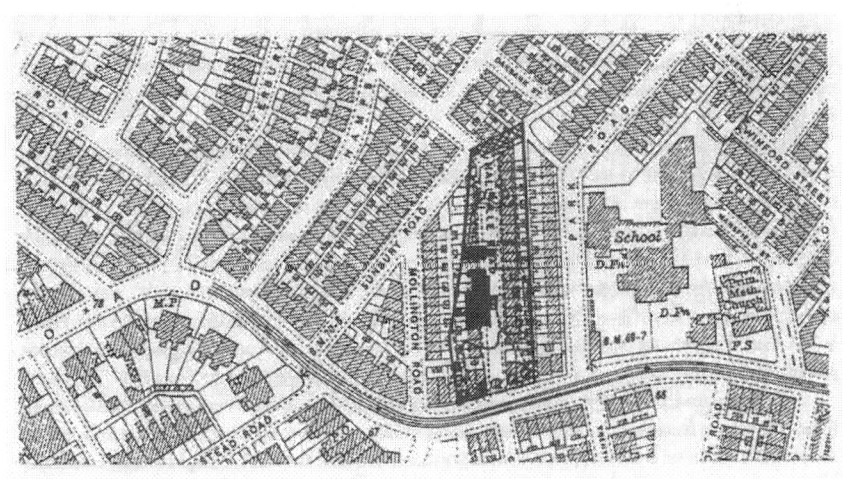

SITE OF "SOMERVILLE HOUSE" IN RELATION TO SURROUNDING PROPERTY IN 1925

Some distance down Poulton Road, almost opposite to Halestead Road, was 'Somerville House'. Built by James Finlay, a Tea Merchant, prior to 1860, it was his residence until the early 1870's, although he had a sad life inasmuch as he lost an infant son in 1855, and five years later his wife, who died at Clifton, Bristol, at the early age of 35. His successor was Lawrence Keizer, founder of the well-known glass firm of L.Keizer & Co., which later became part of a large company. Mr Keizer's stay at 'Somerville House' lasted nearly thirty years, but after the Poulton-cum-Seacombe School Board erected what was then the Somerville Elementary School close by, in 1892, the character of the neighbourhood began to change, and although we find Mr William March in residence at 'Somerville House' as late as 1905, it was probably soon after this that the demolition squad moved in.

Poulton Manor House

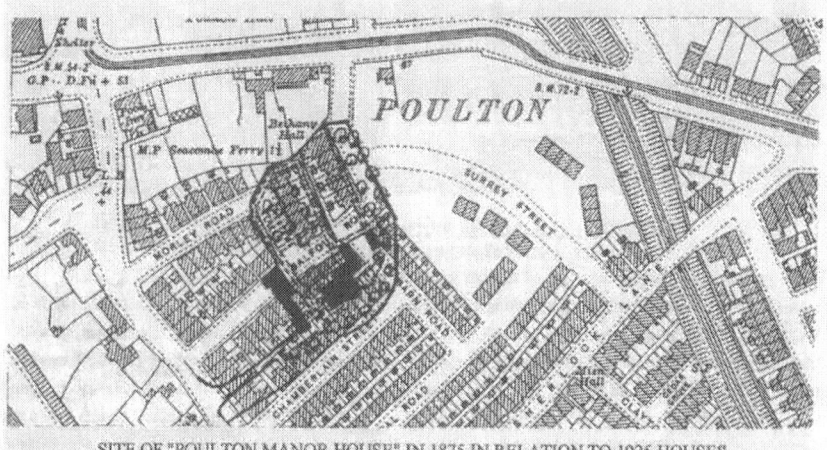

SITE OF "POULTON MANOR HOUSE" IN 1875 IN RELATION TO 1925 HOUSES

In Sherlock Lane, which runs between Poulton Road and Limekiln Lane, stood Poulton Manor House, which dated from the late eighteenth century and in its day was quite a stately edifice. In 1841 there appeared to be several people resident there, particularly one Henry Meadows, who farmed the adjacent Manor Farm. and they were followed in 1860 by Mr James Clerk Boyd, a Liverpool Merchant, formerly of 'Bird's House' and Chairman of the Wallasey Local Board for several years. He spent some ten years at the Manor

House before giving way to a Mr F.B Salmon, an Iron Merchant, also a member of the Local Board. A later occupant was John Robinson, a Sand and Gravel Merchant, who had previously lived at the Manor Farm, but he died in 1900, and in 1904 the Manor House, which had become involved in a large sale of land in the area to the Progressive Land Company, was demolished to make way for the small houses which now stand on the site.

Hope House

SITE OF "HOPE HOUSE" (LATER "IRVING THEATRE") SHOWING "WINCH HOUSE" AND "BROUGHAM HOUSE"

When walking down Liscard Road towards Seacombe over 100 years ago, people would have approached what is now Brougham Road and they would have seen on the north-west corner, 'Brougham House', known to the locals as 'Frog Hall', possibly named because of the nearby duck pond. For many years the house was the residence of Mr Thomas Parry, proprietor of the old Seacombe Ferry and the Seacombe Hotel, and it eventually passed, with other land in the area, to his daughter, Lady Crichton-Browne. A little further on they would have reached 'Winch House', built about 1840 and approached from Brougham Road along a noble avenue of trees. 'Winch House' occupied what is now the site of Edith Road and Florence Road, and it was demolished about 1894, when houses were built there. The builder and original occupant Mr Henry Winch, founder of Peek Bros. and Winch, a wholesale provision firm in a large way of business. A later resident was Captain Askew, a one-time harbour master of Liverpool, who had earlier built himself a house in Tobin Street which he called 'Egremont', after his birth place in Cumberland, with the result that the area became known by the same name.

Turning down what was then Victoria Road, known now as Borough Road, they would have reached this charming house, hardly a mansion perhaps, but representative of many similar houses existing in Wallasey at that time. Its name was 'Hope House', and as far back as the 1860's it was occupied by Mr Samuel Wright, Secretary and Manager of the West India & Pacific Steam Navigation Company. In 1867 or thereabouts the property was purchased, probably as an investment originally, by Mr George Hulse, a turtle merchant, with one of the largest businesses of that type in England. He had a shop in Dale Street, Liverpool, near Manchester Street, with a huge tank in which turtles could be seen swimming about, and he was able to meet the great demand for turtle soup, which in those days appeared on the menu at most restaurants and any public or private banquet worthy of the name. The turtles were apparently brought from their West Indies island homes on the decks of steamers, lying on their backs, and were regularly hosed down with sea-water by the sailors as they flushed the decks.

About the time he bought 'Hope House', George Hulse also purchased and occupied 'North Meade', a mansion in Brighton Street subsequently demolished to make way for the Town Hall. It cost him £4,000, but three years later he died and was buried at St. Hilary's Churchyard. There was an unusual story attached to this, inasmuch as Mr Hulse had a great friend, William Manders, who was the proprietor of a travelling menagerie which pitched its tent in William Brown Street, on the site of the Walker Art Gallery. Apparently, in addition to turtles, Mr Hulse's importing activities also extended to young lions, which he sold to his friend and to various other menageries. When William Manders died in 1871, a grave was prepared for him in St. Hilary's Churchyard immediately in front of that of George Hulse, but it's said that Manders was actually buried in Hulse's grave, and his own grave lacks an occupant. Time has rendered the inscription on the Marsden illegible and even the Hulse tombstone does not incorporate any reference to him.

George Hulse had a son, George Hulse Jnr, who followed in his father's footsteps as a turtle merchant, and continued to live at 'North Meade', after his father's death, in company with his mother and his brother Richard. George Jnr, was in some respects lucky to have reached manhood, as he once entered a den of lions when he was a boy, and was badly clawed but escaped with his life, although he bore claw marks until his dying day. The Hulse's ownership of 'North Meade' ceased in 1898, when the Trustees of the father's estate sold the property, consisting of two houses and over 9,000 square yards of land, to a Mr James Kiernan, a Councillor, for £5,000. Kiernan, who already owned two places of entertainment in Liverpool, the Palace of Varieties in Paddington and the Park Palace in Park Lane, had plans for demolishing 'North Meade' and building a theatre on the site, but the Corporation prevailed on him to sell to them at a premium, and so the land became available for the Town Hall.

In the meantime, Samuel Wright, the occupant of 'Hope House', had moved across the river to Erskine Street, Liverpool, and was succeeded by various tenants; among them was a Mr John Begg in 1875 and a Mr Joseph Jones in 1880. However, it would appear that in 1885 or thereabouts Mrs Anne Hulse, George's widow, and another son, John Edwin Hulse, decided to return to 'Hope House', and the photograph illustrated in this paragraph was probably taken about that time. it shows Mrs Hulse, John Edwin Hulse, and a granddaughter, who later married a Mr Edward Ward Williams and had herself become a grandmother in the 1930's.

The next development was in 1897, when James Kiernan, whose plans to build a theatre on the site of 'North Meade' had fallen through, bought 'Hope House', demolished it in 1899 and replaced it with a theatre which, in deference to his friend, Sir Henry Irving, who performed the opening ceremony, he named 'The Irving Theatre'. Much of the stone-work for the theatre came from St. George's Church, Lord Street, Liverpool, then in the process of demolition. Sir Henry made it a condition that the theatre should only bear his name as long as legitimate drama was performed there, but in the ensuing years that commodity must have run short, as in 1912 the theatre had been renamed 'The King's', and since then it has functioned under various names and in varying capacities.

Mrs Hulse died in 1897 at the age of 80, and was buried in a separate grave in St. Hilary's Churchyard. Her son, John Edwin, moved to 'Wallasey View', St. George's Road, a house was later incorporated in the English Martyr's complex, but his health deteriorated, and in 1900 he went to Canada to undergo an operation, which was not successful, as he died later the same year at the age of 50. His body was brought back to the country at a cost of £300, and was buried in St. Hilary's Churchyard, on the north side of the church. He was a quiet, unobtrusive man, well-known in Wallasey, and it caused considerable surprise among his many friends when it was announced that the value of the estate was £147,000. it appears that he had indulged, successfully it would seen, in a certain amount of property speculation, in fact it was said that one morning he bought a stationer's shop in Castle Street, Liverpool, for £45,000, and sold it back to a Bank for £52,000 the same afternoon.

Seacombe Pottery

Towards the end of Wallasey is the borough of Seacombe. The Seacombe Pottery, Wallasey factory was established by John Goodwin in 1852. J. Goodwin was considered a prestigious potter during the 19th century and his goods were in high demand all over the world. He moved the Seacombe pottery to Liverpool to be closer to the docks for export trade to the Americas, Russia, Colonial Canada and Asia. Once the factory was set up, which consisted of six (6) domed shaped kilns and several workshops located near the Seacombe Smelt Works.

He sent for the workers from his Staffordshire pottery, which operated from 1840 - 1850 at Lane End. The Seacombe pottery gained widespread popularity, along with the demand for his crockery. In 1870 a large consignment of cargo being sent by ship to America was ship wrecked during a violent storm somewhere in the Atlantic and sunk with all its precious cargo on board.

The Seacombe Pottery was not able to recover from this great loss and voluntarily liquidated the business in 1871. Today, Seacombe Pottery is highly prized and sought after by collectors and a large part can be found in the National Canadian Museum.

Penny Bridge

The Half Penny bridge began in 1843, so called because of the half penny toll to cross it. It was situated in Wallasey Pool on the road between Bidston and Poulton. The Bridge was made of wood and it opened in the middle to allow ships to pass through. On 1st September 1896 the fare was increased to one penny, the bridge is still known as "Penny Bridge" to this day. In 1926 it was replaced by a modern swing bridge by the Mersey Docks & Harbour Board. The Penny Bridge is the furthest upstream Bridge, which crosses the head of Wallasey Pool to connect Poulton with Bidston, Birkenhead. The pool itself has been filled in and the bridge was replaced by a fixed roadway in 1996.

The picture below is how the bridge looks today, somewhat different to that of yesteryears which no longer carries a fee to cross.

The Mariners Homes

Another Wallasey Sea-fairing establishment that was lost in the twentieth century was the old Mariners home on Seabank Road. The building was built in 1880 by William Cliff who was a local ship owner and merchant, whom according to the inscription, built the home in memory of his daughter Rosa who had passed away. The imposing building stood over 130 feet above the Mersey with its impressive clock face on display from all four sides. When the building was opened in 1882 its formal name was The Roger Lyon Jones Park.

The Grounds of Mariners Homes, New Brighton

The original entrance to the building was via a large gate from Maddock Road which was replaced 80 years later. In 1925 Seabank House was sold off with its surrounding ground from the Penkett family to the Trustees of the Mariners home. With this new land they soon demolished the building and created a new wing for the Mariners home.

Mariner's Home, New Brighton

Many of the residents lived in small villas within the grounds of the home whom upon becoming a widow, would transfer to the Andrew Gibson Home for seafaring widows which was situated next door. The villas were in the surrounding drives of: Ismay, Cliff, Cunard and Webster which are still present today.

Like all places connected to the seas. There were of course several recordings of ghosts and spooky activities occurring within the building. There is a story of one mariner falling from the clock tower after over turning the mechanism which resulted in his death. The Mariners home eventually closed down in 1977 and due to lack of interest in a property so large, it was eventually demolished in the 1983.

However, the grounds are still occupied and the surrounding gardens are still one of the beauty spots remaining in Wallasey. (See below shown in an aerial view of the grounds.)

Gibson House

Gibson House which is situated next to the Mariners Homes is the former home for the widows of seafarers, built at the turn of the twentieth century and stands overlooking Egremont Promenade with unrivalled views towards Liverpool. The imposing red brick property was built with a substantial donation from Andrew Gibson, a wealthy Liverpool cotton merchant in 1906.

The generous Mr Gibson and many others from the era also provided money to help build some of the houses next door in Mariners' Park, providing homes to retired seamen and their next of kin. They also provided a welfare funds for former seafarers. Gibson House was built in 1906 to contain 28 self-contained flats for seafarers' widows, who were moved there after the deaths of their partners. Sadly it has been the subject of repeated vandalism since the residents were removed and the building was boarded up. Not only has the building since been vandalised, it has also had the lead stolen from the roof, copper piping ripped out and a fire started in the main lobby.

For many years very few people even knew what the huge building was called Gibson House or what it was for, because the covenant imposed that it included a clause that no sign be put outside saying what it was called or why it was built, to protect the widows who lived there.

The Current owners, Nautilus UK, have previously submitted a planning application to Wirral Council to convert the building into 34 apartments. Nautilus, the union which represents shipmasters, officers, cadets and other staff serving in the UK and international merchant shipping fleets, also wants to build town houses into the sloping grounds to help pay for the cost of refurbishment. The building had become a magnet for antisocial behaviour and squatters after it was closed and every window in the three storey edifice has been smashed in the years it has been left empty.

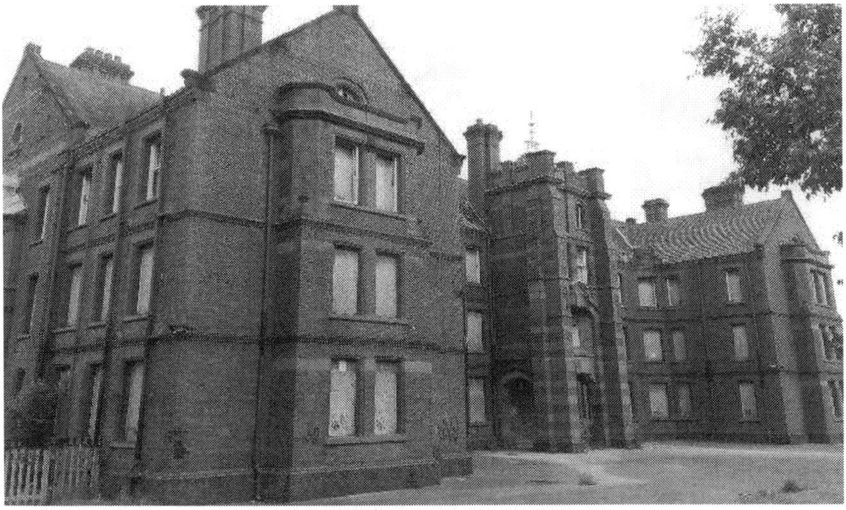

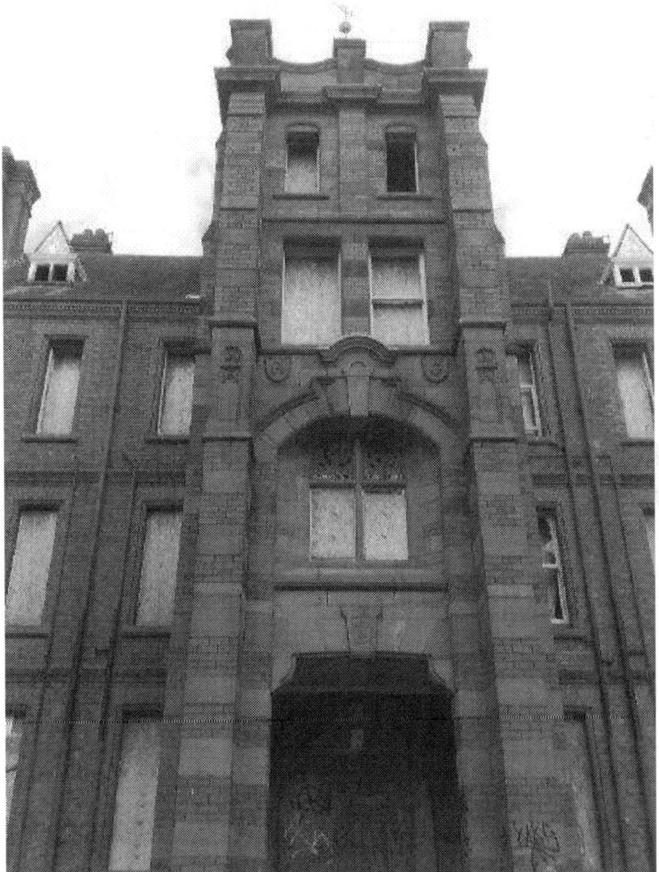

East Float Flour Mill and Dock

The Flour Mill building has a fascinating history; it's thought to have been designed by G.F. Lister, the architect responsible for Liverpool's Waterloo Warehouse. Throughout the 1850's East Float Mill was used as a departure point for emigrants on ships bound for Australia In 1866 Alfred Dock was built providing access for cargo ships bringing grain into East Float Mill and as demand for grain increased this became the busiest time for Wallasey Docks

In 1879 the world's first ever submarine "Resrgam II" was launched into the waters next to East Float Mill. This vessel had the capacity to stay underwater for up to four hours but unfortunately sank near Rhyl in North Wales a year later; the wreck was discovered in 1995.

By 1893 a further four mills were built in Birkenhead and Merseyside became the largest flour milling centre in Europe. Even when trade began to decline, the major flour milling Company Rank Hovis (Spillers) still used East Float Mill almost throughout the twentieth century and this operation only closed in 1999.

Seacombe Ferry

In 1724 Daniel Defoe in his book *A tour Through England and Wales* wrote: *"This narrow strip of land, rich, fertile and full of inhabitants, is called Wirral, or by some Wirehall. Here is a ferry over the Mersey, which at full sea is more than two miles over"*.34

Seacombe Landing 1785. (From a print published by Messrs Longman & Co. in 1815.

---

34 Daniel Defoe, *A tour Through England and Wales, 1724*

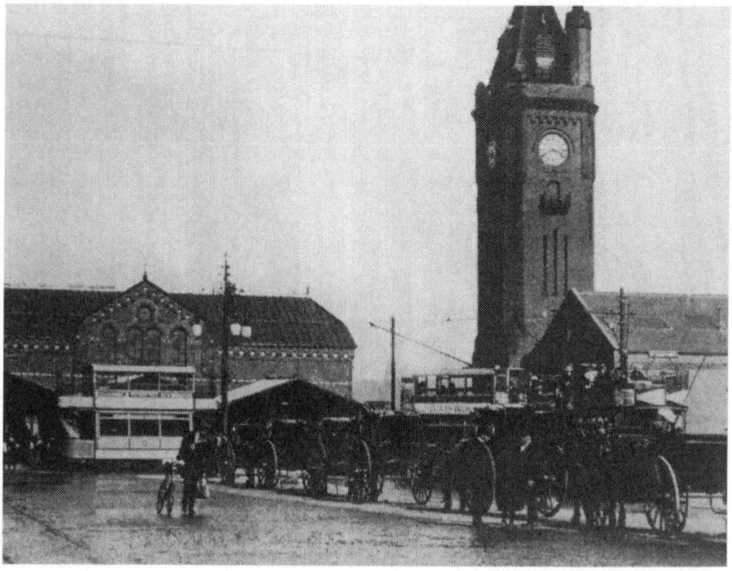

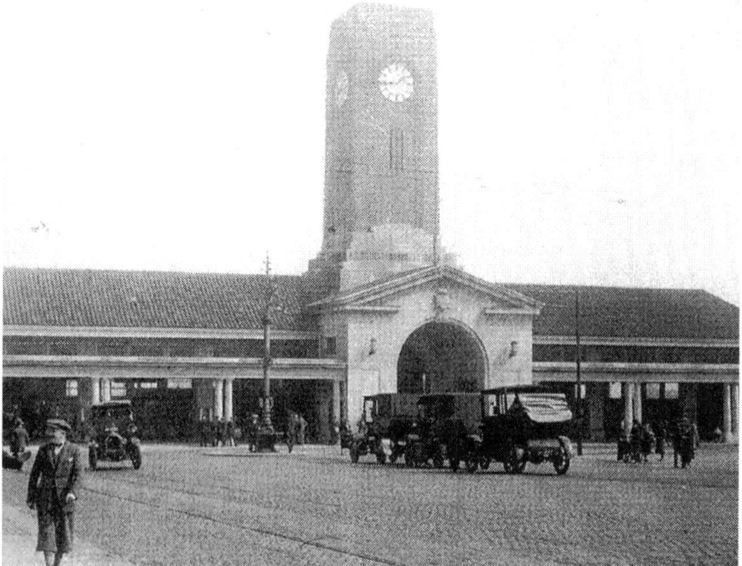

An account from 1750 also mentions using the Mersey ferry: "Here is a ferry over the Mersee…. You land on the flat shore on the other side, and must be content to ride through the water for some length, not on horseback but on the shoulders of some Lancashire man who comes knee-deep to the boat's side to truss one up …" By 1753 Wirral had at least five ferryboat houses at Ince, Carlett or Eastham, the Rock, Woodside and Seacombe. Seacombe Ferry began to operate steamboats in about 1823. The ferry rights were sold to the Local Board under the 1861 Wallasey Improvements Act.

With the increasing number of passengers (1 million per annum by 1876) the ferry terminus was greatly improved, as it has been several times since then. In 1947 Wallasey Ferries were the first in the world to have radar installed. In 1934 the ferry service from Seacombe lost two million passengers because people started to use the new tunnel rather than the ferry. A ferry service still runs between Seacombe on the north side of Birkenhead Dock and Liverpool.

Ferry routes from the Wirral to Liverpool across the River Mersey operated from various places, including New Brighton, Egremont, Seacombe, Woodside, Monks Ferry, Birkenhead, Tranmere, Rock Ferry, New Ferry, Eastham, Ince, Frodsham and Runcorn.

The image above is dated 1908 but the image is a year or two earlier due to the Liver Buildings (being constructed in the background) was already in use from 1908. Seacombe Ferry can be seen in the distance.

There's no better way to experience Liverpool and Merseyside than from the deck of the world famous Mersey Ferry, finalist in Merseyside's Large Visitor Attraction Award, while listening to our commentary.

You'll learn about the city and the region's fascinating history, see its spectacular sights and discover its unique character. The Liverpool waterfront is now a UNESCO World Heritage Site so there is even more reason to take a leisurely 50 minute River Explorer Cruise. River Explorer Cruises depart hourly from Pier Head, Liverpool and from Seacombe or Woodside, Wirral.

Egremont Ferry

Egremont Ferry was started in 1830 by Sir John Tobin and Captain John Askew. As this place had no name it became known as 'Egremont' after the name of Askew's villa, named after his birth place in Cumbria. The pier was built in 1828 and was the longest on
344

the Mersey. Thousands of day trippers tramped along it, as did bowler hatted businessmen. The pier had to be scrapped in 1946 as it had been badly damaged and, as a result, the ferry had to cease operating.

The image above is the bottom of Tobin Street with the ferry terminal situated in the background.

This stone, situated on the site of the old Egremont Ferry, is designated as an area for public speaking. The view from the stone looks out across the Mersey towards Bootle in Liverpool. The rock sits on the roundabout in the middle of the promenade just in front of Egremont Ferry pub and denotes that *"This area is designated for us of public speaking"*. The area just behind the Egremont Ferry pub is the site of the old House which John Askew owned and was simply named "Egremont".

Cheshire Observer, Saturday, 12th July, 1862

The Suspected Child Murder at Egremont, Cheshire

On Thursday afternoon the coroner for the district, H. Churton, Esq., held an inquest, adjourned from Wednesday, the 2nd instant, on the body of a male child, which had been found in a heap of night soil, collected from one of the Seacombe hotels, by the night-soilman, on the Monday previous, a fact sworn to in evidence at the previous inquest by a man named John Hodson.35 The only witness examined on Thursday was Samuel Wagstaff Smith, member of the colleague of surgeons, who deposed – I am the medical officer of the Wallasey dispensary, and on the 2nd July, in virtue of instructions, made a post mortem examination of the body of a male child, found amidst a heap of night-soil. The body somewhat decomposed and could not have been more than a few days old. It was not full-grown, but an eight-months'child. There was no external marks of violence about the body, except blood about the right ear : that the umbilical cord was about fourteen inches in length, somewhat shrunk, no way tight, and very dry; that it was rough at the extremities, as it torn, not cut. On opening the chest I examined the lungs and found them of a pink colour, which floated when immersed in water, even when cut into pieces, from which I inferred that the child had inspired slightly. There was evidently atmospheric influence on the lungs; the left side of the heart was full of black blood; all the other organs appeared healthy and natural. In answer to the coroner, the witness said, I do not think that the child could be said to be born alive; the lungs were imperfectly distended. Cases have occurred where prior to birth the child has breathed : it might have died during parturition; or the child's head, which naturally comes first, might have been alive, and then instantaneous death followed. The body was so fresh when I examined it that I do not think it could have been born more than

---

35 Cheshire Observer, Saturday, 12th July, 1862

three days. On this evidence being given, the coroner addressing the jury said. From the statements now made by the medic I gentlemen, it's clear the case is at an end. He then reviewed the evidence, which he considered clear and highly satisfactory, that the jury could return no other verdict than that the child has been still-born. At first, remarked the coroner, there were many circumstances connected with the finding of the body calculated to arouse the suspicion of Inspector Rowbottom. In the hotel, adjoining the ashpit whence the body had been taken, a woman suspected to have delivered of a child : that the woman had somewhat suddenly left the service of the hotel-keeper, on the 28th May, and had gone to Liverpool, where she consulted a Dr. Waters as to her health, and afterwards was admitted into one of the Liverpool hospitals, from which she was dismissed on the 6th June. The jury, without retiring, returned the verdict – "Still-born."

At the conclusion of the inquest, and while remarking in very complimentary terms on the evidence given by Mr. Smith, the coroner said – Recently I had a very notable instance of the importance of correct medical evidence. In another section of the county I held an inquest on the body of a child found dead under similar circumstances, and on the same day the magistrates held a court, and had signed a commitment of the mother on the serious charge of murder, founding their procedure on the medical testimony given by a surgeon who had been examined before the court. I directed the jury to return the verdict still-born; and on this being told to the magistrates I was sent for. I showed to the satisfaction of the bench that the child had been stillborn, that the lungs being like jelly and adhering to the spine, could never have been distended, and the child could not have been born alive. I had the satisfaction of seeing the murder-commitment paper torn in pieces, and the innocent but unfortunate mother acquitted. So much for perfect and imperfect medical evidence.

In connection with the inquest we were much gratified that the coroner had one of the jurors give a donation to Mr. Smith, for the benefit of the funds of Wallasey dispensary.

New Brighton Railway Station

The station was built as the terminus of the Wirral Railways route from Birkenhead Park station, opening in 1888. Through services via the Mersey Railway Tunnel to Liverpool commenced in 1938, when the London Midland and Scottish Railway electrified the line. The station was used greatly by commuters, heading to the seaside resort of New Brighton for regular days out.

350

Warren Train Station

There was a station known as Warren, it was the station following Wallasey Harrison Drive. Not far from the Red Noses. Warren Station was situated on the Bidston Junctions to New Brighton which opened first to Wallasey Grove Road on 2nd January 1888 and then nearly three months later to New Brighton on 30th March 1888. Warren Station was situated between New Brighton and Wallasey Grove Road and opened with this section of line. The line became part of the Wirral Railway on 1st July 1891. Warren Station was served by trains going to Birkenhead Park, West Kirby and New Brighton. From the 1st June 1895 a service also operated to Seacombe. For most of existence the station only had one train each day per day but occasionally there was a full service (i.e. July 1889) Warren was never well used other than by golfers, it was next to the Warren Golf Course and it was an early closure on 1st October 1916. A little to the east of Wallasey (Grove Road) station the sand trouble was very acute and, after any sort of a wind from the sea, men had to be employed to clear the rails sufficiently for the safe passage of stock, indeed men were nearly always at work on this stretch. A peculiar point about this section of track used to be the silent running of the trains and musically muffled beat of engine exhausts caused by the echo-deadening effect of the surrounding dunes.

Liscard & Poulton Railway Station

Date opened: 1.6.1895
Location: On the west side of Mill Lane (A5088) where it crosses over Kingsway Tunnel approach road.
Company on opening: Wirral Railway
Date closed to passengers: 4th Jan 1960
Date closed completely: 5.12.1960
Company on closing: British Railways (London Midland Region)
Present state: Demolished - the site is now occupied by the Kingsway Tunnel approach road.

Liscard & Poulton station was incomplete when the line opened, and it first appeared in the timetable in October 1895. Its single island platform, with two faces, was in a deep cutting west of Poulton Road. The platform was reached by a covered walkway from Poulton Road, north of the line; it crossed over the Seacombe-bound track, and a covered set of steps led down to the platform. Waiting facilities were in a timber building, the roof of which also provided a canopy. On the island platform a single-storey brick building contained booking facilities, waiting rooms and staff accommodation. The station had a short coal siding with a 5-ton crane at its western end, north of the passenger lines. A short siding on the south side of the station served a quarry and another private siding served the Wallasey Gas and Water Works.

At its opening Liscard & Poulton station was served by nineteen weekday trains in each direction that ran between Seacombe and West Kirkby. There was also a sparse service to New Brighton.

On 1st May 1898 services provided by the Wrexham Mold & Connahs Quay Railway (WM&CQR) also began to call at Liscard & Poulton. The service operated with the agreement of the WR and ran from Seacombe to both Wrexham and Chester Northgate, using a route between Bidston and Hawarden Bridge promoted and built by the WM&CQR and the Great Central Railway (GCR). This endeavour effectively bankrupted the WM&CQR which was absorbed into the GCR on 1st January 1905.

In 1899 the WR made a greater effort to provide a more useful service between Seacombe and New Brighton, which gained the nickname of the *Seacombe Dodger*. In 1902 Wallasey Corporation electrified its tramway system, which passed close to Liscard & Poulton station. This competition reduced the passenger loadings on the *Seacombe Dodger* and, from the end of 1905, it ran only on Bank Holidays; it was discontinued altogether in about 1910. The service between Seacombe and West Kirby remained intensive, and regular GCR services also continued, providing Liscard & Poulton passengers with a variety of journey opportunities.

On 1st January 1923 Liscard & Poulton station became part of the London Midland & Scottish (LMS) railway. The LMS took over the running of the Seacombe and West Kirby service. The former GCR lines from Bidston to Wrexham and Chester became part of the London & North Eastern Railway (LNER) who operated trains on these routes. In the summer of 1932, the LMS operated sixteen trains to West Kirby and eighteen trains to Seacombe & Egremont from Liscard & Poulton on weekdays. The first departure for Seacombe was at 7.11 am and the last was at 9.38 pm. The first departure for West Kirby was at 7.26am and the last was at 08.53pm. The very last departure was for Birkenhead Park and it left at 10.26pm. For most of the day the service was at hourly intervals. The summer Sunday service was almost as intensive as that on weekdays, with thirteen trains in each direction, reflecting West Kirkby's popularity with Liverpudlians as a day trip destination. In addition Liscard & Poulton also had an intensive LNER service both to Chester Northgate and Wrexham Central.

During the 1930s the LMS resurrected a plan first mooted by the WR to electrify the former WR network. As the WR made an end-on connection with the electrified Mersey Railway (MR) which ran from Birkenhead Park to Liverpool Central, through running between the Wirral and Liverpool would be possible.

The LMS drew up plans and started work in 1936. The Seacombe branch was omitted from the scheme as it was not remunerative enough to justify the expenditure; in any case it was well served by LNER trains that afforded good connections with the rest of the system at Bidston. The electrification was completed by the early part of 1938. On 12th March 1938 the LMS ceased to operate the Seacombe - West Kirby service. The following day, a full electric train service began on the other lines. This left Liscard & Poulton, an LMS station, with only LNER passenger services. The LNER route was very popular both with Liverpudlians, who boarded trains at Seacombe, and the inhabitants of Wallasey, many of whom used Liscard & Poulton to travel to North Wales for walking and camping.

On 1st January 1948 Liscard & Poulton station became part of British Railways' London Midland Region. Services from Seacombe to Chester and Wrexham continued to operate throughout the 1950s, but British Railways diverted the services to New Brighton and closed the Seacombe & Egremont branch, including Liscard & Poulton station, on 4th January 1960. Goods services continued to operate through Liscard & Poulton until 1963. The line was lifted shortly afterwards, and the station was demolished. A few years later work began on the construction of the Kingsway Road Tunnel, which used the route of the Seacombe Branch for the approach road and obliterated the site of Liscard & Poulton Station. The Kingsway Road Tunnel opened in 1971.

Seacombe Railway Station

The Seacombe Railway Station was the terminus of a small branch line that ran from Seacombe Junction to opposite the ferry terminal at Seacombe, adjacent to the River Mersey. It was opened on 1 June 1895 as part of the Wirral Railway, with only one other station (Liscard and Poulton) on the stretch of line. The station's single platform was largely of timber construction with a small wooden waiting shelter near the exit. An additional platform was on the site, but was never used as the adjacent line was for the turning round of steam locomotives. The station buildings were constructed of corrugated iron. This was intended as a temporary measure, pending the building of a more permanent station adjoining the ferry terminal.

On 1 July 1901 Seacombe became Seacombe & Egremont; it then reverted to its original name on 5 January 1953. The station saw regular passenger trips to Birkenhead, New Brighton and Chester with occasional specials to Wrexham and West Kirby. However, the line was more focused on goods rather than passengers, so when the majority of the Wirral Railway was electrified in 1938 the Seacombe branch was omitted. Passenger services ended on 4 January 1960, although goods services continued for three further years until the station closed completely on 16 June 1963.

The cutting in which the line was situated is now the approach road to the Kingsway (Wallasey) Tunnel. Traces of the immediate approach to the station can be found at the rear of the supermarket car park in Church Road in the form of bridge stonework and a small section of sandstone wall at the roundabout facing the Seacombe Ferry Terminal.

Fearful Explosion and Loss Of Life At Seacombe

Liverpool Mercury Saturday, 9th November 1850

Between seven and eight o'clock on Wednesday evening last a dreadful explosion of naphtha, attended with fatal consequences, occurred in Mersey Street, Higher Seacombe, Cheshire. The house in which the melancholy occurrence took place is used as a Roman

Catholic School and reading room in connection with St. Alban's Chapel, Liscard, and is under the superintendence of the Rev. Mr. Lennon.36

It appears that on the evening in question, previous to the commencement of the duties of the school, Mr. Johnson, the schoolmaster, and six of the scholars, were in the front room, on the ground floor. The master was engaged in pouring some naphtha into a lamp from a tin can, containing about half a gallon; and a lad named John Crossie, about ten years of age, was holding a candle by his side. Never having before filled the lamp Mr. Johnson was ignorant of the quantity required, and before he was aware, the inflammable liquid ran over, and, coming in contact with the lighted candle, which was held by the boy Crossie, ignited. An instantaneous report, like that of a cannon, was heard, followed by a most tremendous crash, occasioned by the falling of the partition wall, about twelve feet long and nine feet high, which was forced with such violence against the opposite side of the lobby, that several deep indentations were made in the plaster work. In some places large portions of the wall removed, without being shattered, and forced against the wall forming the other side of the lobby. In the reading room, immediately above the scene of the explosion, were fourteen persons, one of whom was in the act of reading aloud an article from the Morning Chronicle. On hearing the report, and the noise which followed, they thought that the arches on which the houses were built, had given way, and a rush instantly took place to the door and window, through which a safe exit was made. Mathew Riley, who lived in the house, got out of the window, and the first person he saw was the lad Crossie, who was enveloped in flames, but his features could not be recognised. Riley immediately clung round the lad, and rolled with him on the floor until the flames were extinguished. The poor little fellow died between eight and nine o'clock on Thursday

---

36 Liverpool Mercury Saturday, 9th November 1850

morning. Mr Johnson, and three lads are lying in a dangerous state, and little hopes are entertained of their ultimate recovery.

Royal Iris & Royal Daffodil

In 1906 two new Mersey ferryboats came into service, the "Iris" and the "Daffodil". Little did anyone realise that these two boats would be remembered more than any other vessels. They were twin-screw steamers, capable of handling 1,735 passengers each. They were built on the Tyne by Robert Stevenson and Company and towed to the Mersey for engines to be fitted by D. Rollo and Sons. They had a single funnel and mast with three separate saloons on deck. The navigation boxes were now on a flying bridge. The "Iris" was 491 tons, while the "Daffodil" was 482 tons. Both were 159 feet in length.

When their Royal Majesties, King George V and Queen Mary came to Wallasey to lay the foundation stone of the Town Hall on 15 March, 1914, they boarded the "Iris" to cross the Mersey. As soon as they were aboard, the Royal Standard broke from the masthead. The boat was decorated with flowers and all was spic and span. They were landed at Seacombe Stage.

New Brighton Life Boat

New Brighton Life Boat Station has a remarkable history of bravery with 48 awards for gallantry. The station is one of four lifeboat stations that operate an inshore hovercraft alongside the conventional lifeboat. The awards history is as follows:

1851 Silver Medals were awarded to Coxswains Peter Cropper, Thomas Evans and Joseph Formby for their long service on the Liverpool Dock Trustees lifeboat.

1863 The RNLI established a lifeboat station and the tubular lifeboat were kept on moorings in the River Mersey.

Silver Medals were awarded to Coxswain Thomas Evans, Thomas Evans Junior and William Evans for their efforts in rescuing 55 people from the stranded *John H Elliot*.

1870 A Silver Medal was awarded to Coxswain Richard Thomas for rescuing two people from the schooner *Elephant* on 19 October 1869. He had jumped aboard and rescued one man from the rigging as it crashed over the side.

1877 A Silver Medal was awarded to Hiram Linaker for 'his long and intrepid services'.

1883 In heavy seas Crew Member Charles Finlay was washed out of the lifeboat and drowned.

1893 The steam lifeboat *Duke of Northumberland* was placed on service.

1894 A Silver Medal was awarded to Coxswain William Martin for his 'gallant services'.

1905 Crew Members Allan Dodd and John Jones, acting as night watchmen, died from the fumes from a fire they had lit to keep themselves warm.

1923 Crew Member WJ Liversage died as a result of exposure on a lifeboat service.

The station's first motor lifeboat was placed on service.

1925 Assistant Mechanic Herbert Harrison drowned after he was thrown out of the boarding boat.

1928 A Silver Medal was awarded to Coxswain George Robinson and Bronze Medals to Crew Members John Nicholson, George Carmody, Ralph Scott, Wilfred Garbutt, Samuel Jones, William Liversage, and John Moore for rescuing 24 men from the steamer *Emile Delmas*.

1938 A Silver Medal was awarded to Coxswain W Jones and Bronze Medals to Second Coxswain J Nicholson, Mechanic W Garbutt and Second Mechanic J Mason for rescuing three men from the fishing boat *Progress* and four men from the schooner *Loch Ranza Castle* that was drifting towards shore on 23 November 1938.

1947 A Bronze Medal was awarded to Second Coxswain WS Jones for evacuating the crew of six from a fort in the River Mersey.

1950 A Bronze Medal was awarded to Acting Coxswain William S Jones for rescuing four people from the schooner *Happy Harry*.

1954 A motor boarding boat was provided for the station from the proceeds of Panto Day, an annual event organised by Liverpool University students; it was named *Panto*.

1957 A Bronze Medal was awarded to Coxswain George Stonall for rescuing the crew from the coaster *J B Kee*.

1962 Second Mechanic FK Neilson lost his life on 6 March when he fell overboard from the boarding boat while approaching the lifeboat.

1963 A Centenary Vellum was awarded to the station.

1973 The all weather lifeboat was withdrawn from service and the station became an inshore lifeboat (ILB) station. An Atlantic 21 B class lifeboat became operational on 19 May.

1974 Silver Medals were awarded to Coxswain Edward Brown and Crew Member Robin Middleton, and Thanks of the Institution Inscribed on Vellum to Crew Members Clifford Downing, Alan

Boult and Ian Campbell for rescuing three men from the fishing vessel *E B H*.

1975 The figure of 100,000 people rescued by the RNLI was reached when the ILB rescued a 13-year-old boy from a rubber dinghy. A Framed certificate to mark the occasion was presented by the boy, Stuart Nixon, to the station.

1976 The Thanks of the Institution Inscribed on Vellum was awarded to Helmsman Edward B Brown for a search for the yacht *Annalivia*.

1982 A Bronze Medal was awarded to Helmsman Edward B Brown and the Thanks of the Institution Inscribed on Vellum to Crew Member Michael Jones for rescuing two crew from the yacht *Ocea*.

1988 The Thanks of the Institution Inscribed on Vellum was awarded to Helmsman Anthony Clare and Framed Letters of Thanks to Crew Members Geoffrey Prince and Anthony Jones for rescuing the three crew from the yacht *Samsal* on 6 October 1987. The crew were also awarded the Ralph Glister Award for the most meritorious service carried out in a lifeboat under 10 metres in 1987.

1990 A new boathouse was built for the Atlantic 21 lifeboat and launching tractor and also provided a souvenir sales outlet and improved crew facilities.

1994 The following awards were made after a car had plunged through the railings at Egremont: Thanks of the Institution Inscribed on Vellum to Crew Members Michael Jones and Tony Clare; Framed Letters of Thanks to Crew Members Neil Jones and Barry Shillinglaw and Shore Helper Tony Jones.

1995 For landing and resuscitating an unconscious man in rough seas the following awards were made: The Thanks of the Institution Inscribed on Vellum to Helmsman Michael Jones; Framed Letters of Thanks to Crew Members Howard Jones, Neil Jones and Michael

Haxby, and the crew of the private rescue service boat *County Rescue,* Richard Finlay and John Goodwin.

1996 An Atlantic 75 lifeboat, B-721 *Rock Light*, named after the lighthouse at the entrance to the River Mersey, was placed on service on 9 January.

2000 After an unconscious man was recovered from the sea early on Christmas morning 1999 the Thanks of the Institution Inscribed on Vellum was awarded to Helmsman Michael Jones for helming the lifeboat at the very limit of the operational capabilities of a B class lifeboat. A collective Framed Letter of Thanks was awarded to Crew

Members Barry Shillinglaw, Paul Wright and Howard Jones. Eight shore helpers received a collective Letter of Appreciation from the Director, and the Station Honorary Secretary received a Letter of Appreciation from the Chief of Operations.

2005 The inshore rescue hovercraft, H-005 *Hurley Spirit*, was placed on service. This is the RNLI's fifth hovercraft and was donated by Mrs Kay Hurley MBE. The hovercraft works alongside the ILB covering the many areas around the coastline where a conventional lifeboat cannot operate.

2007 Lifeboat Press Officer Philip Hockey was awarded the MBE in the Queen's Birthday Honours.

Find out more or get involved with the New Brighton Life Boat Institute www.rnli.org

The Ferry Across the Mersey

There has been a ferry across the River Mersey for well over a thousand years. It's generally accepted that the first ferry was inaugurated by the Benedictine Monks of Birkenhead Priory. In fact, this is not completely accurate. There was a ferry in existence well before the Monks arrived. It ran from a stone slipway situated at Seacombe on an inlet on the northern side of Wallasey Pool close to where Kelvin Road meets Birkenhead Road today. In those days Seacombe consisted of a small collection of cottages that had no other reason for existence other than the ferry and is mentioned in the "Doomsday Book" of 1086.

This ferry may not have been as regular or as reliable as the later Monks' ferry was but it did pre-date it by about one hundred years. Little documentary evidence is available concerning this ferry except for writings stating that the ferryman charged an exorbitant toll for the crossing and that it was not the most reliable of services. It's safe to assume that the ferry took the form of a rowing boat that carried the passengers across the "narrows" of the river to the vicinity of what was to later become St Nicholas' Church. This ferry later became a "feeder" for the Monks' Ferry. The later Monks Ferry used the same location as their Liverpool terminus, either because it already possessed a man-made landing stage or was a natural location that leant itself to the purpose. When the Monks' Ferry was founded, the original Wallasey Ferry at Seacombe transported passengers to the Priory landing stage in order for them to ferried to Liverpool by the Monks.

Birkenhead Priory was founded in 1150. The Benedictine Monks who lived at the Priory offered food and shelter to travellers on their way to Liverpool. When Liverpool became a Borough in 1207, traffic increased and the unreliability of the existing ferry caused the Monks to start rowing (or, when weather permitted... sailing) travellers over the river using their own boat. By 1330 the Monks' Ferry was well established and was granted a Royal Charter by King Edward III allowing them to charge a toll for the crossing (the Royal Charter is still in force today).

King Henry VIII's religious reforms in 1536 caused the dissolution of the Priory. The Priory buildings including the ferry rights passed to the Crown and were eventually sold to a Ralph de Worsley in 1545. The ferry remained in his family for the next two hundred and eighty eight years. The ferry at Tranmere (close to today's Woodside Ferry terminus) was leased to John Poole of Sutton by Queen Elizabeth the First in 1586.

There were other ferries established in the Birkenhead area, the history of which is long, protracted, confusing and contradictory (based upon the research that I have made on the subject). It's a subject that has filled whole books and I have no intention of boring the reader with it. The highlights of this history are documented in the chronology at the end of this piece.

The Birkenhead Ferry, as we know it today was inaugurated in 1820 at Woodside. A George la French obtained the consent to start the service by Mr F R Price, who was the then Lord of the Manor. There had previously been a primitive landing stage at this location, which was developed and expanded taking in the existing Tranmere Ferry landing stage.
Alderman John Cleveland MP of Liverpool bought the Powell (direct descendants of Ralph de Worsley) Estates that also included the ferry rights in 1833, the same year that Birkenhead Town Council was founded. After this, the ferries lacked stability and structure,

changing hands many times. At one point they even belonged to the Birkenhead and Chester Railway Company. By 1842, Birkenhead Council controlled all the ferries except Wallasey, which passed into the control of Wallasey Local Government Board in 1862.

The ferry boats of the time took the shape of large rowing boats capable of carrying thirsty passengers and propelled by four oarsmen. The introduction of steam-powered vessels coincided with the ferries acquiring the stability required for a reliable service. Whilst steam powered vessels had previously operated on the river experimentally (the "Etna" in 1817 and the "Gem" of 1820), the first steam powered Mersey ferryboats were wooden paddle steamers called "Royal Mail" on the Birkenhead service and the "Seacombe" on the Wallasey service. Both were introduced the same year… 1822.

Slowly, the smaller, less popular landing stages that had sprung up (sometimes unofficially and illegally) along the banks of the river as far as Runcorn, operated by both Wallasey and Birkenhead started to be closed down. Tranmere Pier was rebuilt as part of the Tranmere Oil Terminal, the original Monk's Ferry was eventually made into a coaling stage for ferryboats and tugs when it was superseded by a rebuilt Woodside Ferry Landing Stage. In 1939, the Rock Ferry service closed. The ferryboat "Upton" was built specifically for this route and was transferred to the Woodside service. As well as ferry duties, she also acted as tender to the training ship, H.M.S. Conway and the quarantine ships "Akbar" and "Indefatigable" moored in the river above Rock Ferry.

The Wallasey Ferry's three landing stages dwindled to one with the closure of the Egremont Pier stage in 1939 due to a drop in traffic and New Brighton following in 1971 for the same reason. Egremont Pier was rammed by the tanker "Empire Commander" on 21st May 1932 and repaired at a cost of £7340. In 1941 another collision took place when the coaster "Newlands" rammed the pier which was dismantled in 1941. New Brighton landing stage was removed in 1973 and the pier was dismantled in 1978.

In 1947, Seacombe Ferry became the base for the World's first commercial radar station. The equipment was supplied by electronics manufacturer; Cossor, and enabled the Wallasey ferryboats to cross the river with complete safety when fog would have previously effected the service. So successful was the installation with its large revolving scanner on top of the terminal building's clock tower that it was later extended to include the Birkenhead service.

The Wallasey and Birkenhead Ferries were absorbed into Merseyside Passenger Transport Executive in 1969. They continued to operate independently until they were amalgamated in 1974. The Wallasey boats were sold one by one leaving the three Birkenhead craft and Wallasey's "Royal Iris". It was decided to operate a triangular service (Seacombe – Woodside – Pier Head) in addition to river cruises and the occasional excursion through the Liverpool Docks Complex or up the Manchester Ship Canal to Trafford Park.

A new ferry terminus was built at Otterspool Promenade in Liverpool to serve the site of the 1984 International Garden Festival. Due to the lack of depth at that part of the river a channel to the new landing stage was dredged. Even then, the service only operated at high tide. The service was operated almost exclusively by the "Overchurch" but the whole ferry fleet sported a red, white and blue colour scheme. When the Festival was finished, the terminus was dismantled and the site became derelict.

In recent years, considerable investment has been made in replacing the original landing stages, Woodside in 1989 and Seacombe in 1999.During both the First and Second World Wars, Mersey Ferry boats saw active duty. In 1917, plans were drawn up to curtail the German U-Boat activities based at Zeebrugge in Belgium. A raiding party was formed which included the Wallasey ferryboats "Iris" and "Daffodil". They were chosen for their strong double hulls and shallow draught, which would enable them to negotiate enemy minefields with reasonable safety.

They were prepared for war by the fitting of bullet proof plating to their exposed upper decks and padded cladding around the wheelhouses and flying bridges in an effort to help protect against enemy gunfire. They sailed down south to join the rest of the flotilla and on the allotted day, crossed the English Channel to Zeebrugge. Their tasks were to help manoeuvre other craft into position and to carry troops for what was the first Commando raid in history. The raid was a success after which, the valiant ferryboats limped to Dover. Urgent repairs were then made before the duo returned to the Mersey and a hero's (or should it be heroine's) welcome.

In recognition of their gallant contribution to the war, King George V recommended that the names of the ferryboats be changed to "Royal Iris" and "Royal Daffodil". For many years, the bullet-holed funnel of the "Royal Daffodil" was on display at Seacombe Ferry.

During the Second World War, the Birkenhead luggage boats "Bebington", "Oxton" plus Wallasey's "Liscard" were fitted with large cranes on their wide, open decks. They were then used for unloading cargo and aircraft necessary for the war effort from the decks of merchant ships in the Mersey. The "J Farley" and "Francis Storey" were also commandeered. They were both employed in laying torpedo nets, the "Francis Storey" was based secretly at a location somewhere in Liverpool Bay and the "J Farley" went to Milford Haven and the River Clyde. The "Royal Daffodil was used as a troopship support vessel, standing by in full steam at Seacombe should one of the troop ships moored in the Mersey suffer a direct hit from enemy bombers. This would have necessitated their subsequent rescue and evacuation.

It was during one of these periods in 1941 that the "Royal Daffodil" herself received a direct hit at Seacombe Landing Stage. Thankfully, there were no casualties although; the engineer did lose his false teeth as he was blown against a bulkhead during the blast from the bomb, most of which went up the funnel. She remained where she sank at Seacombe for more than a year until, after great difficulty (due to the amount of silt that had collected inside her) she was raised and rebuilt, returning to service in 1943. The "Upton", meanwhile, was used to service the many anti-aircraft defence units situated throughout the Liverpool Bay and North Wales coastal area.

One of Wallasey Ferry's most famous and favourite craft was the 1951 "Royal Iris". She was the third ferryboat to posses this name, the first diesel-electric craft to operate as a Mersey ferryboat and was built by Denny's of Dumbarton for Wallasey Corporation at a cost of £400,000. Her primary function was that of a cruise boat but she did operate as an ordinary ferryboat when required. In the early nineteen seventies, she starred in a Saturday morning children's TV series called "The Mersey Pirate". For the series, an odd-looking structure was added to her top deck, which was supposed to be the "pirate's" lookout. When the series ended, the structure was removed.

She has been an ambassador for Liverpool and the Merseyside area on many occasions and in May 1985, even went as far as London for a Merseyside promotion, mooring on the River Thames close to H.M.S. Belfast. This was to be the only time that she left the Mersey during her career as a ferryboat. Her nickname was the "Fish and Chip Boat" due to having a restaurant on board that sold excellent fish and chips during the evening dance cruises. An alternative nickname was the "Booze Boat" as there was also a bar on board. When the "Q.E.2" first came to the Mersey in 1990, the "Royal Iris" was used as a tender, ferrying dignitaries and passengers alike to and from the giant ocean liner. Sadly, she was retired soon afterwards and put up for sale. An unusual spin-off from the "Royal Iris" was a Wallasey Corporation Motors bus styled similarly to the ferry boat. It travelled far and wide promoting the area and the ferries.

After lying in Birkenhead docks, mothballed, she was eventually sold and her new owners had plans for converting her into a floating nightclub and conference centre in Liverpool's Stanley Dock, to where she was moved. This was to be the last time that she sailed under her own power and on leaving the entrance locks at Birkenhead; Captain Peter "Paj" Jones turned her to pose for the many photographers (myself included) and onlookers who had gathered to witness the sad event. It must have been an act of defiance when, halfway across the river, one of her engines failed and she limped into Stanley Dock unaided.

The nightclub and conference centre plans didn't work out and on the 23rd August 1993 she was towed to Cardiff, South Wales for a similar venture, which also collapsed. On the day that she was towed to her new home, she left Stanley Dock and the tug towed her past the Princess Landing Stage for the last time. The fog bell tolled mournfully and the ferryboat on duty sounded her horn as a farewell gesture. After passing the Pier Head the "Royal Iris" was towed across the river to the Wallasey side and passed the Seacombe landing stage before heading downstream and out of the Mersey forever.

On a few occasions, non-ferry craft have operated the service across the Mersey in order to evaluate their suitability on the service. Such a craft was the "Channel Belle"... an ex-naval Fairmile Launch more at home in the Devon and Cornish bays than the unpredictable River Mersey. This craft was used for a number of years from 1949 to 1953. She was eventually sold as a leisure cruiser when she reverted back to her original name.

Another experimental craft was the "Highland Seabird", a high-speed catamaran, which was leased to the Ferries and used for a short while in 1982. Like the "Channel Belle" she was small, highly manoeuvrable and very economical. It was hoped that this type of craft, if the trials were successful, would form the next generation of ferry boats but unfortunately, her size and stability (or lack of) especially in rough weather, were her downfall. On one occasion, when operating in gale force conditions, she became trapped behind the Princess Landing Stage at Liverpool's Pier Head and the "Royal Iris" came to her (and her passengers') rescue. Needless to say, the trials were unsuccessful. Soon after, she was returned to her owners. Hovercrafts have also been tried on the service but they also proved to be unsuccessful.

There have been many threats to the Ferry's existence over the years… railway and road tunnels (which robbed the ferries of foot passengers and road vehicles on the "luggage Boats"), bridge and barrage plans to span the estuary carrying a road on top of it that never materialised and the threatened closure in 1977 by MPTE due to financial losses. With regard to the latter, due to the 1330 Royal Charter still being in force, an act of Parliament was promoted by the MPTE to "authorise the discontinuation of the Mersey Ferries". Local MP Frank Field took an active part in the proceedings and the bill ultimately failed. This failure secured the immediate future of the ferries.

The three craft remaining in service today are… "Royal Daffodil", (formally the "Overchurch" - renamed in 2000) built by Cammell Laird of Birkenhead and the first Mersey ferryboat of all welded construction, "Royal Iris of the Mersey", (formally the "Mountwood" - renamed in 2002) and the "Snow Drop" (formally the "Woodchurch" - renamed in 2004). The latter two being the "twins" built by Philip and Son of Dartmouth, which have been in operation since 1960, and the "Royal Daffodil" came into service two years later in 1962. Now over fifty years old, although in good condition, regularly dry-docked and refitted, consideration may now have to be made as to the future of these craft and what will take their place when they eventually reach the end of their lives.

It's ironical that the complete fleet of ex-Birkenhead Ferries craft have now been renamed after previous members of the Wallasey Ferries fleet… arch-rivals in their heyday. Experiments with craft such as the "Channel Belle" of 1949 ("Wallasey Belle"), the "Highland Seabird" of 1982 and the hovercraft have proved that smaller craft are unsuitable for the Mersey Ferry service. There is a case for the existing craft being refitted again and again but as new legislation and specifications are introduced, their implementation on the current fleet becomes increasingly more difficult and expensive. Maybe their successors will not be all that far removed, design-wise, from the craft in service today.

Warrenside

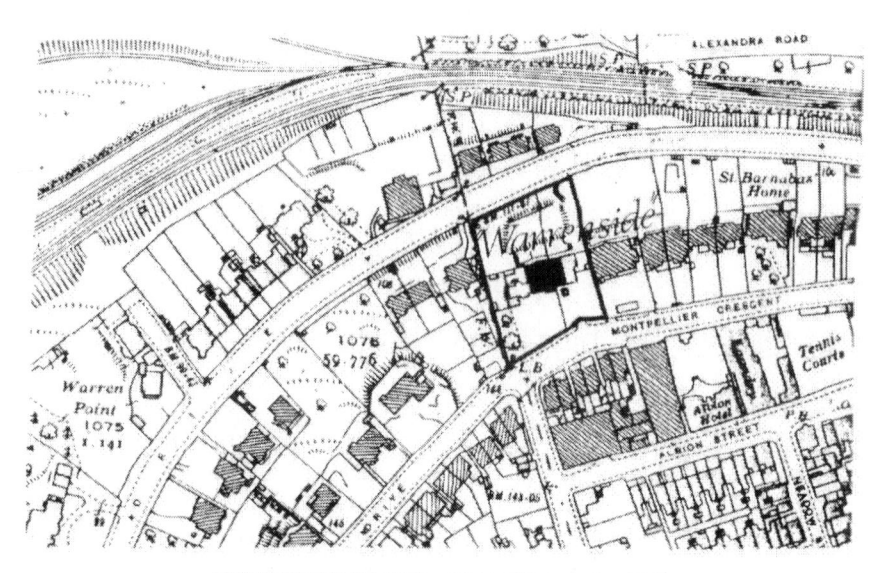

SITE PLAN 1935 "WARRENSIDE" (NOW DEMOLISHED)

'Warrenside', situated in Montpelier Crescent, opposite the end of Mount Road, survived until nearly the end of the 20th Century to remind us of the past glories of the area. It was an ashfar faced building with a porch of four fluted Ionic columns and a pediment above facing the Crescent and on the elevation facing the sea there was a curved centre section and a curved bay window each side. The building was admired for its architectural qualities until alien additions were made.

In the late 1970's the house was the subject of a Public Enquiry it being a listed building and the owners seeking approval for demolition for redevelopment were opposed by the Council who wished to see it preserved and perhaps restored. By then the once stately building had been mutilated inside and outside and also split into two dwellings, so it was perhaps felt that what was left was not worth saving and too costly to restore. It was of course demolished and the site is now 'Redstone Park' a development of houses facing on to Warren Drive and flats were facing on to Montpelier Crescent.

The earliest occupant appears to have been Mr W.H Gilliant, a Merchant, who was there as far back as 1842. By 1855 he had been replaced by Mr J.K Gilliant, presumably his son, who in turn was followed in 1860 by Mr George Booker, one of the founders of what is now the well known Liverpool Company, Booker Bros. McConnell & Co. He died in 1866 at the age of 67, and was succeeded at the house by Mr Thomas William Bouch, son of Thomas Bouch of 'Stoneby Green', a mansion previously where Lansdowne Road is now. There seems to have been a consolidation of family interest in as much as, in 1859, an elder brother of Thomas William Bouch, in the person of John Bouch, had married Margaret Booker, daughter of Rich Booker, also of Wallasey, at St. Hilary's Church. John Bouch died in 1882, at the age of 50, his wife in 1897 aged 63, and they both buried in St. Hilary's Churchyard.

Later residents of 'Warrenside' were Mr B. Strauss, a well known Liverpool Cotton Broker, and Arthur Bradbury, a merchant, at one time of 'Holly Mount', in Mount Road, the site of which later was occupied by a school. From 1935 onwards the owners of 'Warrenside' were the Scott family, of bakery fame, and they remained there until the house was sold for demolition.

Warren Golf Club

Founded in 1911 and situated adjacent to the River Mersey and the Irish Sea, Warren Municipal Golf Club is a short (9-hole) undulating, sandy links course with a first class green open all year round. It's believed that the Club is one of the oldest in England playing over a Municipal Golf Course.

The Wallasey course is the oldest nine-hole municipal golf club in England and it's one of the few municipals on Merseyside still with a junior golf section, reinforcing its position as an active supporter of golf for boys and girls.

Its long history was recalled by Kevin McCormack, captain in 1988 and now again for century year, at a centenary lunch.

The gathering was attended by the President of the English Golf Union, Anthony Abraham, Cheshire Union president, Roger Fielding, county secretary Stephen Foster, local civic officials and 21 past captains of the Warren.

The EGU presented Warren with a centenary plaque which will find a special place in club records and mementoes. They include a minute book of 1916 which reveals that the profit the previous year was £5 12 shillings and two pence, a pewter tray which was the captain's prize of 1939-40, the year World War II started, and the putter that belonged to George Jellicoe, Warren's first professional who retired in 1933.

Warren is well known as a nine hole course, but less well-known is the fact that it was, briefly, 18 holes.

The roots of the club can be traced back beyond 100 years. It was about 1896 when the residents of the prosperous area of Warren Drive, Wallasey decided to buy the farm land at the back of their homes to make a golf course.

That same year the golf course was in full use and in the years ahead the layout was extended to 18 holes.

The club remained an 18 hole course until the 1920s when George Jellicoe became concerned about the possibility that the club could lose control of part of the course on land that had been opened to the public.

It was Jellicoe's solution to revert to a nine-hole course, in effect giving the golf club tighter control over its smaller area of land.

As with many municipals, the war brought changes. Warren was actually closed during the war when the RAF used the land for a rocket site. But it was restored to its original condition two years after the end of the war in 1947 and has continued to progress.

It's believed to be the oldest nine-hole course on municipal land in England, an interesting claim but unproven, like the idea at the Warren that Frank Stableford, who devised the points system of scoring, played at the Warren before joining Wallasey and so giving that club the proud title of "the Home of Stableford."

The Warren members met originally in a New Brighton hotel before moving in the 1950s into a room at the Grange, a school that had closed in 1913. In the 1970s, the club applied for permission to build a club house, but when that was refused some of the past captains asked the local council if they could rent a basement area of the Grange. The council agreed and the members spent many months clearing and cleaning the area, installing new fittings and the new premises were officially opened in 1981.

This self-help effort was in the best traditions of the Warren. It operates on a system of unpaid volunteers taking care of the cleaning and other tasks around the club, such as administrative work or staffing the bar.

Also, although nine holes, its fine reputation as a great test of golf is underlined by the fact that the course record for a professional or amateur – a 68 in 1986 set by Nicky Brace, a club member who became a professional – has not been broken.

Indeed, during the centenary celebrations the captain of the private club at Crewe, also celebrating its centenary, came to visit and paid Warren the tribute of saying it was a greater test than his own club.

The Warren has produced players who have brought success on the tournament scene.

Its players won the Cheshire County Victory Foursomes in 1963 and in the following year club players came first and also second in the Cheshire Handicap Trophy.

This year it organised a visit for members to play at Myrtle Beach in South Carolina against the Kings of Soy Golf Society, who have among their numbers Michael Jordan, the basketball player and Warren member, Andrew Warrington who works in Philadelphia.

Kevin McCormack says that Warren is now one of only two municipals on Merseyside with a junior section.

The club is linked to a tri- golf scheme in Wirral and as part of its support for junior golf Tom Mather, son of the club's junior organiser, has this year set off on a golf scholarship in America with financial support from club members.

McCormack is rightly proud of the club's attitude to juniors. As he told his audience as the centenary dinner: "Golf is one sport that brings out the best in children. As one past captain said, golf has not only taught his boys the art of golf but also, self-discipline, etiquette, and integrity, to be able to mix not only with his peers but also with adults from various backgrounds.

McCormack concluded: "If you wish to improve society you do not need to look any further than the game of golf. We send our juniors to tournaments around Merseyside and not once have they let us down."

The club motto on the badge, designed by the late Charles Mitchell who died in 2010 aged 98, is Floruit Floreat. Kevin McCormack provided the translation: "So we (the Warren) have flourished, so may we continue to flourish."

Wallasey Golf Club, Home of Stableford

The Stableford scoring system was devised by Dr Frank Stableford, a member of and Club Captain (1936) Wallasey. The first Stableford competition was played at Wallasey on 16th May 1932. Visitors to the club will be able to see the famous painting of Bobby Jones, by artist and Wallasey member J.A.A.Berrie, RA. Jones sat for the painting during his 'Grand Slam' year of 1930, when the Open was held at nearby Hoylake with qualifying at Wallasey.

Wallasey is a classic links, originally designed by Tom Morris Snr., but with many later alterations influenced by such illustrious names as Hilton, Hawtree and James Braid. Recent improvements were designed by Donald Steel. Most of the course is played through sand dunes, with few flat lies on tight, running fairways. The greens are firm and fast, and constant sea breezes make clubbing difficult. Wallasey provides a stern but fair challenge, and is a superb test of golf for players of any standard. Wallasey was a Final Qualifying course for the Open Championship when it returned to Royal Liverpool (Hoylake) in 2006.

The clubhouse was opened on Christmas Eve 1892, the clubroom (present lounge) commanding magnificent views over mighty sand dunes and the Mersey Estuary. The opening was recorded in a January 1893 issue of *Golf* which described the clubhouse as "a handsome structure built at a cost of nearly £3,000, delightfully situated and designed to fulfil every possible requirement from both a social and golfing point of view". A point of view, that still holds true to this day. The original clubhouse was somewhat different from what we see today, although as with older Golf Clubs there has been a slow evolution of the layout and facilities. The spike bar was an extension built in the sixties and the snooker room, with two full size tables, used to occupy what is now the dining room. The front of the clubhouse was upgraded as part of a Millennium project; however the layout of the main lounge area has changed little over the years.

The late Tom Morris is reported to have said quite reverently and appropriately, that there were certain golf courses obviously made by the Creator, and others equally made by man. There can be no doubt as to the class to which Wallasey belongs." The original pioneers must have been men of vision to have pictured from the wilderness of scrub and drifting sand the dramatic course that was eventually constructed.

Just two weeks after these pioneers met to explore the possibility of forming a links course Old Tom Morris who had been employed to carry out a survey, reported to a meeting that…"at Wallasey there are all the conditions at hand to form a first class links". Tom Morris was authorized to lay out a course of length 5,175 yards. Less than four months after the first General Meeting the links were open for play for the then 212 members.

Little of the 1891 course remains intact. Gales, blown sand, War Office requirements and the desire for extra length have led to several reconstructions. Only four of the original greens haves stood the test of time and are incorporated in the present layout: 'Stableford' (2nd), 'Lane' (7th), 'Hummocks' (8th) and 'Old Glory' (12th). Several architects have been used over the years, most notable Harold Hilton (four time's Amateur champion and twice Open champion) and James Braid (five times Open champion).

Ashville Football Club

John Dennett Was Born on 23rd July 1924 in Bramham, Yorkshire but soon moved to Somerset with his parents as a child. John grew up in a town called Melksham and spent most of his youth there. Upon leaving school he was not one to sit around and with the outbreak of the Second World War he enlisted to join the Royal Navy, even though he was only aged 17 this did not prevent him from joining the allied forces. Photo is S/M John Dennett Founder of Ashville Football Club

John Dennett served on board LST 322 (a Landing Ship, Tank). Before D-Day both he and the ship had already participated in the landings at Sicily, Salerno and Anzio in Italy. They loaded tanks and Lorries in the Portsmouth area, and then waited in the Solent. The LST landed her troops on Sword Beach in the late morning of D-Day. After 6 June, LST 322 made another estimated 15 trips to pick up more Allied troops from Portsmouth, Southampton or Tilbury. They often carried wounded men on the return journey, and there was a temporary operating theatre set up on board. After the end of the war John moved to Wallasey where he met Joyce and they later married. Just four years after the end of the war came the birth of Ashville Football Club.

(Pictured above far right and centred below, with the Normandy Vets Association)

(At War on his AA Gunner aboard LST322)

Ashville Football Club was founded in 1949 by John and Joyce Dennett, (Pictured Below) from 25 Ashville Road Wallasey. From that humble beginning they had immediate success in the Wallasey Youth league, before progressing to the Bebington league in 1951.

After winning the championship, Ashville moved to the Wirral Combination and won the league for three consecutive seasons.

In the 1955-56 season Ashville were voted into the West Cheshire League Division Two, and in their first season won both the championship and the West Cheshire Bowl. In the following season they were promoted to Division One, and amongst the honours collected at their Wallacre Park ground were the Wirral Amateur and

Wirral Senior Cups. In 1962, Ashville moved to their present ground 'Villa Park', where they have had some success, notably the First division championship in the 1967-68 season and more recently, 1997/98 season, winning the coveted 'Cheshire Amateur Cup' whilst finishing a creditable, Runner-Up in the Division One championship.

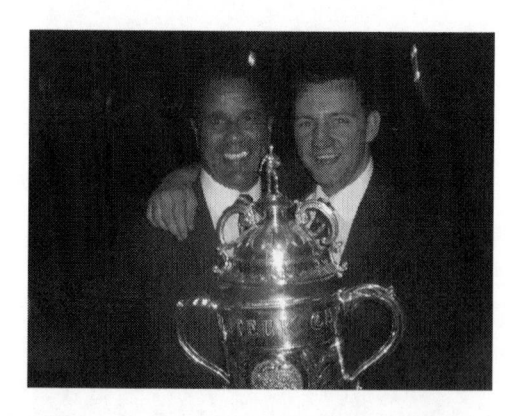

CORINTHIAN'S AMATEUR ROUND-UP

West Cheshire League first division team Ashville are through to the semi-finals of the Pyke Cup and have collected eight of the la points at stake. Back row (left to right): R. Steele, J. Cadden, P. Galagher, D. Radcliffe, G. Fennah, C. Copple, R. Wilkie, P. McN (assistant manager). Front row: J. Dennett (honorary secretary), K. Baker (manager), S. McCann, T. Roberts, T. Fawdrey, D. Thom (captain), R. Stuart, F. Nelson (trainer).

In the Picture above Lifelong Member Kenny Baker can be seen as his stint as manager. Kenny later went on to become club Chairman along with his long servant wife Josie whose endless time and effort towards Ashville still see's them involved today.

Ashville FC, who play in Division 1 of the West Cheshire League (left to right), back: John White, Daniel Mulla, Paul Benson, Richard Hawitt, Anthony White, Kevin Anderson, Lee Atherton, Dave Anderson (manager); front: Peter Bowden, Neil Burdett, Peter Haddock, Gary Jones, Anthony Taylor, Brian Johnson, Paul

The picture above is from the 1995, many of the players stayed for the majority of their careers, but one man didn't. Gary Jones, just a young lad on the photograph, went on to play for professional football with teams such as Rochdale, Barnsley and later Bradford City.

In the season 2002/03 having been re-instated in Division One after finishing in a relegation place the season before, Ashville went on to win the Pyke Cup for the first time In 2009/2010, Ashville Reserves defied the odds to win the Auto Focus Challenge Shield 1-0 under the guidance of manager Mike Melling.

In 2010/11 came a new era at Ashville Football Club with the appointment of Joint Managers Steve Platt & Jason Aldcroft bringing in a new batch of players and exciting football. Ashville stormed to victory in the West Cheshire League Division 2 title as well as winning the prestigious Cheshire Amateur Cup for the second time in the clubs history. Ashville also won the Howarth & Gallagher Bowl and suffered defeat in the final of the Wirral Senior Cup. Ashville Reserves also secured promotion from Division 3 into Division 2.

In 2011/12 Season, Ashville had returned to Division 1 and finally secured the First Division title for the first time in 44 years. Ashville also went on to win the Wirral Senior Cup along with the Bill Weight Trophy. Ashville Reserves also secured silverware with manager John Graham leading them to victory in the Wirral Amateur Cup as well as becoming runners up on goal difference in West Cheshire Division 2.

Ashville have been part of the Wallasey Community for over 60 years and have had long and new serving senior members who have helped make Ashville the Club it's today such as The four Trustees John Dennett, Joe Mallon, Ken Baker, Josie Baker, President Dave Walton, Chairman Bill Graham, Vice Chairman Ray Reid and Secretary John Lawrenson. There is that many people that have been part of the club to mention, nearly every family in Wallasey has had somebody connected to Ashville. Ashville are always looking for new members to get involved in the club. Ashville offers youth football for all ages as well as boasting 2 successful senior sides.

The picture above is the Ashville Committee receiving the trophy haul of 2010/11 season at the West Cheshire Awards night. The Cheshire Amateur Cup seen above is the most Prestigious trophy to be won in the North West of England, Ashville have won the competition on two occasions.

Another lifelong servant of Ashville is Joe Mallon who played in his younger years and later became the clubs grounds man and is now a club trustee and still attends the games. (See below with his hand on the prestigious Cheshire Amateur Cup in 2011.)

Ashville continues to serve the community of Wallasey and Wirral, why not pop down there on a Saturday afternoon and watch them play. (Picture below was from 5-0 friendly win against AFC Liverpool)

New Brighton Football Club

New Brighton 1948-49

In 1921, physician Dr Tom Martlew launched New Brighton FC following the demise of South Liverpool FC, whose place in the Lancashire Combination they took over. This was the second attempt to host a League club in the struggling Wirral resort, New Brighton Tower FC having foundered 20 years earlier. In 1923 the club was elected to one of the vacancies arising when Division Three (North) was extended to 22 clubs, changing from hooped to plain white shirts. In 1925 New Brighton achieved their best ever position, finishing third in Division Three (North) but never finished higher than tenth after that and had to seek re-election four times.

In October 1934 the team adopted red and white quartered shirts, prompting a satirical cartoon in the local newspaper, showing a player mincing onto the pitch under the caption "Isn't it chic?" Three years later they changed their colours again, this time to maroon and white. New Brighton were known as "The Rakers" after their ground, Rake Lane but Football League matches were played at the Tower Grounds, home of the former New Brighton Tower: they moved permanently into this ground after the Second World War because Rake Lane had been destroyed by air raids.

In 1951 they failed re-election and were replaced by Workington FC. The club returned to the Lancashire Combination until 1965 when they moved to the Cheshire County League. In 1983 they were wound up. The current New Brighton club was founded in 1997 and plays in the West Cheshire League at Harrison Park in Wallasey Village. However following the 2011/12 season, the committee stepped down with nobody filling the void which has seen the withdrawal of both senior teams from the West Cheshire Divisions.

Horse Racing in Wallasey

One of the most famous races in the Horse Racing calendar is the Derby. But the origins of the race are to be found here at Leasowe Castle. The first "Gentleman's Racecourse" was established here. The actual year is unknown but must have been soon after 1593, when Leasowe Castle was erected. William Webb, writing in 1662, refers to the 'fairlands or plains upon the shores of the sea which for fitness for such a purpose allure the gentlemen and others oft to appoint great matches and venture no small sums in trying the swiftness of their horses.'

In the autumn of 1682, the race meeting held here had an illustrious visitor and jockey in the person of the ill-starred Duke of Monmouth who, attended by many of his friends, was on a tour courting popularity in this part of England. On Sunday 10th September he arrived in Wallasey. Next day Monmouth went to Wallasey, and the day following he was joined there by the Mayor with a troop of forty horsemen, and a large concourse of people from Chester eager to see the running horses, and the Duke. The First Plate, value £60, was won by the Duke riding his own horse. Monmouth offered to lay £1000 on his horse, but no one would take him. Later, the Duke had two foot races with Mr Cutts of Cambridge, the first stripped, the second in his boots, both of which he won. The Duke, after the race, crossed over to Liverpool with his party. When the news came to Chester that he had steered his own horse to victory at Wallasey (though some hinted that it was by the contrivance of the gentlemen who rode against him) the populace were immensely elated, bonfires were lighted, the church bells rung, and nothing was heard in the streets but shouts of 'A Monmouth! A Monmouth!' The Mayor's house was illuminated and the Duke and his friends were entertained right royally.

In the Eaton Hall Account Books the following entry occurs: 1st September, 1696. Peter Pemberton, a bill of charges at Wallasey at Juggler's match, £1.12. 6 September, 1696. Paid a bill of charges at

Wallasey when Meale ran with ye Lord Ross his white horse Davies.11th September, 1682, Monday. On Monday mid-day he started for Wallasey to be present at the races next day.

The course, according to a map which still exists, seems to have extended for nearly five miles, running from the village out towards the Castle and back again, finishing near the present Wallasey Station. As the races were run in heats, and a win could only be obtained by the first horse leading throughout the last 240 yards, it sometimes happened that the distance had to be traversed two or even three times. Forty years later the popularity of Wallasey had so far increased that it's said that the most considerable stake in the kingdom was run for over this course. The names of the winners give some idea of the importance of the event. We find among them the Duke of Devonshire winning in 1725. About this time Lord Molyneux transferred his training stud to Wallasey. Lord Gower was a winner in 1723 and 1730, the Duke of Lancaster in 1728, and Sir Richard Grosvenor in 1724, 2726 and 1727. Blundell of Crosby, under the date February, 1727, records in his Diary (p. 223): 'Coz. Butler went to Wallasey Race where Sir Richard Grosvenor's horse beat a Black Horse of My Lord Molyneuxe's.' Was this a favourite that gave the name to the Black Horse Inn which on a carved stone bears the initials and "D with W.M. beneath it then 1722" and was it built to accommodate 'the gentlemen and others' referred to by Webb?

Around 1732 the more important events were discontinued, though for some years afterwards a race was run at Newmarket called 'The Wallasey Stakes.' But if the great race was no longer run on the Leasowe's, other events took place there during the latter half of the eighteenth century, as is evident from some inscriptions cut on the old door of the Racing Stable which stood in Wallasey Village, on the site of Sandyways Road. When it was built is not known, but probably between 1600 and 1642, possibly by William, sixth Earl of Derby. Soon after the latest of the dates recorded on the old door, namely 5 April 1785, Earl Grosvenor sold the stables and the adjoining land to one John Zewill, whose ownership was commemorated by the initials M and IZ beneath then the date 1787 cut in stone over one of the doorways. Here he and his wife are said to have lived for many years. The place afterwards came into the possession of someone of the name of Wotherspoon, who sold it to Mr Barton, who inhabited part of the house and intended, it's said, to repair the whole of it, but did not owing to the expense it would involve. At that time it was known as Sandfield Hall popularly called the King's House. After Mr Barton's death in 1851 it was allowed to fall into decay until demolished in 1895. The old oak was utilised in building some of the houses on the site, but the old door above referred to was presented to the Historic Society of Lancashire and Cheshire, and afterwards housed in the Liverpool Museum, only to be destroyed during the war by bombing. It was given by Mr Madders, one of the owners of the property, in 1892. It was an iron-studded oak door, showing marks of four horseshoes. In the centre of each of the marks the following inscriptions were cut into the wood:

Black Slave won 200 guins at Walazey 1778

Ingram Esqr. Tripod won 50 at Conway 176 - Ingram Esqr. Lady Day won 200 gs. at Preston 1767.

Smiling Molly won 5 Walazey 1770 - 50 at Preston

Upon each mark, until within a few years of 1893, a small, beautifully-made racing horseshoe was nailed. All that is left in Wallasey to remind us of its bygone glories as a racing centre is the Black Horse Inn. The racing stables have passed away, and even Jockey Lane has been rechristened Sandcliffe Road. Williamson's Liverpool Advertiser for August 1792 mentions that some horse races were to be run at Seacombe on August 20, 21 and 22. Three prizes were offered of £10 each, the second a subscription purse by five 'gentlemen' of £10 each, and the third a sweepstake by ten 'gentlemen' of £5 each. All horses to be entered at the house of Mr Smith, Seacombe

Guinea Gap Baths

Guinea Gap Baths in Seacombe is the oldest pool on the Wirral. Seacombe promenade was the third stage linking Seacombe and New Brighton by one long continuous promenade. Before the promenade was built (1901), there was a break in the riverbank known to locals as "Guinea Gap". This was a popular place for anyone wishing to go for a swim as it was free from dangerous currents that lurk in the river itself. It was in this place that Seacombe and Egremont Swimming Club was founded back in 1890, they held meetings and competitions there as often as possible. The name of the club was later changed to Wallasey Swimming Club in 1913 and has remained as that since.

The area where Guinea Gap Baths now stands was bought by the council in 1905. Originally there were four houses on this site, these buildings where demolished and the construction of Guinea Gap Baths began in 1906. Guinea Gap Baths where opened by Mr.T.V.Burrows, Chairman of the Health Committee on the 7th April 1908.

For many years this was a favourite local swimming venue and family meeting place, this elegant Edwardian building has graced the

Mersey riverbank and still does today instead of what could have been (maybe those nasty "luxury flats" that nobody likes). Almost all local people share memories of learning to swim there, of taking their children to be taught how to swim there, of joining a swimming club there, or of taking part in their first swimming gala there.

There are various rumours as to how Guinea Gap received its name, the most popular theory being an account of the amount of golden guineas from the reign of William III and others found by workmen around 1849 (possibly a pirate's treasure, wouldn't that be an exciting thought!). Another explanation for the name "Guinea Gap" comes from the word "Gyn" meaning "gap in the cliffs"; a small river once ran into the Mersey from this point.

Since 1908, Guinea Gap Baths has enjoyed a colourful history. It has miraculously survived two world wars and during World War I even served as a rehabilitation hospital for the wounded soldiers being cared for at a makeshift hospital in Wallasey Town Hall. That is one of the things we at Wallasey Swimming Club are most proud of.

Guinea Gap originally had sea water in it rather than the chlorinate water pools have today. Its supply of sea water was drawn from the Mersey estuary. This fact may have been the key to the mystery that grew up around the baths. Although there were other saltwater pools, Guinea Gap alone became famous throughout the country for the huge number of national and international swimming records broken there. Excellent coaching and supreme effort from all the swimmers led to these record breaking results. Between 1908 and 1957 no fewer than 205 world and national swimming records were achieved at Guinea Gap Baths. Believe it or not, Guinea Gap Baths has also been a temporary home for some dolphins. If you don't believe it, just scroll down to the bottom of this page to see the video!

In 1990 Guinea Gap underwent an ambitious refurbishment. The Gala Pool was converted into a freshwater leisure pool for family swimming. A Riverside Conservatory was also added, where you can sit and enjoy the views over the Mersey to Liverpool, while watching your children having fun in the pool, or perhaps just sit and drink a cup of coffee after a nice relaxing swim. The 25yard Training Pool was upgraded and extended to 25 metres, this was to improve facilities for serious swimmers wishing to compete and those of special needs alike. A new Sauna and Fitness Suite was created to replace the old sauna, originally built in an old air raid shelter.

New Brighton Bathing Pool

New Brighton Bathing Pool was opened on 13th June 1934 by Lord Leverhulme at a cost of £103,240 it was the largest aquatic stadium the world. 12,000 people attended the opening. The pool was built on sand, covering an area of approximately 4.5 acres and was constructed of mass concrete, with the floor reinforced with steel mesh. It was covered with a rendering of white Portland cement with a skirting of black tiles. The pool was designed as to gain as much sunshine as possible, therefore south facing and was sheltered from the Northerly winds. The exterior walls were coated with Snowcrete, with special fine sand from Leighton Buzzard. Lights which lit up under water were placed at the deep end for night bathing.

The Pool contained 1,376,000 gallons of pure sea water, which could be filled or emptied in eight hours. The Pool was filled through the ornament cascade and the water was constantly changed and purified, filtered and chemically treated, at a rate of 172,000 gallons per hour. The plant included chemical tanks, aerator, ammoniator, chlorinator, air compressor, and electric motors for the pumps, etc. A regular supply of water was obtained from the adjoining Marine Lake, which acted as a huge storage and settlement tank. The total filter area equalled 861 square feet. The rate of filtration was 200 gallons per square foot per hour.

The Pool was designed to allow for Championship swimming events, on the south being 165 ft (32 laps to one mile) by 60 ft. The central part of the Pool for general swimming was 330 ft by 60 ft (16 laps to the mile). The overall measurements of the Pool: 6,500 square feet, 330 feet by 225 feet wide. On the north side the shallow area was 330 feet by 105 feet. The Pool could hold 4000 bathers and some 20,000 spectators. The depth of the Pool had an average of 5 feet, but at the diving end was 15 feet.

Bathing Pool, New Brighton
www.tonyfranks-buckley.com

The Baths were also famous for annual events that were held within the complex most notably the "Miss New Brighton" contest. The Miss New Brighton Bathing Girl Contest started in the Pool in 1949 when the first heat attracted only nine entrants. The following heat saw an increase to 23 entrants. The final was won by Miss Edna McFarlane and as the rain teamed down she collected her cup and a cheque for £75, 15,000 people paid to watch the event. Among the winners of Miss New Brighton, Violet Petty became the holder of the title in 1950 entering whilst on a day trip from Birmingham at the age of 18, she later became known to millions as Anne Heywood the Rank film actress. The last Miss New Brighton contest was held in 1989. Not only did the baths hold local events, there was a major rock event also held on the premises. In May 1984 Granada

Television staged a £100,000 Pop Spectacular under the title of "New Brighton Rock" with leading groups taking part. It was attended by large crowds and screened on ITV on Saturday 23rd June 1984 at 10.30 pm.

The admission fees were 6d for adults in the week and 1/- on Sundays and Bank Holidays. Children paid 4d and 6d. Non-bathers were charged 2d. At the end of the opening week over 100,000 people had paid to go into the new pool and on the Saturday, a record was set when some 35,000 people went through the turnstiles. During the first four weeks 350,000 people went in, of whom 87,400 were bathers.

Unfortunately like many old traditional building in Wallasey, the Baths took a direct hit from violent storms. The storms in February, 1990 with hurricane force winds of almost 100 mph caused very severe damage to the Pool when seas forced a hole into the foundations of the Northwest corner of the complex causing the upper structure to cave in. With the cost of about £4 million to repair the damage it was decided by the authorities to demolish the building. The Merseyside Development Corporation bulldozers levelled the site in the summer of 1990.

The Derby Pool Swimming Baths

The famous Derby Pool stood on Harrison Drive in New Brighton and was named the race course built in the area by Lord Derby around the turn of the 17th Century. Centuries later the race course has long since disappeared but the remains of the Art Deco swimming built in the early 20th century still remains.

BATHING STATION AND CAFE, HARRISON DRIVE WALLASEY

The huge pool provided many hours of fun for the locals of Wallasey and the day trippers of Liverpool. Its huge outdoor swimming area made the pool an attraction during the summer months and was often the scene of vast overcrowding. Despite its popularity the pool was damaged several times by storm damaged and was eventually shut down due to lack of funds to repair the building in the 1980's.

OPEN AIR BATHS, WALLASEY.   No 3234.

The building was refurbished many years later and some of the original areas still stand. Today the building is a Harvester restaurant overlooking the bay area and has been given the deserving name of "The Derby Pool".

Wallasey Road Names & their Meanings

Poulton Road - led to Poulton at the head of the Pool.
Bellevue road - was the site of Belle Vue Gardens
Demesne Street - ran through the demesne of Rear Admiral Smith, Lord of the Manor of Poulton.
Beaconsfield Road - Lord Beaconsfield
Beatrice Street - Princess Beatrice
Leopold Street - Prince Leopold
Gladstone Road - Prime Minister Gladstone
Byerley Street - Dr Isaac Byerley
Nelson Street - Philip Nelson, Liverpool Ship Owner of the firm Nelson, Ismay & Co
Ellis Street - John Ellis
Littledale Road - Harold Littledale, son in law of Sir John Tobin
Rappart Road - D B Rappart
Mainwaring Road - Mainwaring family
Vienna Street - Mr Emmanuel Kopetzki, built the Vienna Hall, Brighton Street, came from Vienna
Cinder Lane - corruption of Sunderland, name of local field
Creek Side - When the Pool was not restricted by dock walls.
Sherlock Lane - nothing to do with Sherlock Holmes, but Capt Sherlock, the last captain of the sailing bots between Seacombe and Liverpool
Chamberlain Street - Joseph Chamberlain
Breck - Norse word, natural scrub, ferns etc
Harrison Drive - local family who donated local land for public parks
Claremount Road - after the school. Clare College, Cambridge, school founders own school
Hose Side road - corruption of hoose, itself a corruption of Hoes, or sandhills
Broadway Avenue - nicknamed Suicide Lane after a visitor, Mr Munro, shot his two children them himself, formerly Townfield Lane.
Seaview Road - Formerly Marsden's Lane after a Mr Marsden who lived in Liscard "castle" - not actually a castle but a villa nicknamed

thus due to its battlement frontage.

The Laund - built on The Laund, or town fields known as lands or launds.

Kirkway - Modern(ish) road, takes its name from a legendary church (kirk)

Vyner Road - named after the Bidston family

Meddowcroft road - William Meddowcroft - landowner

Love Lane - once a charming rural "walk"

Cuffy Lane - Cuff Hey Lane, local field

Mill Lane - an old mill stood near Eric Road

Monk Road - Thomas monk. Built the Great float and Seacombe Ferry approaches

Urmson road - Old Wallasey family

Rake Lane - Rake means lane, therefore Lane Lane

King Street - formerly Barn Lane. Named after Ellen King who owned the land

Withens Lane another lane named after local field The Withens. A cul de sac leading off known as Withensfield

Trafalgar Road - formerly Abbott's Lane (After Mrs Abbott).

Stringhey Road - field name String Hey

Zigzag Lane - purely from it zing sag route!

Magazine Brow - The powder magazine. Once had a fearsome reputation known locally as "Hell's Brow"? Fishermen lived there.

Holland road - The Holland family who had house in what is now Vale Park.

Atherton Street - James Atherton, creator of New Brighton.

Rowson Street - his son in law

North Drive - Frederick North

Fowell Road - Rev Richard Drake Fowell - 1st Vicar of St James

Molyneux Drive - Molyneux Family

Dalmorton Road & Sudworth Road - named after large houses in these roads, now demolished

Other Wallasey people's names are also associated with roads including Maddock, Penkett, Steel, Walmsley and Tobin.

Bibliography

1 The Rise & Progress of Wallasey - E.C Woods and P.C Brown

2 Almost an Island - Noel E Smith

3 The Wirral Peninsula - Norman Ellison

4 Wallasey Now & Then - Irene Birch. Wendy S Bennett, Paul E Davies and Sheila Hamilton

5 A Perambulation of the Hundred of Wirral - Harold Edgar Young

6 Liverpool Mercury Friday, 8th May 1846

7 Liverpool Mercury Friday, 6th November 1846

8 Liverpool Mercury Thursday, May 18th 1899

9 Liverpool Mercury Friday, 7th March 1856

10 Liverpool Mercury Friday, 4th August 1871

11 Liverpool Mercury Monday, 25th July 1887

12 Liverpool Mercury (2nd Edition) Friday, 28th February 1851

13 Liverpool Mercury Monday, 4th March 1851

14 BBC News Tuesday, 8 July 2008

15 Liverpool Daily Post Feb 2nd 1857

16 Liverpool Mercury Tuesday, 3rd February 1857

17 Picture, painted by C. H. Scott

18 Liverpool Mercury Wednesday, 8th January 1890

19 Liverpool Mercury Saturday, 30th January 1897

20 Liverpool Mercury Friday, 3rd September 1824

21 The Penny Illustrated Paper and Illustrated Times, Saturday 28th May, 1887

22 Berrow's Worcester Journal Saturday, July 30 1887

23 Liverpool Mercury, 22nd March 1883

24 'The Making of Seamen' by Norman W Howell, 1997

25 'The Old Mansions of Wallasey' by J.S. Rebecca

26 Personal recollections - Noel. E. Smith, Harry Nickson and Dr. Peter S. Richards

27 Gavin Chappell - Wirral Smugglers, Wreckers & Pirates, 2009

28 Kenneth Burley, Philadelphia: A 300 Year History, 1982

29 Wirral Globe, 22nd November 2012

30 *Dacie* and *John,* Agents, No September 4, 1813

31 Picture provided by www.historyofwallasey.co.uk

32 Cheshire Observer Saturday, 2nd January 1892

33 Almost An Island - Noel E Smith

34 Daniel Defoe, *A tour Through England and Wales, 1724*

35 Cheshire Observer, Saturday, 12th July, 1862

36 Liverpool Mercury Saturday, 9th November 1850

Index

Adelaide Street, 251
Adventureland, 234
air-raid, 19, 78, 107, 149, 163
Albert Docks, 8
Alfred Dock, 7, 8, 336
Art College, 50
Ashville Football Club, 384, 385, 386, 390
Atherton Street, 149, 200, 203, 205, 228, 242, 411
Barclays Bank, 84
Bathing Pool, 402
Birkenhead, 4, 5, 6, 7, 8, 9, 12, 14, 15, 24, 36, 47, 64, 70, 85, 86, 106, 110, 111, 113, 208, 224, 237, 244, 251, 277, 303, 307, 308, 313, 327, 338, 342, 349, 351, 354, 355, 358, 366, 368, 369, 370, 371, 372, 373, 375
Birkenhead Road, 366
Black Horse Inn, 303, 304, 398, 399
Blackpool, 11, 158, 159, 174
Borough Road, 19, 56, 59, 86, 216, 322
Breck Road, 27, 74, 102, 116, 117, 118, 153, 154, 199, 264, 265, 266, 267, 306
Brighton Street, 18, 34, 35, 58, 207, 323, 410
Cammell Lairds shipyard, 244
Captain Alexander McGachen, 57
Carlyle cottage, 73
Central Library, 147, 150, 205
Charles Holland, 143
Chatsworth Avenue, 55, 56
'Cheshire Cheese, 294
Church, 17, 24, 28, 54, 55, 57, 58, 59, 62, 63, 66, 68, 69, 71, 75, 78, 81, 82, 108, 111, 112, 153, 201, 203, 204, 241, 242, 252, 260, 267, 268, 273, 292, 319, 324, 358, 367, 377
Clifton Hall, 65, 66, 67, 68, 69, 70, 83, 259
Concert Hall, 231, 315, 316
Cotton Broker, 57, 66, 79, 83, 151, 153, 156, 266, 267, 318, 377
council, 12, 30, 50, 53, 143, 144, 156, 173, 175, 177, 178, 186, 380, 400
D-Day, 4, 10, 384
Demesne Street, 29, 410
Derby Pool, 407, 409
Docks, 6, 7, 8, 10, 15, 86, 105, 107, 180, 327, 336, 371
Doomsday Book, 366
dwellings, 39, 61, 376
Earlston House, 147, 149, 205
Education, 4, 26, 70, 260, 262
Egerton Grove, 89
Egremont, 11, 12, 15, 17, 28, 30, 35, 36, 37, 43, 49, 55, 58, 68, 76, 78, 108, 137, 173, 178, 179, 180, 181, 182, 271, 282, 322, 333, 342, 344, 345, 347, 354, 356, 358, 364, 370, 400
Eiffel Tower, 159
'Elleray Park', 75, 156, 157
Empress of Ireland, 243
Eric Idle, 269
Fairground, 158, 164
First World War, 18, 92, 163, 185, 186, 204, 238, 244, 294
Flight Sergeant Ray Holmes, 248
Floral Pavilion, 11, 221, 222
Fort Perch Rock, 182, 183
Gibson House, 333, 334

414

Glasgow, 67, 249
Golf Club, 266, 378, 381
Grannies Rock, 101
Grosvenor Ballroom, 317
Guinea Gap, 12, 178, 400, 401
Harold Littledale, 48, 49, 75, 119, 120, 410
Harrison drive, 135
Harrison Park, 135, 293, 396
Highfield House, 57, 79
Hope House, 59, 322, 323, 324
Horse Racing, 397
Irving theatre, 218
Joe Mallon, 392, 394
John Dennett, 384, 392
John Marsden, 45, 155
John McInnes, 76
Kenny Baker, 388
King George V, 17, 18, 29, 59, 360, 372
King Street, 12, 35, 92, 411
La Scala, 218, 219
Laburnum Cottage, 61
Lady Tobin, 47
Leasowe, 6, 8, 18, 27, 34, 102, 148, 263, 264, 271, 273, 276, 277, 303, 304, 318, 397, 398
Lifeboat, 366
Lighthouse, 187, 189, 313
Liscard, 14, 16, 17, 19, 23, 24, 31, 40, 43, 45, 47, 48, 53, 54, 55, 56, 57, 58, 62, 63, 64, 66, 69, 71, 75, 77, 84, 85, 86, 87, 88, 90, 91, 92, 101, 105, 108, 119, 137, 139, 140, 142, 144, 147, 150, 153, 154, 173, 174, 176, 180, 181, 190, 191, 192, 258, 259, 261, 271, 280, 284, 306, 315, 316, 322, 352, 353, 354, 355, 356, 357, 359, 372, 410
Liscard Battery, 191, 193
Liscard Castle, 45, 85

Liscard Hall, 16, 47, 48, 53, 55, 56, 58, 75, 101, 137, 180
Liverpool, 4, 5, 6, 7, 8, 12, 14, 15, 19, 23, 24, 25, 30, 32, 34, 35, 36, 37, 38, 39, 40, 42, 44, 47, 48, 49, 53, 55, 58, 59, 62, 63, 66, 67, 68, 71, 74, 75, 76, 77, 79, 80, 81, 84, 106, 111, 112, 113, 114, 119, 136, 137, 138, 139, 140, 143, 144, 148, 150, 151, 152, 153, 154, 156, 173, 174, 180, 181, 182, 186, 187, 188, 190, 193, 194, 195, 199, 200, 201, 203, 204, 205, 229, 232, 235, 236, 241, 244, 245, 247, 250, 251, 254, 258, 259, 263, 266, 273, 275, 277, 282, 283, 284, 286, 290, 291, 292, 306, 316, 320, 322, 323, 324, 325, 333, 336, 342, 343, 344, 345, 348, 349, 355, 358, 359, 361, 363, 367, 368, 369, 371, 372, 373, 374, 377, 382, 394, 395, 397, 399, 401, 408, 410, 412, 413
Lusitania, 244, 245, 246
Magazine Hotel, 296
Manor Lane, 62, 63, 148
Margaret Boode, 263, 264
Mariners, 31, 64, 76, 199, 282, 329, 330, 331, 333
Marsden Castle, 45
Maternity Hospital, 57, 79
Merchant Navy, 69, 260, 262
Mersey Beat, 165
Mersey Ferry, 12, 343, 371, 375
Mill Lane, 16, 32, 71, 79, 119, 120, 137, 244, 251, 310, 318, 352, 411
Millthwaite, 118
Mockbeggar Hall, 263
Model Farm, 119
Monkey House, 84, 161

Monte Bello, 200, 201, 202
Moreton, 18, 34, 86, 272, 301
Morpeth Dock, 8
Mother Redcaps, 272, 278
Mount Pleasant, 32, 63, 68, 76, 85, 150, 155, 156, 232
Navy, 4, 67, 69, 70, 257, 258, 259, 260, 261, 283, 287, 384
Nelsons gutter, 27
Nelsons Gutter, 73
New Brighton, 11, 12, 16, 17, 32, 36, 43, 44, 47, 108, 137, 139, 140, 142, 152, 156, 158, 159, 165, 166, 167, 168, 170, 171, 172, 173, 177, 178, 182, 184, 186, 187, 190, 191, 196, 198, 199, 221, 223, 224, 227, 229, 231, 232, 234, 235, 240, 242, 281, 293, 299, 342, 349, 351, 353, 354, 356, 358, 361, 366, 370, 380, 395, 396, 400, 402, 404, 407, 411
New Brighton Tower, 158, 159, 395, 396
North Meade, 18, 55, 58, 59, 323, 324
Palace, 87, 167, 221, 231, 232, 233, 234, 235, 236, 237, 238, 239, 240, 248, 249, 250, 323
Pavilion, 198, 221, 223, 224, 226, 232
Pavilion theatre, 198
Penny bridge, 327
Perch Rock Light, 182
Pier, 11, 12, 196, 221, 224, 225, 226, 275, 344, 370, 371, 374
Pier Head, 12, 275, 344, 371, 374
Pilot Boat, 191, 299, 300
Plough Inn, 309, 310
Pool inn, 314
Poulton, 11, 12, 13, 15, 16, 17, 33, 43, 66, 74, 79, 105, 106, 154, 174, 251, 252, 294, 314, 318, 319, 320, 327, 352, 353, 354, 355, 356, 357, 410
Powder Magazines, 190
Prenton, 6
Public Health Act, 1848, 15, 16
Railway, 164, 168, 208, 247, 349, 351, 352, 353, 354, 355, 357, 358, 370
Rake Lane, 43, 80, 243, 244, 245, 247, 251, 255, 396, 411
Red Noses, 280, 282, 292, 293, 351
Rev. John Tobin, 49, 55
River Mersey, 6, 8, 9, 12, 168, 190, 191, 241, 257, 261, 271, 342, 357, 362, 363, 365, 366, 374, 378
Royal Navy, 69, 258, 260, 262
Salisbury's cottage, 73
school, 23, 26, 27, 29, 43, 50, 55, 58, 64, 69, 77, 88, 104, 118, 149, 153, 156, 157, 170, 206, 259, 261, 262, 269, 316, 359, 377, 380, 384, 410
Seabank House, 59
Seabank Road, 31, 244, 329
Seacombe, 7, 10, 12, 14, 15, 16, 17, 19, 33, 36, 38, 40, 41, 42, 43, 56, 71, 76, 78, 81, 105, 108, 140, 173, 174, 178, 180, 181, 207, 208, 216, 220, 254, 281, 285, 289, 308, 318, 320, 322, 325, 326, 339, 341, 342, 343, 344, 347, 351, 352, 353, 354, 355, 356, 357, 358, 360, 366, 368, 370, 371, 372, 374, 399, 400, 410
Seacombe Pottery, 7, 325, 326
Seafield House, 154, 155, 156
Seaview Road, 32, 85, 86, 87, 149, 155, 410
Sebastopol Inn, 103, 116

Second World War, 69, 86, 87, 88, 156, 163, 185, 186, 238, 239, 372, 384, 396
Sherlock Lane, 320, 410
Sir Henry Irving, 216, 324
Sir John Tobin, 47, 48, 53, 54, 55, 58, 75, 101, 105, 119, 180, 181, 344, 410
Smithy, 79, 104
Somerville, 16, 33, 206, 320
St George's Mount, 199, 202, 251
St Georges Road, 27
St Hilary's church, 10
St John's Church, 54
St. Hilary's Brow, 102
St. Hilary's, 62, 63, 66, 69, 75, 76, 77, 81, 82, 107, 148, 149, 153, 156, 199, 201, 268, 319, 323, 324, 377
St. Mary's Church, 63, 260
The Beatles, 165, 317
The Breck, 100, 101
Thomas Peers, 57, 79, 311
Titanic, 243, 246, 247
Tivoli Theatre, 223, 224, 233
Tommy Mann, 168
Town Hall, 11, 18, 28, 29, 55, 59, 251, 253, 318, 323, 360, 401
Traveller's Rest, 314
Tudor Tower, 115
Vale House, 143, 144, 146
Vale Park, 11, 66, 142, 143, 144, 145, 256, 411
Wallasey Corporation, 77, 79, 151, 157, 196, 199, 227, 237, 262, 354, 373

Wallasey Cricket Club, 76, 203
Wallasey Dispensary, 39, 76
Wallasey Dock, 8, 9
Wallasey Grammar School, 27, 43, 69, 199
Wallasey Grove Road, 351
Wallasey Mill, 102, 116, 118, 120
Wallasey Pool, 6, 7, 8, 11, 14, 16, 194, 195, 266, 327, 366
Wallasey Village, 7, 10, 25, 27, 79, 103, 116, 178, 267, 289, 294, 312, 396, 398
warehouses, 9
Warren Station, 351
Warrenside, 376, 377
Wellington Hotel, 85
West Cheshire League, 387, 390, 396
Wilkes, 233, 234
Wilkie, 220, 234, 237, 238, 239, 240
William Laird, 7
William Peers, 57
Willow Cottage, 61
Winter Gardens, 159, 221, 224, 227, 228, 229, 230, 235
Wirral Peninsula, 6, 13, 22, 412
Withens Lane, 27, 65, 70, 77, 83, 200, 259, 287, 411
Woodchurch, 6, 375
Woodside Ferry, 9, 369, 370
World War II, 4, 30, 50, 201, 206, 234, 379
World War Two, 10, 221, 251
Zig Zag Lane, 80

This page intentionally left blank

Printed in Great Britain
by Amazon.co.uk, Ltd.,
Marston Gate.